12-15-71

The English Country Pottery

The last of the 'bigware' throwers—Mr G. Curtis of Littlethorpe at his wheel

The
English Country Pottery
Its History and Techniques

Peter C. D. Brears

CHARLES E. TUTTLE COMPANY: PUBLISHERS
Rutland, Vermont

Published by the Charles E. Tuttle Company, Inc.
of Rutland, Vermont & Tokyo, Japan
with editorial offices at
Suido 1-chome, 2-6, Bunkyo-ku, Tokyo, Japan

© *Peter C. D. Brears 1971*

Library of Congress Catalog Card No. 78-152115

International Standard Book No. 0-8048-0986-0

First Tuttle edition published 1971

PRINTED IN GREAT BRITAIN

1633831

Contents

List of Illustrations

Plates

In Text

7

Introduction

The term 'Country Pottery' may sound romantic, conjuring up a picture of some aged artisan plying his time-honoured craft in a never-never land of thatched cottages and perpetual sunshine, but it is by this title that the coarse domestic pottery of England has come to be known over the last fifty years. In this book, therefore, an attempt has been made to trace the history of those small craft potteries in which the local clays were transformed into useful earthenware vessels for the use of the surrounding communities.

At first sight the potter's craft appears to be little different in its scope from any other of the creative crafts, but it does possess two very important attributes: firstly, it gives the craftsman a unique choice of shapes and styles due to the plasticity of its materials, and, secondly, the finished article is virtually indestructible, for, although it may be broken, it will neither rot away when discarded nor be collected for re-forming into another product. When writing the history of any other craft we are largely limited to documentation alone to determine what the wares were like, when and where they were used, etc, a virtually impossible task. With pottery, however, it is possible to combine all the wide-ranging disciplines of the archaeologist, the art historian, the sociologist, and the economic historian to produce a complete picture of the craft's development over the last 500 years.

The study of pottery and its history has proved an engaging pursuit both for the connoisseur and the dilettante for well over 300 years. At first only the curious, the exotic, or the magnificent pieces were collected, but in the mid-nineteenth century, with the Gothic revival, interest was eventually directed to the native English productions of the medieval and post-medieval periods. Once this interest had become established collectors and museums throughout the country began to acquire any available examples from old households or excavations as new building works progressed. As these collections grew, so did a scientific approach to the subject, with such techniques as documentary research and chemical analysis often being employed. Most of the information gained from these researches was published during the late nineteenth century in a series of classic volumes which included such works as the *Catalogue of British Pottery & Porcelain in the Museum of Practical Geology* of 1871, Llewellyn Jewitt's *Ceramic Art of Great Britain* of 1878, Sir Arthur Church's *English Earthenware*, and Louis Marc Solon's *Art of the Old English Potter*, both published in 1885. From that time almost to the present day, this body of material has formed the basis for all works on the subject, the only major exceptions being the superb catalogues to the Schreiber and Glaisher collections by Bernard Rackham.

The modern study of post-medieval English pottery, though grounded on the earlier work, has really expanded as a result of the great developments that have taken place in archaeology since the Second World War. Archaeologists specialising in pre-history, Roman, or medieval studies found ceramic material of a later date in their excavations. Where was it made, by whom, and when? To answer these questions a few interested individuals throughout the country have been carrying out their own programmes of research, publishing their findings either in local journals or in the publications of the newly formed Society for Post-Medieval Archaeology. By these means a growing corpus of new material is slowly being formed, much of it printed here for the first time. The subject is still in its infancy, however, and a tremendous amount of work still remains to be done.

Among further sources of information, perhaps the most important of all are those potters who were trained and work on in the traditional manner. Although there are many people who understand the academic aspects of clayworking, there are very few indeed who could demonstrate how to throw 150 good-sized pots in an hour, how to form a hundredweight of clay on the wheel, or how to make pots big enough to plant fully grown trees in. Men with these skills are still alive, but their numbers are greatly depleted, and unless the knowledge they possess is recorded within the next few years it will be lost for ever. Within the last year Isaac Button, last of the Halifax potters, has died, and his workshop is now dismantled; the photographic records of the Verwood potteries have been destroyed; and the kilns at Littlethorpe have been demolished. It is hoped, therefore, that this history will not only stimulate an interest in the country pottery and its wares, but will also help to preserve them.

Chapter One

Developments
from the Medieval Tradition

During the late fifteenth and early sixteenth centuries in England
many important social and economic changes were taking place.
The dissolution of the monasteries, the final collapse of demesne
farming, the break-up of the great feudal households, and the
waning power of the guilds all mark the closure of the medieval
period. Its place was being taken by a new form of society, based
on the expansion of industry and trade rather than on the land
and a largely agrarian economy.

This change was not confined to politics and economics alone,
but was also reflected in the country's domestic life. Growing
trade with the Continent brought with it not only the importation
of Continental pottery, but also the adoption of Continental
habits of cooking, eating, and drinking. In medieval England
the cooking pot, jug, and (to a lesser degree) bowl were almost
the sole products of the potter, but by the end of the sixteenth
century an extremely wide range of wares, largely modelled on
Continental originals, was in production in most of the potteries
throughout the country. Of these new wares, the individual pottery drinking vessel, the cup or mug, was perhaps the most
important. Up to the early sixteenth century earthenware cups
were extremely rare, wooden cups being most commonly used:
as late as 1552 communities such as the Draper's Company of
London were still using at their feasts 'green pots of ale and
wine, with ashen cups set before them at every mess'[1], but by
the later 1550s these wooden cups were falling into disuse, most
of the great houses and colleges placing their orders with the
potter rather than with the turner. Sir William Petre of Ingate-

stone, for example, was ordering 'a dozen cups for the butler' from Prentice, the potter of Stock, Essex, in 1550, a further twenty being supplied in 1552[2]. A few years later, in 1559, the gentlemen of the Inner Temple ordered 'that from henceforth there shall not any ash cups be provided, but the House be served in green cups, both of winter & summer'[3], thus illustrating the contemporary change in drinking habits. The advantages of these green-glazed cups over their wooden predecessors are obvious, for, though a little more expensive, they could be easily cleaned, were pleasant to drink from, were visually attractive in their shiny glazes, and were not subject to the staining, splitting, or splintering encountered with turned wooden vessels.

As might be expected, this change to earthenware drinking cups brought about great changes in the pottery industry, potteries specialising in cup-making alone springing up in many parts of the country at this period. Often the site of a medieval pottery was retained for cup-making, as at Nuneaton in Warwickshire, for example, but in other cases new potteries were built. Groups of potters, or 'cuppers' as they were usually known, frequently formed themselves into small industrial communities wherever suitable conditions existed. Their activities, such as clay-digging or firing smoky kilns were unpopular, as was the fire hazard they created, so they were not encouraged to work near the larger towns and villages, and we find the potteries on the perimeter of the wastes, where they were of little nuisance, and within easy reach of their fuel.

The only potting community of this period to have been studied in detail is that at Potovens in the West Riding of Yorkshire, where at least six kilns operated during the sixteenth century. From its situation and the available documentation it would appear to be typical of many such potteries. The kilns were built immediately outside the enclosed fields of Wakefield in the Out-wood, a waste area of poor scrub which, though unsuitable for agriculture, was well supplied with clay, fireclay, coal, stone, and water, all of which were utilised by the potters in their craft. Even though a number of kilns were being worked simultaneously, there was little competition between the individual potters, for each had his own speciality, some producing coarse wares, while others concentrated on making plain or decorative cups, etc. This specialisation of individual kilns illustrates the danger of assuming that the excavation of a single kiln will give a comprehensive range of wares for the whole of that particular kiln group.

Once made, the pottery had then to be sold, most of the potter's produce being retailed through the local market towns. In York, in 1495, 'It was enact that if any citicine or inhabitaunt in Ousegate frome hensfurth set any erth potts . . . without the gutters tofore theyr shopps, . . . to the nusaunce of theyr nebours or the Kyngs people passyng that way, they to forfet at every tyme al the said potts . . . And if any man or woman set any erth potts to sell, upon the payment at any day in tyme of market ther they to forfet and loese al the said potts'[4]. By selling their pots in this way, the potters were able to distribute their wares over a comparatively large area. Excavated sherds from the Potovens area have shown that the market towns of Wakefield, Pontefract, Leeds, and Dewsbury, together with the great annual horse-fair at Lee Gap, some three miles away, were all used by the potters, who thus developed an effective marketing area of about fifteen to twenty miles radius. It is also likely that the Potovens potters supplied some establishments individually, possibly even to order. For instance, the pottery excavated from the Priory of St John, Pontefract, which was approximately equidistant from the Potovens and the Potterton kilns, contained 'cistercian' wares from certain of the Potovens kilns alone, and not pieces from a variety of local kiln sites.

The map (p 16), showing the known pottery sites of the late sixteenth century, illustrates that there was a fairly even distribution of potteries throughout the country, except for a slightly greater concentration round London, as might be expected. This distribution was necessitated by the lack of both long-distance transport facilities for such fragile merchandise and also a countrywide system of marketing. Fig 1 also shows that each pottery served an area of approximately twenty miles radius, as the excavations in the Potovens area suggested.

After this general introduction, the following sections each deal with one of the characteristic regional varieties of pottery made in England during the sixteenth century.

Potteries working in England, 1530-1630

Reduced Greenware

In the counties of England north of the River Humber the local late-medieval pottery tradition continued with but little change into the post-medieval period. As early as the mid-thirteenth century[5] a variety of ware made in this region had a hard, slightly gritty reduced grey fabric, which appeared a dull olive green beneath its yellow lead glaze. Frequently, however, pieces of this ware were accidentally oxidised in the firing, thus causing the fabric to burn to a brown or orange colour. The *reduced* greenwares were entirely different from the southern greenwares, where the colour depended on an artificial stain in the glaze and not on the state of reduction of the fabric. By the early fifteenth century reduced greenwares had become fairly common throughout the North of England, usually in the form of storage jars[6] or bung-hole pots[7], the latter having a spigot hole just above the base from which its contents might be drawn. Both varieties of vessel were characterised by two or three broad vertical handles which radiated from the rim to join the main body of the pot a few inches beneath. If any form of decoration was used at all it was restricted either to a series of narrow bands of horizontal grooving thrown into the shoulder of the pot, or to the application of coarsely thumbed rolls of clay about the rim or neck. Although a few money boxes[8], salts[9], and pitchers[10] were made in this fabric, there is a surprising lack of plates, cups, and bowls. One would have expected an increased demand for these wares from the mid-sixteenth century to the end of the seventeenth, as in other parts of the country, but this was not so. Any cups of this period found in Durham, Cumberland, Northumberland, or even parts of North Yorkshire, appear to have been imported from the kilns to the south of the region. The two Cistercian-ware Type 4 cups from Finchdale Priory, for example, are completely different from the products of the local potters, and were presumably brought into the area. Perhaps this lack of ceramic cups, plates, and bowls, can be explained by the remote and conservative nature of these northern counties. The competition of the wood-turner as a producer of these particular wares must also have been considerable, for even as late as the 1830s unusually large numbers of wood-turners are listed in the local directories, demonstrating that wooden vessels were still very widely used. The conservative aspect of domestic life in this area is also shown by the way in which the major products of the reduced green-ware potter became set in their fifteenth-century form. Storage jars and bung-hole pots almost identical to their late medieval forbears were still being made on the outskirts of York as late as the 1840s, though in the remainder of the country they had fallen out of use many years before.

Cistercian Wares

Throughout the English Midlands the transition from the medieval to the post-medieval period in pottery is marked by the introduction of a range of finely thrown redware cups. These were first noted in the dissolution débris of the Cistercian monasteries in Yorkshire by J. T. Micklethwaite, who published a paper on them in the *Proceedings of the Society of Antiquaries* of 1893. At first it was thought that these cups were made exclusively for and by the prosperous Cistercian establishments, but further research over the last decade has shown that the pottery (Plate p 33) was made by independent professional potters for all sections of the community. The convenient title 'Cistercian ware' is still retained, however.

The origins of this ware are as yet unknown, but from various excavations it would appear that it was introduced during the late fifteenth/early sixteenth centuries into England north of a line running approximately from London to Bristol (though it was not necessarily made throughout this area). The largest concentration and the greatest variety of shapes are to be found in central Yorkshire, where, it is suggested, it was first made. The introduction of these small drinking cups, never made in England before, would have meant the development of new techniques of throwing and firing, and so one might expect that vessels illustrating the transition from earlier wares would have been found, but they have not. On kiln sites such as that at Nuneaton in Warwickshire the Cistercian wares arrived suddenly in a fully developed form. It is possible that some forms of proto-Cistercian ware may be discovered in the future, but it is strange that none have yet.

Perhaps the change in contemporary drinking habits, combined with the influence of the handled stoneware drinking vessels which were then being imported from the Rhine in relatively large numbers, gave rise to this new type of pottery quite suddenly about the end of the fifteenth century[11].

Cistercian wares are normally characterised by their smooth red fabric, thrown into a specific range of shapes and finished in brown or black by a lead glaze. Many examples, particularly those from Yorkshire, Derbyshire, or Lancashire, are decorated with white clay applied in the form of strips, pellets, or modelled details. This decoration appears to have been used for only a short period before and after the dissolution of the monasteries, as has been proved by the excavations carried out on the Nuneaton kiln-sites into the earliest Cistercian wares and those at Potovens and Wakefield in Yorkshire into the later (third quarter of the sixteenth century).

'Reversed' Cistercian ware was also made throughout the north Midlands. As its name implies this ware had the red and white clay fabrics in the reverse order, the pot itself being made from an off-white or cream-coloured fabric while the decoration, if any, was applied in a red-firing fabric. From the types of Cistercian ware made in this manner, and the sites from which it has been excavated, it must have been a high-quality ware, often closely following the designs of contemporary silverwares. Although one kiln in Yorkshire, at Potterton, specialised in this ware almost exclusively, it appears to have been made in only limited quantities at most kiln sites, probably because the light-coloured clay was hard to find and difficult to purify.

After much research into this subject, Mrs J. Le Patourel of the Extra-mural Department of Leeds University has established a Cistercian ware type-series, which, extended and modified by the author, is here given in full.

THE CISTERCIAN-WARE TYPE-SERIES

Type 1. Posset Pots

These pots, made in both the normal and the reversed fabrics, have a squat body with two opposed handles and a seating at the rim to take a shallow conical lid. The body and lid are often decorated with identical patterns in a contrasting clay, which is

The Cistercian-ware Type-Series

usually applied in a series of narrow vertical stripes rouletted into place (see p 20), though other patterns made up of pellets, stamps, etc, are frequently found[12].

Type 2. Three-handled Cups

These cups are characterised firstly by the number of handles, and secondly by the shape of their bodies. They have a slight constriction round the pot, level with the topmost handle junction, and also a slightly belled rim[13].

Type 3. Tall Two-handled Beakers

These vessels have a tall cylindrical body with two opposed handles and a rim formed to receive a lid. They are often decorated with applied stag or goat heads, trefoils, quatrefoils, or stripes, in applied white clay[14].

Type 4. Two-handled Cups

This is the most common type of Cistercian ware, and was made in both the normal and the reversed fabrics. The cups have two opposed handles, a slightly bulbous body constricted near the top of the handles, and a belled rim, often decorated with a number of horizontal grooves. Occasionally, applied pellet designs in the contrasting clay are thumbed round the lower portions of the cups[15].

Type 5. Flasks or Costrels

These pots, made only in the normal fabric, have a bulbous body, a narrow neck bearing two pierced lugs for suspension, and a flared mouth[16].

Type 6. Basket Pots

These pots have a bowl-shaped body with a concave rim, and are characterised by their arched basket-like handles[17].

Type 7. Two-handled Cups

Such cups (including the former Type 14) have a convex-sided body, the diameter being approximately equal to the height, and are constricted at the level of the top handle junction. The rim, which is also convex, may be either vertical or slightly flared. This type was made in both the normal and the reversed fabrics, and occasionally has pellet decoration applied to it in the contrasting clay[18].

Type 8. Pedestal Cups

These cups have a hollow-thrown pedestal base supporting a wide cup-shaped body with two opposed handles. Occasionally these cups bear applied clay pellet decoration[19].

Type 9. Two-handled Cups

This type of cup has straight sides tapering slightly towards the base, and two handles placed closely together at one side in the manner of the later blackware mugs. Type 9 cups are usually undecorated[20].

Type 10. Two-handled Cups

They are similar in shape and fabric to Type 9, but have opposed handles[21].

Type 11. Small Bottles

This type (including the former Type 21) consists of small bottles with narrow necks, and single looped handles[22].

Type 12. Multi-handled Cups

These cups have a similar body to that of Type 1, but have numerous handles (up to eight) and no decoration[23].

Type 13. Ridged Cups

This type (including the former Type 16) are characterised by their unusual section, being divided into three, four, or even more corrugations by a series of horizontal constrictions. They also have two opposed handles, and are made in both the plain and reversed fabrics, occasionally being decorated with pellet decoration in the contrasting clay[24].

Type 14. Short Two-handled Cups

These cups (formerly Type 20) are similar to Type 4 cups, except that their height is less than their rim diameter. They are usually found at kiln-sites where Type 4 is absent, and are to be regarded as a separate type[25].

Type 15. 'Altar Vases'

These are copies of the southern Netherlands majolica altar vases, which were imported into this country c 1475-1525[26].

Type 16. Cup-salts

This type (formerly Type 19) was produced solely in the reversed Cistercian-ware fabric, and was copied from either contemporary metalwork (in which case knife-cut facets and lids imitate the metal forms) or imported Flemish examples. A cup-salt of the latter type is shown in Pieter Breughel the Elder's 'Dance of the Peasants', c 1568. Frequently pieces of this type go unrecognised, and appear inverted as lids[27].

Type 17. Chalices

Copied from contemporary metalwork designs, this type has the faceted base and knob of Type 16, but possesses a globular body, often furnished with a lid-seating at the rim. It was made in both the normal and the reversed fabrics[28].

Type 18. Figures

Anthropomorphic vessels taking the form of bottles, salts, or ornaments. They are usually executed in the red fabric, but have details added in white. The most common variety of this type is composed of female figures modelled in mid-sixteenth century costume[29].

Tudor Greenware

Although green-glazed pottery had been produced in many parts of England during the medieval period, it was in the West Surrey potteries of the early fourteenth century that the Tudor greenware tradition originally developed[30]. Here the pottery had a sandy-textured off-white to pale buff fabric, patchily glazed to a bright green by means of a copper-stained lead glaze. These wares developed throughout the fifteenth century, specially round Cheam, where the major products consisted of cooking pots and jugs having the green glaze extending halfway down their bodies. During the late fifteenth and early sixteenth centuries, however, there was a great increase in both the range and quality of the

wares, due to the new demand for drinking cups and the influence
of imported wares from France and Germany. Typically French
items, such as chafing dishes and lobed cups, were copied by the
Surrey potters, and recent excavations at the Farnborough Hill
kilns have shown that it is virtually impossible to distinguish between a genuine French import and a contemporary English
copy. The ware, developed Tudor green, is characterised by its
hard fine-textured white or off-white fabric, which is covered
with a smooth rich green glaze frequently having a lustrous or
slightly iridescent finish. Tudor green, of either English or
French origin, has been found in the excavations of late fifteenth
to early seventeenth-century deposits in many parts of the
country, but mostly in the south Midlands, the central south
coast, and London. The best groups were in London, Southampton, Oxford, Winchester, and Worcester[31], and in most of them
there are a number of pots showing a marked similarity to the
contemporary Cistercian wares: the cups from Worcester have
a number of applied clay stamps impressed with a 'cartwheel

The Tudor greenware Type-Series

design', identical to those applied to Cistercian-ware types 1, 2, and 4, while at Winchester there are Tudor green cups in the shapes of Cistercian-ware types 4 and 14. At present it is impossible to state why these similarities exist, but perhaps the Cistercian wares exerted an influence on the southern greenwares, for the former was basically a cup-making tradition, in contrast to the wide range of the latter.

THE TUDOR GREENWARE TYPE-SERIES
Type 1. Tall Jugs

These jugs are developments of the medieval Surrey greenware jugs, such as those made at the Cheam kilns. The earlier jugs held from one to two pints, and had a comparatively heavy rim of almost square section, in contrast to the later jugs, which had finely thrown rims and a capacity of from three-quarters of a pint to one pint. Vessels of this type were still in use in the late seventeenth century[32].

Type 2. Squat Jugs

The shape of these jugs (Plate p 33), with their slightly flared cylindrical necks and bulbous bodies, was copied from that of the stoneware jugs imported from the potteries of Cologne and Frechen during the latter half of the sixteenth century[33].

Type 3. Tall Cups

This form of cup[34], probably originating from the imported stonewares in common with Type 7, appears to be the prototype of the later yellow-ware Type 2.

Type 4. Two-handled Cups

Almost identical in shape to Types 4 and 14 Cistercian wares, so it is possible that all originated from a common source; but as this source is unknown at present, it might be assumed that the comparatively rare Tudor greenware examples extant[35] were in fact copied from their numerous Cistercian-ware contemporaries.

Type 5. Corrugated Cups

Cups of this type, having a cylindrical body ridged with

numerous constrictions, and a single handle, have been found on various sites in Hampshire and Surrey[36].

Type 6. Tall Corrugated Cups
These vessels are characterised by their narrow pedestal bases and flaring corrugations[37].

Type 7. Wide Cups
This form of cup[38] was almost certainly copied from late fifteenth-century stoneware cups made in the Siegburg potteries, an example of which is to be seen in 'The Holy Family at a meal' painted by Jan Mostaert (c 1475-1555).

Type 8. Lobed Cups
Cups of this type have been found in deposits ranging in date from the early fifteenth to the seventeenth century in England[39]. Although some rather coarsely potted examples were almost certainly made in England, it is still virtually impossible to distinguish between a French import and an English contemporary copy; but this difficulty might be resolved by further research in the future.

Type 9. Cups
Type 9 cups, with their S-sectioned profile, have been found on sixteenth- and seventeenth-century sites in London, Surrey, and Hampshire[40].

Type 10. Inkpots
As these pots had a fairly restricted market, they are comparatively rare, but examples have been found in Lincoln's Inn and the Middle Temple in London, the former pot still retaining an ink-stained interior[41].

Type 11. Money Boxes
Onion-shaped money boxes with a vertical coin slot were made at the Ash and Farnborough Hill kilns in West Surrey, and were fairly common throughout the London area during the sixteenth and seventeenth centuries[42].

The Netherlands Influence

As we have seen, most English pottery of the early sixteenth century was made either in the form of cups and jugs, which often imitated those of the Continent, or in the form of large storage jars, which were developments of the native English wares. During the latter half of the century, however, an increasing number of new varieties of vessel appeared, most of them showing a strong Netherlands influence. Although the growing trade in wool and woollens between England and the Netherlands had provided an excellent medium for the casual importation of foreign wares for some time, the main reason for the appearance of the new vessels was the sudden arrival of tens of thousands of Protestant Flemings, fleeing from religious persecution in the 1560s. These refugees, who probably included a few earthenware potters, were allowed to settle in England, and also to practise their own religion and trades. Even if they did not bring their own pottery with them, they would certainly have wanted to use similar vessels in their new homeland.

Sixteenth-century Dutch pottery copied from contemporary Dutch paintings

Fortunately the mid-sixteenth century also saw the development of the Dutch school of painting, its numerous scenes of everyday life recording the contemporary earthenwares in perfect detail. Most of the vessels shown in these paintings were almost unknown in England until the arrival of the Flemings, but from that time they grew in popularity, becoming part of the normal potter's produce by the early seventeenth century. The drawing on p 27 shows a number of these wares, redrawn from contemporary Dutch paintings.

Chamber, or stool pots, such as one from Pieter Breughel the Elder's engraving of 'Indolence' from 'The Seven Deadly Sins' of 1557 (p 27—1) were only used by the wealthy in England at this time. Sir William Petre of Ingatestone Hall, for example, ordered four stool pots, at twopence each, from Prentice the potter of Stock in 1550. It was not until the last quarter of the century that chamber pots slowly came into general use, but by the early seventeenth century they were commonplace. In the recent excavations at Sandal Castle, near Wakefield, which was destroyed by siege in 1645, it was noted that every room in the castle, with the exception of the stables, contained a yellow-ware chamber-pot, thus proving how widely accepted they had become.

The illustration of the firepot (2), chosen for its clarity of detail rather than its date, is taken from Vermeer's 'Maidservant Pouring Milk' of c 1660. A similar pot is shown in use in Breughel's 'Battle between Carnival and Lent' of 1559, but is not so closely observed. The pot, complete in its wooden case, was filled with hot ashes and placed under the long skirts of ladies, such as lacemakers, who required some form of 'central heating' when sitting at their work for long hours. Ralph Thoresby, the Leeds antiquary, had one in his collection, describing it as 'A *stove* used by the *Dutch* women at Church and Market' in his catalogue of the *Musaeum Thoresbyanum* which he published in 1712. Pots of this type would certainly be used by the immigrant laceworkers, and English-made examples have been excavated in this country in early seventeenth-century contexts[43]. Firepots continued to be made, particularly in the lace-making counties of Bedfordshire, Buckinghamshire, and Hertfordshire, until the late nineteenth century, when they gradually fell out of use. Perhaps this was to some extent due to the habit of small boys silently approaching the user from the rear, placing a few raw chestnuts on top of the hot ashes, and swiftly withdrawing before the ensuing explosion.

Tripod pipkins (3) are shown in a number of Dutch paintings: in the 'Battle between Carnival and Lent' of 1559 Pieter Breughel the Elder shows a small circle of peasants throwing them one to another in sport, while one lies broken in pieces at their feet. In a later painting, 'The Numbering of the People at Bethlehem' of 1566, Breughel shows the same vessels in use, standing by a fire where cooking is in progress. Although tripod cooking vessels, including skillets, had been used in the Middle Ages, their real period of popularity was the late sixteenth and early seventeenth centuries, due to the Netherlands influence, and examples have been found in most parts of England[44].

Handled bowls (4), also from Breughel's 'Carnival and Lent' of 1559, were unknown in England until the late sixteenth century but, together with a wide range of plates and bowls, they soon became part of the average potter's range of wares[45].

In addition to these distinct types of vessel, the Netherlands influence also showed itself in the details of many others. The use of the horizontal strap-handle, as seen on the handled bowls, became a fairly common feature, as did the application of small pulled feet round the bases of large jars, etc.

The opening years of the seventeenth century saw the increasing importation of a new type of ware from the Continent. Instead of being plain, as all the previous earthenwares had been, it was decorated with coloured solutions of clay known as slips. These were piped on to the raw ware through fine quills, thus appearing in a variety of geometric or naturalistic designs. One of the main sources of import was the province of North Holland, where certain potteries made attractive two-handled bowls in a red fabric, with white slip decoration, and a yellow lead glaze that was often stained green in patches by the addition of copper. The subjects, including cockerels, peacocks, or deer, were positioned in the centre of the bowls, and were usually surrounded by one or more concentric borders of slip (see p 30). Imported bowls of this type have been found in seventeenth-century contexts throughout the south and east of England, on sites ranging from Boston in the north to Plymouth in the west.

A second source of slipware imports was Wanfried-an-der-Werra, near Kassel in Germany, whose potteries produced dishes and bowls of a very high quality. The fine-textured fabric of a buff or pink-buff colour was first given an internal coat of red or white slip, on top of which the decoration was trailed in orange, yellow, and green slips. Often the design was based on a star-shaped motif. Finally the bowl was given a coating of pale yellow lead glaze before being fired. Many Continental examples of these wares have dates ranging from 1604 to 1632[46], and it is likely that many were imported into England during this period. Certainly they have been found on early seventeenth-century sites ranging from Hartlepool in the north to Cornwall in the west, and are relatively common around the London area. As could be expected, the English potters were not slow to adopt

A typical sixteenth-century slipware bowl from North Holland

these simple slip-trailing techniques, and so by the 1630s at the latest, they were producing their own, competently decorated, wares.

Having discussed the major influences on English domestic

pottery during the late sixteenth and early seventeenth centuries, the following sections each deal with one of the characteristic wares produced during this period. The potters had no hard and fast rules as to the shapes of the pots they were going to make in a particular type of ware; so if a vessel is classified as a yellow-ware Type 2, for example, it only means that this particular shape was made *most commonly*, and not *exclusively*, in the yellow-ware fabric.

Midlands Yellow-ware

Early post-medieval excavations in the Midlands frequently produce quantities of a characteristic type of pottery having a fine

The Midlands yellow-ware Type-Series

off-white to pale buff fabric and a golden yellow lead glaze. This is Midlands yellow-ware (Plate p 34). At present this ware would appear to spread itself from Yorkshire in the north (where it takes on Cistercian-ware shapes, becoming reversed Cistercian ware) to Surrey in the south. The greatest concentrations are round Nottingham, Leicester, and Coventry (in the north of the region), and London and north-west Surrey (in the south). Perhaps these concentrations were only to be expected, for both areas lay within easy reach of light-firing clays, the northern potters drawing their supplies from the local coal measures, and the southern using the outcrops of the Reading beds round Farnham.

During the mid-late sixteenth century, yellow-wares were only produced in comparatively small quantities, their shapes being governed by the regions in which they were produced—Cistercian wares to the north and Tudor greenwares to the south—but by the early seventeenth century yellow-wares had become much more popular, for they had adopted many of the freshly introduced Netherlands forms, in addition to those of the Cistercian and Tudor greenware traditions. Many potteries throughout the Midlands now went into production. It has even been suggested that where no suitable clays could be found, as at Potterspury in Northamptonshire, the common red clays were soaked in horse urine to 'leach' them of their iron content and bring them to the colour required, but this must have been a prohibitively expensive process. When the white clay was not easily to be found pottery was often made in the red-firing fabric and then covered with a disguising coat of white slip, making it almost indistinguishable from the true yellow-ware when glazed. Once trade and transport had begun to develop in the mid-seventeenth century most of the makers of yellow-ware were driven out of business by the Staffordshire potters, who, with their abundant supplies of both white throwing-clay and coal, were able to sell their products at a much lower price. Thus, by the late seventeenth century most of the English yellow-wares were being made in Staffordshire, though the potters working other light-coloured clays in the south were far enough from the Potteries to be unaffected by their competition. The Surrey potteries lasted until the eighteenth century, while those of Verwood continued to make a variety of yellow-ware up to their closure some twenty years ago. In the remainder of the country, however, the yellow-ware made was more or less

Page 33 (above) Early sixteenth-century Cistercian wares from York; (below) a group of Type 2 Tudor greenwares from London (see notes on page 163)

Page 34 Typical wares of the mid-seventeenth century: *(above)* Midlands blackwares; *(below)* Midlands yellow-wares (see notes on page 163)

confined to a limited number of semi-ornamental pieces from the coal-measure potteries of the eighteenth and nineteenth centuries.

Although much more work is required before the development of the Midlands yellow-ware is fully elucidated, the following type-series covers the common varieties from c 1575 to c 1650.

THE MIDLANDS YELLOW-WARE TYPE-SERIES

Type 1. Carinated Cups

Characterised by their slightly squat shape, single handle, and ridged walls, these cups probably originated from the sharply ridged Tudor greenware cups of the early sixteenth century; but they were still being made throughout the Midlands by the time of the Civil War[47].

1633831

Type 2. Tall Cups

The earliest cups of this type were made in the Tudor greenware fabric at such potteries as Farnborough Hill, Surrey, during the mid-sixteenth century. The yellow-ware type 2 had already developed from these greenwares by the early seventeenth century[48].

Type 3. Handled Bowls

These vessels, made up to the mid-seventeenth century, have a fairly deep convex body surmounted by a tall finely thrown rim, and show a strong Netherlands influence. The handle is applied horizontally in the Dutch manner, rather than vertically in the English[49].

Type 4. Handled Cooking Vessels

These vessels, in common with those of Type 3, have a horizontal loop handle applied to their cylindrical bodies. They were used for general cooking purposes, one from Coventry being fire-blackened round its base. A further example, probably of the 1640s, has been excavated from Basing House, Hampshire[50].

Type 5. Cup-salts

These are identical to Cistercian ware Type 16 (ref 27).

Type 6. Candlesticks

These candlesticks, with their deep convex bases, are probably earthenware copies of contemporary metalwares[51].

Type 7. Candlesticks with Wide Trays

These have been found in Civil War débris of the 1640s on various Midland sites. Later examples are frequently decorated with a series of black slip dots round the edge of the tray[52].

Type 8. Candlesticks with Double Wax-trays

Thrown hollow from a single piece of clay, they have been found on the same Civil War sites as Type 7.

Type 9. Drug Jars

Jars of this type were most likely copied from Lambeth Delft originals of the mid-seventeenth century, and they were in turn copied from imported Continental originals[53].

Type 10. Drug Pots

Small drug pots of albarello shape were copied from either Continental originals, such as those imported from Ger in France[54] or from Holland; or from the products of the English-based Dutch Delft-ware potters like Jacob Janson, who set up his pottery in Aldgate about 1570, or Christian Wilhelm, who lived in Southwark from about 1617[55].

Type 11. Copies of Sieburg or Cologne Jugs

From the early sixteenth century quantities of tall baluster-shaped stoneware jugs were imported into England from the potteries of Sieburg and Cologne. They were copied by the English potters, who used a pale yellow lead glaze to imitate the buff-coloured stonewares of the Continental originals, thus producing some of the earliest English yellow-wares[56].

Type 12. Tripod Pipkins

Yellow-ware pipkins of this type, with a tubular handle and a lid-seating at the rim, became popular during the period of Netherlands influence in the late sixteenth century. Some examples, such as one excavated from Hungate, York, copied the small suspension loops seen on the Dutch example on p 27 (3)[57].

Type 13. Chamber Pots

Chamber pots as we now know them, with a single handle

near the rim, also owed their popularity to the Netherlands influence. Compare, for example, the Dutch example on p 27 with that on p 31. Yellow-ware pots of this type have been found on many sites of the Civil War period[58], but it is noticeable that the chamber pots made in the eastern Midlands are mainly in red-wares at this time, in contrast to the normal yellow-ware fabric.

Midlands Blackwares

By the early seventeenth century a range of wares having a smooth brick-red fabric and a glossy black iron-stained glaze had come into general use throughout a triangular area extending from Yorkshire in the north to Herefordshire in the west and Kent in the south-east. These were the Midlands blackwares (Plate p 34), which, like their yellow-ware contemporaries, appear to have been the result of a combination of the native Cistercian-ware cup-making tradition with imported European stonewares. Technically these wares were superior to their predecessors, usually having smooth turned rather than coarse wire-cut bases, and a much improved glaze—uniformly coloured, evenly applied,

The Midlands blackware Type-Series

and accurately fired. This well made ware continued to be made in this country up to about 1900, but the term 'Midlands blackware' is best restricted to such types as those listed below, all made during the early to late seventeenth century.

THE MIDLANDS BLACKWARE TYPE-SERIES

Type 1. Tall Two-handled Beakers
Beakers of this type are characterised by their tall flared bodies and twin-looped handles placed close together at one side. Around the London area the handles tend to be circular in section and are particularly long and thin in relation to the remainder of the pot, but in Yorkshire the handles generally have a flat lozenge-shaped section and are almost circular in profile. One example of the Yorkshire type in the British Museum is dated 1599, but as none have been excavated from pre-1645 sites, its authenticity is doubtful[59].

Type 2. Tall Single-handled Beakers
These beakers have a similar body to those of Type 1, but have only one handle and are usually a little shorter in height. Most finds have been made to the south of the region normally covered by the blackwares[60].

Type 3. Two-handled Mugs
Having two handles placed close together at one side and a pronounced rilling round the centre of their bodies, they mostly originate from the London area or from the potteries serving the London market[61].

Type 4. Copies of Sieburg Mugs
These mugs are characterised by their tall bodies, single handles, and two bands of heavy rilling (one round the base, and the other at the height of the top junction of the handle with the body). Examples have been found from London to Cambridgeshire[62].

Type 5. Short Single-handled Mugs
They have a relatively plain cylindrical body, occasionally ornamented with slight bands of rilling, and a single handle.

They have been found in the area bounded by London to the south, Oxford to the west, and Cambridgeshire to the east[63].

Type 6. 'Delft-shaped' Mugs

Their shape was obviously taken from that of the Delftware examples made at Southwark or Lambeth. Mugs of this type have been found in an area ranging from Nottingham in the north to Gravesend in the south[64].

Type 7. Small Three-handled Cups

These well made cups occur only in the north of the blackware region[65].

Type 8. Small Costrels

Costrels, with their two pierced lugs for suspension, were used either for drinks or for medicines. One group of these vessels from York formed the medicine-chest for a chemist, from whose shop they were excavated complete in their wooden rack. Examples have been found in most parts of the blackware region, but they appear to be rather more common towards the north[66].

Type 9. Jugs

A great number of different styles of jug were made during this period, but only one, which had more than a local distribution, was suitable for inclusion in this type-series[67]. This type had an S-shaped profile, with a flaring mouth, and a single handle that sprang from the rim to the broadest point of the body. Similar wares were made throughout the eighteenth and nineteenth centuries.

Notes for this chapter are on pages 153-9.

Chapter Two

The Effects of Trade

Throughout the sixteenth and early seventeenth centuries the technique of the pottery industry had developed greatly; the simple forms of the medieval period had been discarded for a wide range of new wares. Only one side of the industry remained unchanged: the method of sale and distribution. Even though the potter now made a greater variety of cheap good-quality wares, he still sold them only at the local market. The defects of this system were numerous: if the local clay was poor, the local people had to make do with poor-quality wares; in areas where fuel was scarce, the wares would be expensive; if the winter was hard, no pots could be made, and, therefore, as the potters could not afford suitable warehousing facilities, none would be on sale.

If the industry were to flourish, a more efficient marketing system had to be evolved. About the second quarter of the seventeenth century such a system slowly emerged through the services of the pot-monger, the pot-seller, or the crateman. These men of the rapidly forming merchant class would buy the products of a particular group of potteries, and arrange their own methods of transport and marketing. Apparently this could be quite a lucrative business, for when Robert Morris[1], of Halifax, 'Pottseller', died in 1679 he left over £50 in cash, besides other personal property—far more than any of his suppliers could ever hope to have accumulated. Contemporary views of such merchants were not entirely favourable. Petty, in his *Treaty of Taxes* of 1662 thought that they were unproductive, and that 'a large proportion of these . . . might be retrenched, who properly and originally earn nothing from the Publick, being onely a kinde of Gamsters',

40

even though they did act as 'veins and arteries to distribute back and forth . . . the product of Husbandry and Manufacture'. Their effect on the contemporary pottery trade was considerable, for their skilful marketing, well organised transport, and provision of warehouses, allowed pottery to be sold all the year round, and for the first time brought the country's potteries into open competition with one another. Now each pottery had to rely on its own ability for its survival, and, naturally, the potteries in the best geological situations rapidly expanded, forcing their less fortunate competitors out of business.

The greatest of these fast-growing pottery centres in the North of England were undoubtably Burslem, near Newcastle-under-Lyme in Staffordshire, and Ticknall in Derbyshire. Geologically Burslem was unique, for nowhere else in the country could such a great variety of potter's clay be worked in one place, besides which the town lay on a rich and easily accessible coalfield. From the early mid-seventeenth century the wares from this pottery were distributed by 'poor CRATE-MEN, who carry them at their backs all over the country', as Dr Plot described it in his *Natural History of Staffordshire*. Ticknall, while not possessing the same range of clays as Burslem, had the advantages of a few good potting clays, ample coal, an established community of potters, and a good location for distributing its wares to all the eastern counties. Philip Kinder, in his collections towards a history of Derbyshire, c 1650[2], described how the 'earthen vessels, potts, and pancions [were made] at Tychnall, and carried all East England through'.

The combined activities of these two potteries, and the efficiency of their merchant pot-sellers, soon put the remainder of the Midlands pottery industry out of business. By 1700 the potteries of Lincolnshire, Cambridgeshire, Leicestershire, Bedfordshire, Oxfordshire, and Northamptonshire had nearly all ceased production, as had many others in the surrounding counties. John Morton, in his *Natural History of Northamptonshire*, published in 1712 but written some time before, gives typical reasons for such closures. Referring to the Potterspury potteries he complains:

> The depth of the bed [of clay] is uncertain; tis scarce above two feet at most. It is a yellowish clay, dense and firm, and free from mixture. Yet notwithstanding its density, the ware made of it is of a brittler and less enduring nature than that of Ticknall in Derbyshire; tho'

equal care and skil have been used in the managing [of] it; an effect, which we may therefore reasonably suspect, proceeds from some salt embody'd in the clay. The garden pots made of it tho' never so well baked, are very apt to scale, and be broken in pieces by foul weather and frosts; but being sized, that is, laid in oil, will abide the weather as well as any whatsoever as the sellers of them say; but others who made that experiment have found it fail them. Nevertheless it is the largest as well as the oldest pottery in all those parts . . . Were our materials never so good, [it] is never likely to flourish very much with us because the way of living here is more expensive than in Derbyshire and Staffordshire, and the potters of those two counties who bring hither their wares upon little horses or asses, usually begging their victuals, do on that account afford their wares at such under-rates as our potters here cannot live so well upon the trade.

In the South of England few potteries had any outstanding geological advantage, and so the effects of competition between them were minimal. Even so, the geographical situation of some southern potteries ensured their success. The potteries of the London area naturally benefited from the growing metropolitan trade, for example, while those of North Devon, and probably South Hampshire, were able to develop a profitable export trade through their respective sea ports. The majority of the southern potteries, however, were unaffected by the new marketing methods, and continued much as before. Compare the distribution maps showing the potteries working between 1530 and 1630 (p 16) and between 1700 and 1720 (p 43). The former shows the potteries distributed fairly evenly throughout England; but the latter shows that, though the southern potteries remain almost unchanged, those of the Midlands have largely disappeared. In fact, only those protected from the competition of Staffordshire by the high moors of the Pennines had survived.

Decorative Wares

Two of the major advantages of the new marketing system were (1) that a single community of potters could now supply a much greater number of households than before, and (2) that there was now a merchant whose sole object was to develop a market for the potter's wares. Under the old system of local sale there would only be a handful of people who would want, or could afford, anything but the commonest varieties of earthenware. Even if a

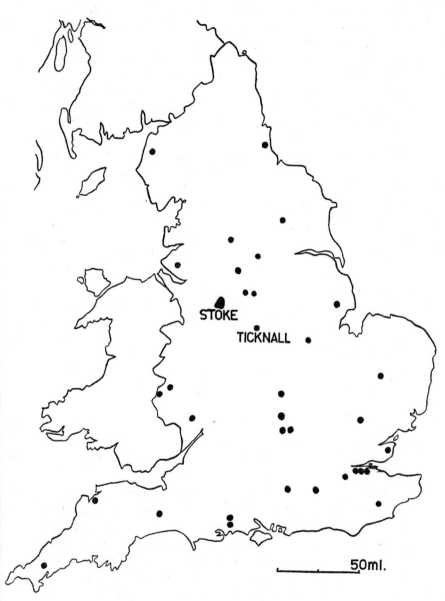

Potteries working in England, 1700-1720

43

better-quality piece was required, it would have to be specially ordered, for there was no one to promote a market for better-quality or decorative wares. Once the merchant pot-seller had established himself, however, the position was much more favourable. In the new enlarged trading area he created there were many who could afford decorative wares and it became profitable for potters to specialise in it. Now, instead of being considered merely utilitarian, pottery came to be appreciated for its ornamental or symbolic qualities. Large slipware plates in particular, with their royalist, religious, moral, or naturalistic designs, soon became prized possessions, illustrating as they did their owner's wealth, political leaning, and possibly even his good taste. In 1907 Marc-Louis Solon, the ceramic artist and historian, discovered a contemporary collection of these plates at Chirk Castle, Denbighshire, which included the following designs[3];

Design	Initials	Potter's Name
Charles in the Boscobel Oak		Thomas Toft
Catherine of Braganza		Ralph Simpson
William III	W.R.	Ralph Simpson
George I	G.R.	Ralph Simpson
King holding a shield		William Taylor
A lion rampant		Ralph Simpson
A double-headed eagle		James Toft, 1705
A mermaid		Ralph Toft
The pelican in her piety		Ralph Simpson
A Cavalier		Ralph Toft
A portrait	T.T.	John Osland
A geometric design		
A geometric design with two faces		

This collection was presumably typical of the period, and the Chirk household must have been proud to boast of such a magnificent display.

It is particularly noticeable that the second quarter of the seventeenth century—the period in which the merchant pot-seller came into being—saw this major development of decorative wares in England. It is even possible that the pot-sellers purposely imported Dutch slipwares to stimulate the home market, for in a register of passengers from Yarmouth to Holland, dated 21 August 1673, was one 'CHRISTOPHER HATTON of Norwich, a pottsellers of earthen vessels borne in Bradish in Norff. agreed about 36 years [who] is desirous to passe into Holland to by

44

Commodities and Retorne in a Mounth'. A load of either Dutch slipwares or Delftwares would certainly appear to be the most likely 'commodity' for such a merchant to import.

By the mid-seventeenth century a number of regional decorative styles had emerged, each one utilising either the imported or the native production techniques.

Staffordshire

The most important community of potters to produce decorative wares was undoubtably that at Burslem in Staffordshire. These potters, having used their outstanding natural resources to corner the Midlands pottery trade, then proceeded to improve the quality of their wares still further. Although large quantities of blackwares and redwares were made, most of the finer products followed the Midlands yellow-ware tradition, being executed in either an off-white fabric or in a red fabric covered with an off-white slip to give a similar appearance. The earlier wares were quite simple in their design, often having freely trailed line or dot patterns placed round them in a black slip, but by the mid-century at least the techniques of both slip-trailing and plate-making had developed tremendously (Plate p 51). Instead of each plate having to be thrown separately on the potter's wheel, they were now also made by pressing rolled-out slabs of clay over domed moulds, a much quicker and easier method. It was soon realised that if a large number of these plates were required in a like design, then the mould need only be suitably incised, and an identical raised design would result on the upper surface of the moulded plate. This design could then be filled in with coloured slips with the minimum of effort (Plate p 52).

The excavations carried out in 1969 at St Nicholas's Alms-houses, Bristol, by K. J. Barton, proved that these wares were highly developed by the mid-1650s. A sealed deposit of 1652-6 contained sections of press-moulded plates bearing raised linear designs of peacocks, etc, executed in first-class detail and coloured with orange, red, dark brown, and black slips. Plates such as these continued to be made in Staffordshire from this time until the mid-late eighteenth century at least. For large plates, such as those in the Chirk collection, together with posset-pots, tygs,

45

jugs, and other ornamental wares, hand-throwing still remained the sole method of production. But the quality of the slip decoration used on these vessels now surpassed any others of either English or Continental origin, perhaps because the potters used their own initiative, wit, and practical experience of clayworking instead of attempting to imitate the 'better' classes of ware. Their skills, like their designs, were comparatively unsophisticated, aiming to satisfy the tastes of the average man rather than those of the wealthy aesthete, and it is for these uninhibited and essentially human qualities that the Staffordshire slipwares of this period are chiefly admired today.

Naturally, the exact manner in which the slip decoration was carried out differed from one potter to another, but the most outstanding characteristic of this group was the use of 'jewelled' slipware. This involved trailing an outline of dark slip round the major motifs of the design and then, while this slip was still wet, placing drops of a slightly stiffer white slip along the centre of the dark trailed line at regular intervals. Under a coat of yellow-tinted lead glaze this technique gave particularly rich and sparkling results, which proved extremely popular (see the Toft plate, p 51).

Other slipware techniques pioneered in Staffordshire at this time included both feathering and marbling. To produce a feathered design the potter first dipped or poured a coating of slip over the ware, and quickly trailed a pattern of parallel lines in a contrasting slip on top of it. The two slips were then dragged into one another by a series of long quill or bristle strokes running at right-angles to the parallel lines of trailing. A similar technique is often used today in cake-icing. It is quite likely that feathering was developed from a simple accident in normal slip trailing. By the third quarter of the seventeenth century the Staffordshire potters were producing a wide range of these wares, all exhibiting a superb mastery of the feathering technique.

The process of marbling, in common with that of feathering, demanded that the ware should first be coated in liquid slip and then have a series of lines trailed over it in one or more contrasting colours. The piece was then twisted and jerked to run the colours together, so giving a variegated marble-like finish. Although most marbled wares such as plates or dishes were left in this state, designs of even greater complexity could be produced by running a quill or stylus through the still wet marbled slips, a technique perhaps best used on the owl-shaped jugs made in the Potteries during the early eighteenth century.

These various decorative wares were of a higher quality than any previously made in England, and must have been extremely popular, for they are found on excavation sites throughout the whole of England with the possible exception of the extreme south. The potteries that had managed to withstand the Staffordshire competition frequently imitated its designs, but they could never rival the true Staffordshire products.

The range of wares made in the Potteries during the seventeenth century was so vast that it would be impossible to give more than this brief outline of their characteristic products, but a list of the numerous volumes covering this subject is given in the Bibliography.

Ticknall

It is known from various documentary references that Ticknall near Burton-on-Trent in Derbyshire was one of the largest pottery centres during the middle and later seventeenth century, but surprisingly little has been done on this site, and our knowledge of its decorative wares is small. A number of pieces, however, have been attributed to Ticknall, the majority being large lead-glazed pressed plates with a hard buff to near-red fabric and a black slipped interior on which are trailed either geometric designs or hunting scenes in white slip.

South Wiltshire

From the opening years of the seventeenth century South Wiltshire produced a class of pottery which, unlike the other major decorative wares, relied for its effect on modelling techniques instead of multi-coloured clay slips. The ware itself was of a hard pink-buff fabric covered with a speckled purple-brown manganese-stained lead glaze. Most of the pieces were made in the form of jugs, puzzle-jugs, or covered cups, the latter being modelled in particularly fine detail. Not only were three-dimensional figures of men or birds added as knobs, but details such as the handles were enriched with twisted and plaited ropes of clay, scrolls, and pellets, while any plain areas between the handles or round the lid either had designs scratched into them or were impressed with stamps bearing such motifs as mermaids with mirrors, lions, kings, grapes, or nuts. Frequently the wares also bore dates (usually between 1603 and 1799) and inscriptions such as these, taken from examples in the Glaisher collection: 'MERI MET AND MERI PART I DRINK TO U WITH ALL MI HART 1710', or 'William & mary Goldsmith June ye 7th 1697'. A number of pieces dated 1603, 1609, and 1799 have also the initials 'W.Z.' marked upon them, traditionally the initials of a potter named Zillwood, though there is no real evidence for this.

The site of the pottery is as yet unknown, but it was probably in the Salisbury area, for the majority of the examples extant have been collected from this region. Further evidence was obtained by Mr R. Cook in 1864: having obtained samples of clay from Clarendon, immediately to the east of Salisbury, he proceeded to make them into vessels, which he glazed and fired, discovering that his materials were identical to those used in the seventeenth-century wares. These experimental pieces, together with an excellent collection of the originals, can now be seen in the Salisbury and South Wilts Museum in Salisbury.

Donyatt

Donyatt, near Ilminster in the Vale of Taunton Deane in Somerset, had been the site of a thriving medieval pottery, but by the mid-seventeenth century its wares retained few of their medieval characteristics. Pottery excavated from Bristol and Taunton[4] dating from the period 1652-9 illustrates the range of decorative wares made at Donyatt at this time. Three major decorative techniques were used: sgraffito, slip brushing and trailing, and combing.

In the first, the red fabric of the pot was given a coating of white slip, which, when dry, was incised to reveal the red clay beneath; the decoration was usually restricted to series of S-shaped scrolls, zig-zag lines, or cross-hatchings round plate and bowl rims. The second technique usually involved trailing a series of concentric rings of white slip round the interior of plate bases, etc, and then breaking up the design by pulling a finger through the wet rings in a number of radiating loops. Further decoration might then be added by brushing on white slip dots, asterisks or formalised fern patterns on any remaining plain areas. The third technique consisted of applying a coat of white slip over the pot and running a blunt-toothed comb through it while it was still wet, to produce an attractive pattern of parallel waves or scallops. This method was largely used on hollow-wares, particularly on storage jars or jugs, the shape of the latter being copied from imported Raeren or Grenzau stonewares. Whichever slip technique was used, the wares were always given a yellow-tinted lead glaze, which was often patchily speckled with a rich green by particles of copper in the lead.

By the 1670s, when dated pieces were being made, the Donyatt potters produced many new lines of decorative ware, including puzzle jugs, flower vases, bottles, commemorative plates, covered cups, and 'Jolly Boys' (a type of multi-bodied fuddling cup). As in South Wiltshire, the covered cups were frequently the most intricate products, having free-standing figures of men and birds as knobs, with similar figures modelled in relief round the mural surfaces of the cup itself. The above-mentioned techniques were still used for decoration, but now a much greater degree of skill was evident both in design and execution. Trailing, brushing, and combing were extensively used, but the finest examples were always carried out in sgraffito, as this was the easiest, yet the most precise, method.

Although decorative wares continued to be made at Donyatt well into the present century, the finest wares were produced during the late seventeenth century.

Wrotham

The parish of Wrotham (pronounced Root-ham), Kent, lies some 26 miles south-east of London at the junction of the Gault clays with the Folkestone beds of the lower greensand. Here, from the early seventeenth century at least, a group of potters made a wide range of products, including some remarkable decorative pieces for which the area has become famous.

The wares, with their red fabrics and yellow lead glazes, included large dishes, jugs, candlesticks, and a cistern; but the most common forms were two distinct types of posset pot or tyg. The earlier type, ranging in date between 1612 and 1699, had straight sides and four double-looped handles (see Plate, p 85); while the later, dating between 1687 and 1721, was globular in form and had two or three handles with either single or double loops. These handles were particularly ornate, being decorated with slip trailing, applied clay pellets, or pinnacles, the latter frequently concealing a number of hidden drinking spouts. Pads of white clay were usually placed round their bodies and then overstamped with intaglio seals bearing the relief designs of angels, roses, fleurs-de-lis, lions rampant, of the potter's initials (see the Gazetteer entry for Wrotham, p 190), while the remaining areas of the rim, handles, and base were decorated with details in trailed slip.

Metropolitan Wares

Excavations and casual building works in the city of London have disclosed a distinct regional variety of ware, which has been named Metropolitan ware from its location. It comprises a range of cups, plates, jugs, etc, executed in a light red fabric and decorated with scroll designs and bold legends freely trailed in white slip. Typical inscriptions advise the user to 'BE NOT HY MINDED BUT FEAR GOD', to 'FEAR GOD HONOR THE KING', or to 'FEAR GOD FAST AND PRAY'. Recent work has shown that these wares were chiefly made in Essex, principally at Harlow and Latton, though future research may well reveal other centres.

North Devon

The major pottery centres in North Devon, from the early sixteenth century at least, were situated near Barnstaple and Bideford on the estuaries of the Rivers Taw and Torridge. Here, as at Donyatt, the wares were decorated by the sgraffito technique (Plate p 85), the designs being scratched through a coating of white slip to reveal the dark red fabric beneath. By the mid-late

Page 51 The royal arms on a plate by Thomas Toft, perhaps
the greatest exponent of the Staffordshire slipware technique
(see note on page 164)

Page 52 A Staffordshire pressed-ware plate (*left*) and its mould (*right*), the latter being inscribed 'William Bird made this mould In the year of Our Lord 1751' (see note on page 164)

seventeenth century the sgraffito wares made here had already reached a high standard, and included cups, jugs, and plates decorated with a variety of floral and geometric designs; the plates were particularly attractive, with their borders of scrolls, stylised flower heads, or zig-zag designs executed with narrow five-pointed combs. These wares were not produced solely for the home market, however, for large quantities were made for export to Ireland, Wales, and North America, as recorded by Malcolm Watkins in his *North Devon Pottery and its Export to North America* of 1960. As early as 1635 cargoes of pottery were being shipped across the Atlantic, later shipments being directed specifically to New England, Virginia, or Maryland, but this trade had ceased by the time of the American War of Independence.

By the mid-eighteenth century the skill of the North Devon potters had improved considerably, and a wide range of decorative subjects had been introduced. These included lions and unicorns, ships in full sail, maids and youths, each design often being surrounded by a lush growth of ornamental foliage (Plate, p 85). Similar designs continued to be used throughout the nineteenth century, and Henry Phillips, the last of the true North Devon sgraffito-ware potters, died in 1894.

Up to the late seventeenth century the history of the earthenware potter had been one of continuous development. Gradually overcoming the competition from other materials the craft had flourished, but time was now beginning to run out. The merchant pot-seller had set the craft on a commercial basis in the 1630s and 1640s, promoting competition and thus favouring the potteries making the better-quality wares. But as the seventeenth century progressed, fashion began to ask for wares of a higher standard still. The English and Dutch East India Companies had introduced tea and coffee into Europe, together with oriental porcelain teapots, cups, and saucers necessary for their full enjoyment, and it was obvious that customers would not long be satisfied with less from English potters.

As early as 1671 John Dwight of Fulham had been granted a patent for the manufacture of 'Transparent Earthenware, comonly Knowne by the names of Porcelaine or China, and Persian ware . . .', but his future work was disappointing, and his wares never went beyond the experimental stage. Probably

D 53

the first potters in England to produce effective pseudo-Chinese wares commercially were the brothers John Philip and David Ellers, who used a very fine red fabric to make a so-called 'red porcelain', which was finished either on the lathe or by being pressed into engraved copper moulds. Originating from Holland, they first set up a pottery at Fulham about 1690, where their main products were brown mugs and red teapots, but within a few years they had left the London area and moved on to Bradwell Wood, a short distance from Burslem. Celia Fiennes the diarist tried to visit this pottery in 1698, recording that she—

> went to this Newcastle in Staffordshire to see the making of ye fine teapotts, cups, and saucers of ye fine red Earth in imitation and as Curious as yt wch comes from China, but was defeated in my design, they coming to an end of their Clay they made use of for yt sort of ware, and therefore was removed to some other place where they were not settled to their work, so could not see it.

Meanwhile other potters such as Twyford, Astbury, and the Wedgwoods were also developing finer earthenwares, each trying to imitate the peerless whiteness and high finish of porcelain. By the use of such materials as ground calcined flint and Cornish china clay in the fabric, and flint glass, zinc oxide, and sand in the glaze, they greatly improved their earthenwares. New methods of manufacture, too, such as slip-casting in plaster of Paris moulds, lathe-turning, and engraved transfer-printed decoration, all succeeded in converting the craft into an industrial process. It was now impossible for a single potter and his family to produce the finer wares competitively: he had neither the skill, the time, the labour, the equipment, nor the capital necessary. Pottery had suddenly jumped from being a semi-cottage industry, operated by a craftsman and his family alone, into a fully developed factory-based manufacturing process, employing a large percentage of unskilled or only semi-skilled labour.

Notes for this chapter are on page 159.

Chapter Three

The Urban Potteries

The new wares produced by the Staffordshire potters during the first half of the eighteenth century were of an unprecedented quality, both in design and execution. Their elegant forms, finely modelled details, and light weight, combined with a moderate selling price, ensured their commercial success. By the third quarter of the century pottery such as Wedgwood's 'Queen's Ware', together with its numerous imitators, was not only being marketed throughout the entire kingdom by way of the newly built network of canals and turnpike roads, but was also being exported to Europe and the colonies in vast quantities. At first it might be thought that the introduction and rapid expansion of these factory-made ceramics would have completed the collapse of those smaller potteries still operating on a cottage-industry basis, but this, rather surprisingly, was not so. The reason was that the new wares, being of such a high standard, did not affect the traditional coarse earthenware markets, but tended to replace the contemporary better-class ware, such as pewter.

Pewter plates and tankards had served most better-class tables from the mid-seventeenth century at least, but pewter, though not so easily broken as pottery, had some major disadvantages: it was easily scratched and twisted out of shape, constant attention was needed to remove the knife-cuts it received at table, and it was unpleasant to eat from directly. In contrast, the new fine earthenwares possessed a hard glass-like finish, which was easily cleaned, withstood the action of the knife and fork, and were attractively designed and decorated. No potters objected to the new wares, but the pewterers and their allied tradesmen protested vigorously, as an Exeter paper of 4 April 1776 recorded :

> Last week the tinners in Cornwall rose in consequence of the intro-
> duction into that county of such large quantities of Staffordshire and
> other earthenware. About a hundred in a body went to Redruth, on
> the market day, and broke all the wares they could meet with, the sale
> of which had been intended in that town. From thence they went to
> Falmouth for the same purpose, and because they could not force their
> way into the Town Hall, where a large parcel of Staffordshire and
> other wares were lodged, they were about to set fire to it, had not Mr.
> Allison, the printer and alderman of that town, with another gentle-
> man, pacified them, by promising to discourage the sale and use of
> these wares by every means in their power, and by going to a pew-
> terer's and bespeaking a quantity of pewter dishes and plates to evince
> their readiness to serve them, on which they happily dispersed.[1]

During the latter half of the eighteenth century a number of
major changes were taking place in England, and collectively
they made up the process known as the Industrial Revolution.
One of the greatest of these changes was the rapid growth and
redistribution of the population. About 1700 the population of
8,000,000 or so was mostly based on agriculture and its ancillary
trades, and was most dense in the fertile lands of Lancashire and
Cheshire, Norfolk and Suffolk, and the counties of the southern
Midlands. By the time of the census of 1831, however, the population had grown to some 16,500,000, half of which lived in the
industrial regions of London, the west Midlands, Lancashire,
Durham, and the West Riding of Yorkshire. The communities
that gradually converged towards and expanded round these
industrial centres during the latter half of the eighteenth century
were largely composed of wage labourers, the majority of whom
hardly earned enough to support themselves and their families
at a subsistence level. Even if the growing middle classes were
able to afford the new factory-made wares, the large labouring
classes were not, and so a demand for the cheapest varieties of
coarse pottery grew up as industrialisation progressed.

To satisfy this demand new coarseware potteries sprang up
throughout England, recapturing the trade that had been appro-
priated by the Staffordshire and Derbyshire potteries a century
before. Craftsmen potters from those potteries which had survived the earlier competition moved into the new industrial
centres, there to establish potteries to serve the ever-growing
population. John Catherall, for instance, a potter from the vil-

lage of Buckley in Flintshire, moved to Keelham between the great wool towns of Bradford and Halifax in the 1770s, there to found a number of new and highly successful potteries; while at the same time John Bragg, potter, moved from the failing Potovens potteries to those of Midhope, which served the engineering town of Sheffield. Fortunately most of the new industrial centres were situated close to outcrops of coal-measure deposits. Around these outcrops, particularly where the coal measures lay next to the millstone grits, the potter could usually find ample supplies of potting clay, fireclay, a clay for making white slip, and coal, all of which could be worked within a small area by means of quarrying or simple mining operations.

It must be remembered that no geological maps were published until the late eighteenth and early nineteenth centuries, when there was a growing interest in agriculture. This meant that the only information available on the variations in subsoil from one area to another was that built up by the local inhabitants by means of their own observations. So it is amazing to discover that wherever possible every new pottery fixed on the precise location that gave it the optimum geological advantage. The map on p 58 shows the potteries working during 1800-30 and that the major groups all lay near the perimeter of the coal measures (hatched); the remainder are working chiefly on the London, Wealden, or Gault clays, the Reading beds, or on minor alluvial deposits. This illustration also shows the great number of potteries in production at this period in contrast to the few a century before, as seen on p 43.

The majority of the new urban potteries were fairly small family concerns, often run in conjunction with a smallholding. This dual role of potter and farmer was common in many parts of the country, as can be seen by studying account books. Those of the Farnham Pottery in Surrey show Absalom Harris's dealings in potatoes, barley, and straw, and also give the dates on which his cows and horses were served. Fishley Holland has described how the potters at Fremington grew their own potatoes, corn, and food for the horse, while at Halifax, Nicholas Taylor recorded the potters making hay at Bateain or Howcans late in the last century. From these accounts it would appear that most of the potteries were self-supporting, and that pottery-making on its own was hardly profitable enough to maintain the potters at

Potteries working in England, 1800-1830, showing their concentration in the coal-measure regions (hatched)

a reasonable standard of living. Staff was therefore kept to an absolute minimum, only the potter's family, two or three paid labourers, and a number of apprentices being used to operate the entire undertaking.

Frequently the apprentices were also members of the potter's family, or else were Town's apprentices, put to the craft by the local Board of Guardians when about thirteen years old. During his apprenticeship, which lasted from five to seven years, a boy was taught all the processes of clayworking and potting: starting as a clay-boy, digging, blunging, or treading the clay, and preparing it in balls ready for the thrower, he rose to become a turner or spinner, winding the potter's wheel, and finally a thrower, shaping the pottery on the wheel himself. Throughout this course he was also taught the arts of glaze preparation, decorating, and kiln-firing. On the completion of this formal apprenticeship he became a journeyman, travelling from one pottery to another to gain additional experience before taking up a permanent situation. This movement of journeymen, combined with the movement of trained potters from one kiln to another as their fancy took them, had a unifying effect on the styles of pottery made, thus making it particularly difficult to attribute any particular piece of late eighteenth- or nineteenth-century pottery to one definite kiln on stylistic grounds alone.

Being a fairly small concern, the average urban pottery worked in a partly seasonal and partly weekly cycle. Before the introduction of heated clay-pans, which could dry out the clay irrespective of the weather, most potteries prepared a season's batch of clay in the spring, storing it ready for use in a stone-lined 'dess' or 'clay-ain'. It was hopeless to try and use the sun-pan alone to prepare the clays in winter, for they would never dry out, but then the autumn and winter were the best times for clay digging, as the frost broke down or 'weathered' the clays in an excellent manner. The week was normally the unit of time used for the everyday processes of the pottery, so many days being allocated to throwing, packing, and firing, and so many further days for delivery, either to customers who had ordered pottery or to the local market.

The methods used to distribute the wares were different to those used in the seventeenth century, as new systems of wholesaling and retailing had been established. Whereas the seventeenth-century potter had largely dealt through a merchant pot-seller, it was now no longer profitable for a merchant to handle this class of goods alone, for two reasons: firstly, the value of the goods was now extremely low, as they served only the poorest markets, and there was no margin for a worthwhile profit; and, secondly, the potteries were now situated within easy reach of their markets and the financial gain to be had by transporting the wares to the consumers was negligible. Both of these changes meant that each pottery had to undertake its own marketing, just as it had done in the sixteenth century. In most parts of England the potters personally sold their wares either on stalls at the local markets, or by hawking them round the neighbourhood in horse-drawn carts, selling from door to door. Occasionally these activities were carried out by 'potmen', who hawked the wares along with miscellaneous hardware or groceries. Around the Scottish borders this could also provide a convincing cover for whisky-smuggling, and so prove quite lucrative[2]. If trade was scarce, or if a new area was being tried, the prospective customers' children were tempted by free gifts—specially made whistles, pottery marbles, or small modelled birds—and this practice was apparently quite successful. John Catherall of the Soil Hill Pottery, Halifax, even went so far as to name his house 'Whistle Hall' to celebrate the new trade he had built up by means of these simple introductory gifts. A further outlet for the potter's wares were the earthenware-dealers' shops which sprang up in almost every large village or town during the late eighteenth and early nineteenth centuries. Usually these shops stocked a wide variety of pottery, including creamwares, Welsh-wares, salt-glazed stonewares, and transfer-printed or lustred whitewares, besides the coarse lead-glazed earthenwares. The normal practice was for the potter to visit dealers, showing his wares and taking as many orders as he could. It was a precarious business, for each potter tried to cut his prices to attract the most custom, but any diminution in the quality of his wares led to an immediate cancellation of the order. Price fixing and the terms of delivery were, therefore, of the utmost importance.

The actual units in which the pottery was bought and sold varied greatly throughout the country, but the most common were the 'cast' and the 'dozen', only extremely large or unusual items being sold individually. A cast, as used in the southern counties, was a unit of work and/or clay expended. A single 18in flower-pot, for example, made up one cast, as did seventy-two 2½in or sixty 3in plant pots. Other wares, such as chicken feeders, were also rated at so many per cast. This system greatly simplified both the accounts and the process of bargaining, as only the price per cast need be agreed, and not the price of each item. In the North of England the dozen was the standard unit. This term, first recorded in the North Devon potteries[3], originally referred to the capacity of the vessels—a dozen being the number of vessels which collectively held a dozen quarts, but now a dozen, a long dozen, a short dozen, a sea dozen, or a land dozen, varies from one pottery to another, and has ceased to be a rational standard unit.

Once the potter had gained his orders for so many casts or dozen of a certain range of his wares, he then proceeded to make them, carefully designing the shapes so that the pots would nest into one another for easy transport. If they were only to be carted a few miles, he would pack them carefully in straw in his cart and deliver them personally (p 62, top), but if they were to be transported farther they were usually crated and delivered either by carrier's waggon, canal barge, or very occasionally, by train. The crates (see p 62, bottom) were made of yew by the local basketmakers, though some potteries, such as those in Burton-in-Lonsdale in Yorkshire, employed their own basketmaker, who also wove individual wicker sheaths for large bottles, etc. In Natte's view of Silkstone Pottery of 1806 (Plate p 104) the crating process is shown : a potter in the foreground holds a wide pan which he is about to carry to the crateman, who is seen packing the wares in straw a few yards behind.

The type of ware most commonly made in these urban potteries had a red fabric, covered where necessary with a yellowish lead glaze. This type was made in almost every pottery, but in areas where industrialisation was minimal, particularly in the West of England, the old forms of materials and techniques were still retained : Barnstaple and Bideford still made their sgraffito wares, Donyatt continued its slip decoration, and Verwood went on making its coarse yellow-ware jugs and costrels. In the North, meanwhile, reduced greenwares of sixteenth-century style were still being produced at York up to the 1840s. Redwares, however, were made in the majority of the urban potteries in a great

(*above*) A potter delivering his wares to a dealer in Lower Kirkgate, Halifax, from a drawing by John Horner, 1825; (*below*) a pottery crate of hazel, made early this century

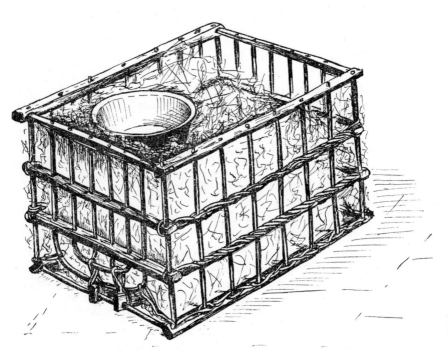

variety of new forms to meet the needs of both the industrial population and the farmers and dairymen who helped to feed them. Each region of the country had its own range of redware forms, suited to local requirements (though, as has been said, the passage of journeymen and potters from one pottery to another did tend to unify the forms more than ever before).

The North-east

Compared with other parts of the country, the wares of the North-east had a very limited range, only pressed-ware dishes, stewpots, and large bread-crocks or brewing-jars being made in any quantity. The pressed-ware dishes, almost exclusive to this region in form, were rectangular in shape, with rounded corners, an optional dividing wall across the middle, and crude white slip scrolls trailed round their internal bases and sides. They were

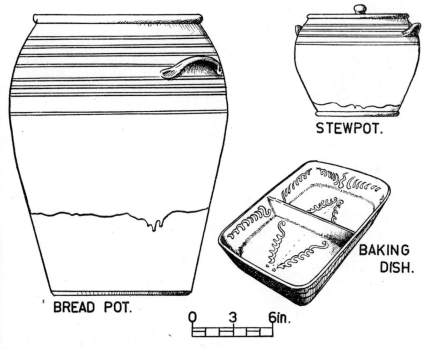

STEWPOT.

BAKING DISH.

' BREAD POT.

0   3   6in.

The wares of the North-east

used mainly as oven dishes for roasting or baking, and are frequently inscribed 'Fireproof' underneath. The stewpots, now called casseroles, had two small opposed handles near the rim, a flat pottery lid, and three or four trailed bands of white slip about their shoulders, a typical North-eastern feature. Bread-crocks or brewing-jars, their exact use being determined by the size and/or inclination of the family, were large convex-sided vessels up to 3ft in height and 2ft in diameter, with wide mouths and two, four, or even six handles spaced round the widest section of their bodies. These, too, were decorated with groups of white slipbands about their shoulders. Very little ornamental ware was made in this region, probably because the Sunderland potteries, with their lustred and transfer-printed whitewares, were better equipped to undertake this type of work. Some decorative redwares were made in the North-east, however, including chests of drawers, salt-kits, money boxes, and mugs, all very like those of the Yorkshire potteries.

The North-west

The North-western potteries made a good range of utilitarian wares (Plate p 103), as shown by the following list of products of the Weatheriggs Pottery, near Penrith:

Barm-pots	Flower-pots
Beetle-traps	Hen and Chickens Money Boxes
Bread-pots	Jugs
Butter-pots	Mugs
Cream-pots	Pancheons
Drain-pipes	Salt-kits

Most of these wares were quite plain, but jugs, mugs, and salt-kits were often decorated with a white slip-trailed design of vertical zig-zag lines ('the sea') between rows of dots ('the fishes') and finally rows of comma-shaped dashes ('the men'). The forms of the bread-pot and the beetle-trap were almost exclusive to this area: the bread-pot was a pure cylinder with two handles and a flat pottery lid, and the beetle-trap had a rough-surfaced stepped outer slope leading up to a highly glazed well. In use the well was partially filled with an aromatic liquid that attracted the insects up the slope, over the brink, and so into the liquid, where they drowned.

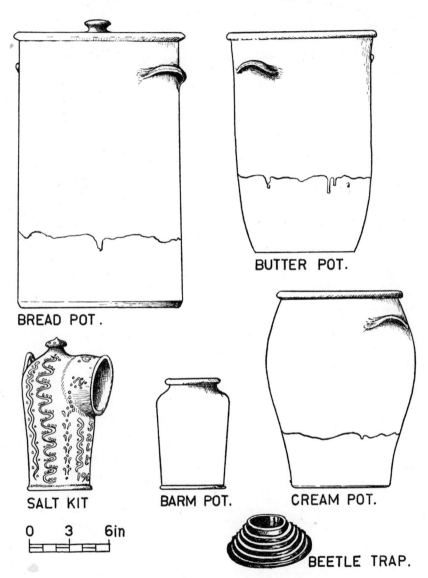

BREAD POT.

BUTTER POT.

SALT KIT

BARM POT.

CREAM POT.

0   3   6in

BEETLE TRAP.

The wares of the North-west, drawn at the Weatheriggs Pottery

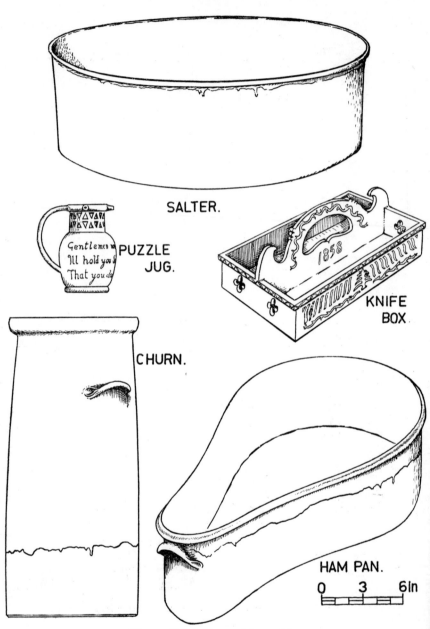

SALTER.

PUZZLE JUG.

Gentlemen
I'll hold you
That you do

1858

KNIFE BOX.

CHURN.

HAM PAN.

0   3   6 in

Wares of Yorkshire and Lancashire

West Yorkshire and East Lancashire

From the middle of the eighteenth century the towns and villages of this region had expanded rapidly as industrialisation progressed. The development of the Lancashire cotton industry and the Yorkshire woollen industry brought together increasingly large working populations, all of whom required cheap coarse earthenwares. The purely functional products made in this region included :

Barm-pots	Ham-pans	Mugs
Bread-pots	Jars	Pancheons
Brewing-jars	Jugs	Plant-pots
Butter-pots	Lading-pots	Plates
Chamber-pots	Milk churns	Salters
Cream-pots	Milk-settling pans	Spittoons
		Stewpots

The bread-pots and stewpots were of a similar shape to those used in the North-east, but lacked the trailed slip bands about their shoulders. A wide range of wares decorated with dipped and trailed slip; sgraffito; inlayed, applied, or stamped clays; and agate ware fabrics were also made in the following forms :

Candle-holders	Knife boxes	Puzzle jugs
Chest of drawers	Loving cups	Salt-kits
Cradles	Money boxes	Teapots
Frog mugs	Plant-pots	

The North Midlands

This region, which included South Staffordshire, Derbyshire, Nottinghamshire, South Yorkshire, and North Leicestershire, tended to continue the pottery traditions of seventeenth-century Staffordshire. Pressed-ware plates were still being made here in the early nineteenth century with Staffordshire-type trailed decoration, marbling, and even sgraffito. Although 'Bargee' wares were introduced in the mid-late nineteenth century, the most common productions were :

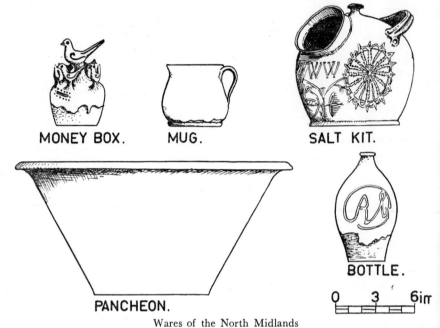

MONEY BOX.   MUG.   SALT KIT.

BOTTLE.

PANCHEON.

0   3   6in

Wares of the North Midlands

Barm pots	Pancheons
Bottles	Salt-kits
Hen & Chickens money boxes	Pressed-ware plates with
Honey-pots	marbled, trailed, or sgraffito
Mugs	decoration

The South

Two main groups of potteries make up this region—those of the Hampshire-Surrey border, serving their own locality and London, and those of Fareham, in South Hampshire, serving the towns of Southampton, Fareham, Gosport, and Portsmouth. These potteries made little or no decorated ware, but concentrated instead on the making of coarse redwares. The following list of products made at the Farnham Pottery late last century is typical:

Bread-pots	Lard-pots	Plant-pots
Chicken feeders	Milk pans	Pork pans
Chimney-pots	Paint-pots	Seakale-pots
Drain-pipes	Pans (misc)	Stands

The southern bread-pots were almost cylindrical, and about as

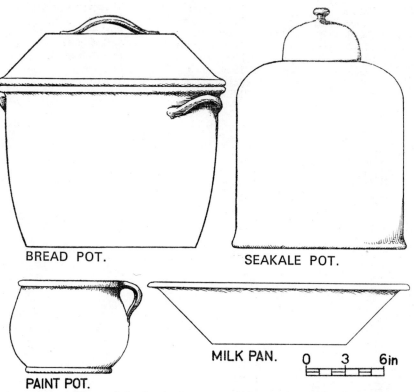

BREAD POT.

SEAKALE POT.

PAINT POT.

MILK PAN.   0   3   6in

Wares of the South, drawn at the Farnham Pottery

wide as they were tall, having two handles near the rim and a deep lid in the form of a truncated cone with a single strap handle across the top. It is noticeable that all the harvest bottles used in the surrounding areas, which were predominantly agrarian, were 'imported' from the Verwood kilns of the New Forest. These kilns had established this monopoly by their good reputation and by long usage.

Sussex

The Sussex potters served most of the rural areas of south-eastern England during the late eighteenth and nineteenth centuries, producing a wide range of utilitarian wares, as shown by the following list from the mid-nineteenth century Brede pottery:

Bottles	Flower-pots	Money-pots
Butter dishes	Flower pans	Pipkins
Candlesticks	Glazed Basins	Pitchers
Chicken pans	Glazed crocks	Seakale-pots
Chimney-pots	Ham pans	Sewer-pipes
Common Chambers	Hand-bowls	Spittoons
Glazed Chambers	Jars	Tongue pans
Dishes	Milk pans	(churns)

BARREL.   FLASK.   JAR.

BOTTLE.   PITCHER.   PIG.

0   3   6in

Wares of Sussex

Often these wares were decorated in applied clays, or trailed or dipped slips. The characteristic technique of decoration was the inlaying of white slip into recesses stamped into the leather-hard pot with printer's type, which technique gave particularly well defined and attractive results, and was extremely popular.

The South-west

The potteries of the South-west, the most important being situated at Barnstaple and Bideford in North Devon and at Truro in Cornwall, made wares for export to Wales and Ireland in addition to those for the purely local markets. Perhaps their most characteristic products were their decorative sgraffito jugs and their 'cloam' ovens, the latter being tempered with coarse grit taken from the River Torridge at Bideford. The following list covers the products made at the North Devon pottery of Fremington:

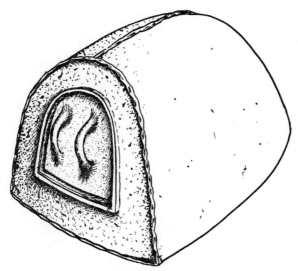

A North Devon oven

Baking dishes, round or oval	Pans: Widebottoms
Bread-crocks	Cawderns
Bussas	Bigpans
Butter-pots	Washpans
Casseroles	Pantiles
Collanders	Pipkins
Cream pans	Pitchers: 1, 1½, & 3pt
Flower-pots	4pt Pinchguts
Gallipots	Gullymouths
Great-crocks	Thirtytales
Ovens, from 2 to 12 peck sizes	8pt Long Toms
Owlsheads	

Notes for this chapter are on page 159.

Chapter Four

Art Wares

Most coarse-ware potters of the eighteenth and nineteenth centuries considered themselves to be craftsmen, and fairly low-grade craftsmen at that. They could not realistically compare themselves with the cabinetmakers, silversmiths or coachbuilders who produced choice items for a genteel and informed clientele, and they did not attempt to ape their elegant styles. The coarse-ware potter was a maker of utilitarian wares, and only made ornamental pieces specifically to order. Any suggestion that the potter was an artist, a creator of beauty, would have been considered ridiculous. This does not mean that the wares he made were necessarily ill-proportioned or ugly, but it does mean that any aesthetic appeal they might have was based on their function: a well proportioned, flowing handle is easier for a skilled potter to make and fire than an angular design, and is also stronger; a graceful spout usually pours best, and vessels with spouts that spurted or dripped just would not sell. By using clay all his life the potter came to know almost instinctively what was 'right' for it, and so worked in complete sympathy with his materials.

From the early-mid nineteenth century there was a great increase in public demand for cheap decorative wares, which were within the scope of most competent earthenware potters. The initial demand arose in the late 1830s. As a result of the industrial legislation of the 30s and 40s, combined with a general rise in the standard of living, the urban population was enabled to look beyond its own cramped industrial surroundings. The countryside, together with all things natural and God-made, which had been taken almost for granted half a century before, now became a constant source of interest. Spurred on by the lectures, books and museum exhibits of the local Mechanics Institutes, working men collected and adorned their homes with all manner of natural trivia, such as stuffed fishes and birds, dried and pressed sea-weeds, flowers or grasses, fossils and birds' eggs. It was the period of the Wardian case and the fern-pot. This growing interest in natural history resulted in the production of fern-stands, plant-stands, and 'Rustic ferneries' at many small urban potteries. As the century progressed these semi-horticultural wares became increasingly popular, so that by the 1860s the range frequently included such vessels as bouquet holders, trellis-work flower-pot holders (bearing a remarkable similarity to the present-day plastic variety), 'Rustic wall-pots', and 'Rustic Epergnes'. The term rustic in most cases meant that the pot had been deeply scored with a fork to give a realistic bark-like finish, and clay 'knots' had been modelled about the form, each one being high-lighted with bands of white slip about its tip. Such wares were exhibited at the Great Exhibition of 1851, which itself acted as a great stimulant to the public's interest in design.

Following the success of rustic wares many potters discovered how enjoyable, and even lucrative, the production of decorative wares could be. Some, such as Edward Bingham of the Castle Hedingham Pottery, Essex, even went so far as to abandon the making of domestic wares, so becoming an artist-potter rather than a local craftsman pure and simple. Two main influences fostered this change in the potter's outlook: firstly, from a chronological point of view, the eclecticism of the mid-Victorian collector, and, secondly, the development of the Arts and Crafts movement.

The mid-late nineteenth century was an outstanding period for collecting. Specimens relating to both natural and local history, coins, stamps, books, and by no means least, pottery, were all eagerly sought after, the size and quality of each col-lection being a source of pride to its owner. One class of material that began to be collected was early English pottery, both medieval and post-medieval. Public interest in these wares was considerably increased by the publication of a number of illus-trated books on the subject, including: *Collections towards a History of Pottery*, by J. Marryat, 1850; *The Catalogue of*

Art Wares

Specimens in the Museum of Practical Geology, British Pottery & Porcelain, 1855 and 1871; *Marks and Monograms on Pottery & Porcelain*, by W. Chaffers, 1863; *The Ceramic Art of Great Britain*, by L. Jewitt, 1878; and *The Art of the Old English Potter*, by L. M. Solon, 1883.

If a particular piece was required, either for decorative purposes or for fraudulent sale to a collector, it was a simple enough matter to order one from the local potter. He still used the same materials and techniques as were employed in making the originals, and his products, modelled from the illustrations in the volumes listed above, were virtually identical to the genuine wares. So convincing were some of these reproductions that they even found their way into the national collections, including those of the British Museum, but recent work by the Museum's staff has now successfully weeded out these spurious pieces[1]. A further source of these wares was the potter himself. If a collector was searching for examples of seventeenth- or eighteenth-century coarsewares, for example, what could be more natural than for him to ask the contemporary potters if they knew the whereabouts of any. An unscrupulous potter would answer that he might be able to locate a suitable pot, and make it himself, adding a suitable date and often abrading the surface slightly to give the impression of age and wear. A piece of this type is now to be seen in the Yorkshire Museum at York. It is a small jug, reputed to have been made at the Woodman House pottery during the early eighteenth century, but actually made by Nicholas Taylor of the Denholme pottery to satisfy the request of Mr Oxley Grabham, the curator of the museum, for a genuine piece of early Woodman House ware.

The Arts and Crafts movement was promoted by such men as John Ruskin and William Morris, who preached a doctrine of beauty through craftsmanship. The Utopia they envisaged was largely based on their concept of the English guild system of the fourteenth century, every craftsman being an artist in his own right, producing each item with loving and unfailing care. As a result of their teachings and copious publications a number of 'guilds' of craftsmen/designers, set up during the 1880s[2] and organised in a pseudo-medieval manner, produced limited quantities of fine hand-made craftwork. Naturally such work was expensive, but the urban potter was perfectly capable of supplying the average household with cheaper substitutes, which, even if they lacked the aesthetic finesse of the guild productions, were certainly well made technically[3]. By the use of metallic oxides, the newly-developed 'Wenger's' colours, and a great deal of personal experimentation with combinations of the traditional materials, completely fresh types of ware were evolved, some potteries building up a considerable reputation for a particular variety.

The Farnham pottery[4], for example, became exceptionally well known for its 'Farnham Greenwares' (plate, p 103). Up to about 1880 the pottery had made nothing but coarse redwares, but then Birket Foster, the watercolourist and illustrator, brought a French green-glazed garden vase to the pottery, asking the proprietor, Absalom Harris, to produce a number of copies for him. After repeated experiments a suitable glaze and fabric were developed, and the order completed. Much to Absalom's surprise the many experimental pieces he had made sold well, and so he began to produce a few 'art' wares in the same materials. His success as a copier also brought in extra business: two Roman jars for the collection of Mr Heath of Hollycombe, and a collection of sixteenth-century Tudor greenwares excavated from the city of London, both being copied in 1885. The owners of this collection, J. C. & B. Hook, had read of the letter, sent from the Inns of Court in 1594, which requested the controller of Farnham Park to allow the potters to obtain their supplies of white clay for making the 'greene potts usually drunk in by the gentlemen of the Temple'[5], and wished to have their copies made from the same materials; fortunately the Farnham Park Claypits were still open, though they had not been used since 1865, and so Absalom was able to produce identical wares.

In 1889 a new master arrived at the Farnham School of Art, Mr W. H. Allen, who had formerly worked as a freelance for the Victoria and Albert Museum, and who possessed a wide knowledge of English ceramics and design in general. Within a few months he had supplied the potters with fresh designs for art wares and also for further 'Tudor greenwares', copied in detail from originals in the Victoria and Albert Museum's collection. In December 1890 the pottery had its first public showing at an exhibition at the Farnham School of Art, at which many orders were taken. The well known London firms, Heal's and Liberty's, and the Rural Industries Society, all began to stock the ware, and the pottery's turnover more than doubled. Extra staff were employed, and a showroom built at the works for the benefit of customers. For the next twenty years the pottery produced ever-increasing quantities of Farnham greenware, but in 1914 the First World War broke out and killed the demand for art pottery within a few months. After the war its popularity revived; the public wanted bright shiny colourful wares, which Farnham made in vivid green, blue, and yellow lead glazes. It was a short-lived popularity, however, for the economic depression of the 20s and 30s ruined the market for purely ornamental pieces, and the sale of art ware came to an end.

The story of the Farnham pottery is typical of many others scattered throughout the country. Most made some form of art ware, as it provided a good alternative source of income at a time when the potter's traditional markets were failing. In nearly every case the potter tried to become a ceramic virtuoso, neglecting his native traditions to demonstrate his skill and versatility. The results were often ghastly. Well proportioned, soundly made wares, the results of a gradual evolvement of style and technique, rapidly degenerated as the potters attempted to become artists. Sussex pottery of this period often sagged under an oppressive weight of over-detailed modelling, while Halifax ware was finally embalmed in massed pink roses, both modelled and transfer-printed. It was fine for the potter while it lasted, specially before the First World War, but in the depression of the late 20s and early 30s, many potters were forced out of business.

Notes for this chapter are on pages 159-60.

Chapter Five

The Decline of the Potteries

The success of the urban potteries depended on the existence of large poorly paid communities who could not afford to buy higher quality wares than they produced. It was for this reason that they had grown up chiefly round the new industrial centres of the late eighteenth century and there made largely functional wares. From the mid-nineteenth century, however, the state of their market began to change as their customers' standard of living improved. Industrially produced wares were also becoming cheaper, and new substitutes for earthenware being developed.

A glance through the lists of wares at the end of Chapter 3 shows that most potteries made a range of brewing-pots, pancheons, barm-pots, pork and ham pans, butter-pots, etc, all designed for the preparation or storage of food in the home. In a rural situation the wife had been expected to produce her own beer, bread, and salted provisions, for which the above wares were essential. Even when the family left the country and moved into the town, these activities were at first continued; but they waned as the advantages of urban life were realised. Brewing, for example, was quite an expensive business, consuming large quantities of both time and fuel, and it was now much simpler to buy one's ale from one of the beer-houses set up after the Beer-house Act of 1830 than to brew one's own. Although half the beer made in this country was still being home-brewed in 1800, by 1850 the proportion was down to one seventh, falling in 1870 to one fortieth[1], thus illustrating the great decline in home-brewing, and in the sale of brewing-pots also. The home-baking of bread suffered a similar fate as new town bakeries were built, so cutting the sales of pancheons and barm (yeast) pots; though the former did remain in production in the West Riding as late as 1964 as many families still retained one for occasional use, particularly the baking of the Christmas cake. Butter salting, in which a stone or two of butter was preserved in a tall butter-pot, and the home pickling of hams and pork joints in brine were also discontinued about the mid-late nineteenth century.

In addition to this loss of trade the urban potter had also to face growing competition from the industrial potteries. Just as the Staffordshire potteries had captured the entire Midlands market in the seventeenth century through their unique geological situation and well developed marketing methods, so the factory potteries, specially those in and round Stoke-on-Trent, began to take over the urban potter's trade in tablewares such as jugs, mugs, plates, teapots, etc. The reasons were three-fold. Firstly, the diffusion of mass-production techniques throughout the pottery factories now made it possible to offer the public cheap good-quality whitewares for the first time. White-coloured cast and moulded pottery had now been placed within reach of the working classes, and so it started out with an immediate prestige value, besides being much superior to the work of the urban potter. The cast bodies of this tableware were bright, clean-looking, and light in weight; their glazes were clear and glossy; and their decoration, either transfer-printed or hand-painted, made them additionally attractive. As the whitewares were mainly retailed through the same channels as the coarsewares, ie, in the town earthenware dealer's shop, on the market stall, or on the cart of the travelling pot-man, they were in direct competition with the redwares of the urban potter, much to the disadvantage of the latter. Secondly, railway transport favoured the factory potters, who, with their reserves of capital, were able to bring china clay from Cornwall, and to deliver their pottery to any part of the country as they pleased. This was entirely beyond the means of the average urban potter with only his horse and cart and limited finance. Thirdly, the average income of the working classes was rising, wages increasing by an estimated 30 per cent between the 1850s and the 1880s[2], so they were now prepared to pay the marginal difference between the cost of the whitewares and that of the redwares in order to secure a much better pot.

As early as the second quarter of the nineteenth century the effects of industrial competition were beginning to be felt, and the urban potters started to make rather different ranges of ware. The growing demand for rustic wares and the rather more mundane flower pots for use in conservatories, etc, was fully exploited, offering as it did a timely substitute for the purely domestic wares. Later in the century some of these potteries went on to the production of art wares, thus being able to keep their staff fully employed.

About the same time a number of redware potteries, sensing the coming decline in their sales, began to make bricks, tiles, chimney-pots and field drain-pipes in addition to their normal product. This was a wise decision, for as the century progressed the building trade and the improvement of land through drainage both flourished, whereas the demand for coarse redwares waned.

This diversification into rustic and art wares, or ceramic building materials and drainage pipes, required both initiative and a certain amount of capital, two commodities which the coarse redware potters lacked. The whole organisation of the industry was anachronistic, still based on the family unit, the head of the family usually being the master potter and his sons acting as his apprentices. Some potters, it is true, possessed sufficient business acumen to transform their potteries into successful small companies, but they were the exceptions. As can be seen from the Gazetteer entries, many potteries were unable to withstand the factory potter's competition, and numerous closures resulted from the 1860s onwards.

The decline of the urban pottery industry was not at all sudden; it was a slow, almost unconscious, change, the gradual falling off of sales of one particular vessel and possibly the slightly increased demand for another. A great deal depended on the community that the potter served. In the North of England and the West Midlands the inhabitants of the large industrial towns were among the first to change over to factory-made wares, while the hill farmers of those regions, together with the agricultural communities of East Anglia, the South Coast, and the West Country were amongst the last. This was only to be expected, for the townsfolk would have had little use for anything but tablewares, which were factory-made, but in the country districts there was still a demand for harvest barrels, bottles, ham pans, and butter- and cream-pots, which no factory could provide. It is particularly noticeable that all the potteries continuing to make their traditional wares into the second half of the present century were all catering to rural areas—for example, the Weatheriggs Pottery, Penrith, serving the Lakeland Hills and the Pennine moorlands; the Littlethorpe Pottery, Ripon (plate, p 104), serving the Yorkshire dales and the North Yorkshire moors; the Wattisfield Pottery, serving East Anglia; the Farnham Pottery, between the North and South Downs; the Verwood Pottery, serving the New Forest and Cranborne Chase; and Lake's Pottery at Truro, serving the Cornish peninsula.

The outbreak of war in 1914 accelerated the collapse of the industry, since the market for art wares completely disappeared and many potters and their apprentices were conscripted into the armed forces. Those potteries that did manage to remain in production throughout the First World War were rewarded, however, with a wealth of new trade in the early 1920s. Art wares, specially if brightly coloured, were more popular than ever before, and bricks, tiles, and chimney-pots were all required as a fresh spate of building ensued. During this period the more successful potteries were able to expand considerably. Steam power and some degree of mechanisation became more common, and the number of employed staff frequently reached a total of twenty or more men. The war was over, and the country was looking forward to a long and prosperous peace.

Gradually this idyllic post-war phase came to an end. One by one the shops began to cancel their orders as economic depression set in, and the potteries were forced to lay off their staff as trade became increasingly scarce. In 1939 war broke out once more, bringing with it further troubles for the potter : fuel rationing, the provision of blackouts for the kilns, the lack of a sufficient market, and again the conscription of the potters and their apprentices. The effects of the depression of the 20s and 30s, combined with the difficulties experienced during the Second World War were catastrophic for the traditional hand-thrown pottery industry. They had finally killed the demand for its product, forced most of its skilled craftsmen to follow other trades as the potteries had failed, and prevented a new generation of craftsmen from being trained. In the opening decade of the present century there were still over a hundred potteries of this type in full operation, but by 1945, when the war ended, there were less than a dozen. Those potteries that did manage to survive into the late 1940s were all owned and worked by potters who had been trained as apprentices in the prosperous periods immediately before and after the First World War. Each of the potteries served a rural area where its products were still required, and each one made a wide range of horticultural wares, especially plant-pots and terrace jars, the latter becoming a particularly successful line. For a while it appeared as if these potteries were going to expand to their former size, and they would have done so had it not been for the shortage of craftsmen. Men returning from the war preferred easier, if less satisfying, occupations, and thus it has proved impossible for the existing potters to train a succeeding generation. If new staff could be found who were willing to be taught the craft the success of the potteries would be assured. Most potters today have more orders than they can handle, but they are growing old, and year by year their numbers are diminishing. In 1955 Meshech Sims, last of the Verwood potters, ceased production; in 1970 Fishley Holland of Fremington Pottery died; in 1964 Isaac Button, last of the Halifax potters, closed the Soil Hill Pottery; and in 1971 it is likely that the last two potteries in the North of England will finally close down also. If this trend continues at its present rate the craft of the English country potter will certainly have ceased by the end of the present century.

NOTE

Perhaps it should be stressed at this point that the writer has been concerned solely with the potters who operated their potteries in a purely traditional manner, digging their clay nearby, processing it themselves with the minimum of mechanisation, glazing it with glazes of their own preparation, and making their wares according to their regional tradition and/or the particular requirements of their own localities. It is true that a great number of new potteries have been opened within the last decade, principally in popular tourist areas, but these are of a completely different variety. They concentrate on making pottery for its aesthetic appeal rather than for its functional necessity, and use mainly bought-in materials. At first sight the difference may seem trifling, but it is just as great as that between a master mason and a sculptor, or between a blacksmith and a precision engineer.

Notes for this chapter are on page 160.

Chapter Six

Clay Preparation

Of all the basic raw materials required by the potter, clay is obviously the most important, for it was the availability of a good clay source that most commonly decided the location of the pottery. The average potter was not competent to choose his site from a geological map, even if he had access to one when they were first issued in the late eighteenth and early nineteenth centuries, and so he must have relied entirely on local knowledge of the subsoil. With no other aid than this, he had to find a site that was also close enough to a cheap supply of fuel and a reasonable market to make his efforts worthwhile. He also had to obtain the permission of the local landowner, usually the lord of the manor, to cut his claypit and extract his clay.

The control of claydigging varied from one area to another, but it was usual up to the eighteenth century on private land to grant claydigging licences, to rent or lease the claypits to the potters at a set sum per annum, or to charge the potters a fixed amount per load of clay extracted. The famous Farnham Park claypits, for example, were dug under licence of the Bishop of Winchester, Lord of the Manor of Farnham. Only licence-holders were allowed to dig and sell the clay, all others forfeiting their lands or paying a heavy fine for so doing. The potters of Potovens, on the other hand, rented their claypits as a group, each potter contributing towards the total rental. In a survey made for Sir Christopher Clapham, Lord of the Manor of Wakefield, in 1666 we find that 'the Potters farm [ie rent] the Clay att £10 pr. Ann. and if my Ld. would have suffered itt to have been ingross'd One Man bid £30 pr. Ann. for a Lease'[1]. On the Gwysaney Estate

83

at Buckley, near Chester, the potters were charged so much per load of clay taken from the pits, a much fairer system.

From the eighteenth century onwards most of the potters throughout the country obtained their clay either by purchasing their own plots, or by making a private agreement with the owner of land on a suitable clayfield. This change was brought about mainly by the various enclosures of the eighteenth and nineteenth centuries, which prevented the potters from digging their clay from pits on the open common, as had been their custom. In some areas the potters were unable to finance this new method of clay purchase, and had to close down. This was the fate of many of the potters in the large potting community of Ticknall, and, as Pilkington noted in his *View of Derbyshire* of 1803, 'the business [at Ticknall] has very much declined. It is said, that, since the land in the neighbourhood has been enclosed, it has been difficult to meet with proper clay'. Many potteries at this period only produced sufficient income to support the potter and his family, and were unable to afford the clay once they had lost the right to dig on common land.

Having obtained a site, the potter then proceeded to dig his clay, the depth and size of his 'pot-hole' or 'potter's pit' being determined by the situation of the clay and the amounts that he required. These pits were a continuing source of trouble for the local community, for the potters appear to have rarely refilled them. These open pits, often flooded with water, were dangerous, and numerous complaints were raised against them. In manorial and burgess courts throughout England there were hundreds of complaints and pains made against the potters, usually because the pits endangered the lives of both the local people and their livestock. In areas where the clay deposits lay just under the surface it was not uncommon for the potters to dig large holes in the roadways, where the clay was rendered down to an excellent consistency by the combined action of the weather and the passing traffic. At Burslem in 1549 Richard Daniel came before the courts for digging in 'the King's Way', and a little earlier, in 1533, the Wakefield Burgess Court ordered that 'the Cuppers from henceforth shall get no clay within eight yeards of the hye waye side.'

Often the claypit was only a matter of yards from the potter's workshop, but at other potteries horses and carts had to be kept

Page 85 Early decorated wares: *(left)* a North Devon sgraffito harvest jug of 1708; *(right)* a typical Wrotham tyg by 'IE' of 1697 (see notes on page 164)

Page 86 (above) A Sussex harvest barrel made by 'H. Foster', inscribed 'Dec th 1865-23' East Grinstead; (below) a Halifax wedding cradle of 1835. Both are decorated in their distinct regional styles (see notes on page 165)

both to transport the clay and to distribute the finished wares. Even this seemingly inoffensive method of transport brought the potters before the courts. At the West Riding Quarter Sessions of 1680-81 the potters were accused of 'driving waynes, Cartes & Carriages crosse over the said common and with horses and breaking ye soyle, making rutts and new wayes, digging and getting of clay for making pipes, potts, and other earthenwares, and making pitts and holes neare ye hye waye to the danger of travellers'. Sometimes the potter's waggons were required for other general purposes, including, appropriately enough, road making. The Burgesses of Nottingham, for example, had to fine Charles Morley the Nottingham potter 25s in 1637 'for being absent with his draught from Common worke 5 dayes, being lawfully summoned'.

For general purposes no clay would be carted for more than two or three miles, but clay for a particular job would be carted much farther. In the early 1840s Absalom Harris, then working at the Bishops Waltham potteries, had to take his waggon over 27 miles to Farnham Park to obtain a supply of white clay, unobtainable elsewhere, which was necessary to whiten the interiors of his milk pans.

In Staffordshire a great variety of clays was required. Details are given by Dr Robert Plot in his *Natural History of Staffordshire* of 1686 :

Other *potters' clays* for the more common wares, there are at many other places, particularly at *Horsley Heath* in the parish of *Tipton*; in *Monway Field* above mentioned, where there are two sorts gotten, one of a *yellowish* colour mixed with *white*, the other *blewish*; the former stiff and weighty, the other more friable and light, which, mixt together, work better than when apart. Of these they make divers sorts of *vessels* at *Wednesbury*, which they paint with *slip*, made of a *reddish* sort of *earth* gotten at *Tipton*. But the greatest *pottery* they have in this *county* is carried on at *Burslem*, near *Newcastle* under *Lyme*, where for making their several sorts of *pots*, they have as many different sorts of clay, which they dig round about the *towne*, all within half a mile's distance, the best being found nearest the *coale*, and are distinguish't by their *colours* and *uses* as foloweth;

1. *Bottle clay*, of a bright whitish streaked yellow colour.
2. *Hard fire clay* of a duller whitish colour, and fuller intersperst with a dark yellow, which they use for their *black ware*, being mixt with the
3. *Red blending clay*, which is of a dirty red colour.
4. *White clay*, so called it seems, though of a blewish colour, and used for making yellow colour'd *ware*, because yellow is the *lightest* colour they make any *ware* of.

All which they call *throwing* clays, because they are of a closer texture, and will work on the *wheel*; which none of the three other *clays* they call *slips*, will any of them doe, being of looser and more friable natures; these mixed with water they make into a consistence thinner than a *syrup*, so that being put into a *bucket* it will run out through a quill, this they call *slip,* and is the substance wherewith they *paint* their *wares*; whereof the

1. Sort is called the *orange slip*, which before it is work't is of a greyish colour mixt with orange balls, and gives the ware [when annealed] an *orange* colour
2. The white *slip*, this before it is work't is of a dark blewish colour, yet makes the ware yellow, which being the *lightest* colour they make any of, they call it [as they did the clay above] the *white* slip.
3. The *red slip*, made of a dirty reddish clay, which gives wares a black colour.

These clay deposits were exceptional, however, and most potteries had a choice of only one or two clays. The great string of potteries lying on the coal-measure pot-clay seams in the North of England were fortunate to be able to dig a red throwing clay, a buff fireclay, and a white clay for slip making, Many other potteries, such as those in Northamptonshire, had only one clay to work from, and this was frequently poor and impure in quality.

Cleaning the Clay

Most of the clays found in England had to be treated before they could be successfully converted into pottery; only a few beds of alluvial clay, such as those of the Ure valley at Littlethorpe near Ripon, are made up of so pure a mixture of clay and sand that they may be used almost straight from the claypit. Most clays used by the country potter are rather coarse, dense, and impure when excavated, and lack the plasticity necessary for good pot-making. To remedy these faults the potters of each area evolved their own techniques.

Unfortunately there are no records of how clays were prepared before the seventeenth century, and no clayworking areas have yet been discovered on any of the kiln sites excavated. Some form of preparation must have taken place, however, for the clay used in making Cistercian wares in particular was well cleaned, all traces of coarse sand and pebbles being removed to leave only the pure red or off-white fabric.

Clay Preparation

Perhaps the earliest account of clay preparation is that of Dr Plot in 1686. After describing the various clays used by the Staffordshire potters he continues: 'Neither of which *clays* or *slips* must have any *gravel* or *sand* in them. Upon this account, before it be brought to the *wheel* they prepare the *clay* by steeping it in water in a square pit, till it be of a due consistence; then they bring it to their *beating board*, where with a long *spatula* they beat it till it be well mix't; then being first made into great *squarish* rolls, it is brought to the wageing board, where it is slit into flat thin pieces with a *wire*, and the least stones or gravel pick't out of it'. This description shows that the clay was softened by soaking and then the process of purification consisted merely of slicing the clay thinly and picking out any stones.

A similar method is still used today at the Farnham potteries. The clay is thrown in lumps into a square soaking pit, together with a quantity of sand, the proportion being one part of sand to five parts of clay. This mixture is necessary at Farnham to ensure a standard shrinkage of one-eighth in the drying and firing of the pots, and also to make the firing easier. After being coarsely mixed and allowed to soak for some time in the pit, the clay is then dug out and beaten to a uniform consistency in a pug mill.

This rather crude method of preparation developed into the sun-pan of the late seventeenth or early eighteenth century. A good description of the Staffordshire sun-pans is given by Simeon Shaw in his *History of the Staffordshire Potteries* of 1829:

The *Sun Kiln* is formed usually square, 16 to 20 feet in extent each way, and about 18 inches deep, having at one corner a smaller place, deeper, and lined with slabs or flags. The clay, after being brought out of the mine is spread abroad on the adjoining ground, and frequently turned over by the spade during two or three seasons, that it may be well exposed to the action of the atmosphere (called *weathering*). Into the smaller vat a quantity of clay is thrown, and by a proper tool *blunged* in the water by agitation, till all the heavier particles and small stones sink to the bottom; the fluid mass is next poured into a sieve, thro' which it runs into the largest vat, or sun kiln, until the whole surface is covered to the depth of three or four inches, which is left to be evaporated by solar action. When this is partly accomplished, another layer, and a third and fourth are added, until the mass is from 12 to 18 inches deep; and the whole is then cut out and placed in a damp cellar for use.

Most country potteries used this technique, each having its own particular method of dissolving the raw clay in water, or blunging.

Perhaps the crudest form of blunging was that used at the Denholm and Burton-in-Lonsdale potteries until machinery was first introduced in the late nineteenth century. The clay was placed in a shallow trough of water that had a flagstone set vertically at one end. A long board with a handle attached to one of its ends rested on the top edge of the flagstone and dipped into the trough. By pushing the board backwards and forwards, the clay and water mixture was slowly broken down to the con-

The steam blunger at the Weatheriggs Pottery, 1970

sistency of thick cream; the clay was then run off through a sieve into the sun-pan where the surplus water slowly evaporated.

At Buckley, near Chester, this process of blunging was worked by a horse. In Warner's *Walk Through Wales* of 1798 we are informed that the Buckley potters placed their clay 'in a circular cistern called a blunging pool, when, whilst it is covered with water, it is kneaded by a cylindrical machine which performs a double revolution round its own axis and an upright pole in the centre, and pounds it completely . . . and lastly it is passed through a fine silk sieve to free it from stones and dirt'.

Claymills of this type, with their two vertical crushing wheels and circular claypan beneath, were later developed for use by both potters and brickmakers by such firms as Messrs Bradley & Craven of Wakefield. When strongly made of cast iron, they could be worked by steam power, and towards the end of the nineteenth century they were to be found in many small potteries, such as that at Soil Hill, where steam was installed in 1898.

A second type is still to be seen at the Weatheriggs pottery near Penrith (see p 90). This steam-powered blunger, built in 1855, consists of a circular brick-lined trough some 14ft in diameter and 3ft deep. Suspended above this trough by means of a massive central axis are two heavy iron frames, each having a number of tines about 9in long stretching down almost to the

The Weatheriggs sunpan with the blunger in the background, 1970

floor of the trough. In operation the trough is half filled with clay and water and the blunger set in motion, the tines rotating and breaking down the clay into a fine solution. Once the lumps have all been dissolved the blunger is stopped, and the stones, etc, allowed to settle to the bottom of the trough. Then, by means of a small sluice, the clay solution is run off down a stone-lined channel into the sunpan (above), where the excess water is naturally evaporated. All the heavy impurities remain behind in the trough itself.

From about 1900 onwards various types of vaned blunger came into more general use. These had been used in industrial potteries from the late eighteenth century at least, but it was not until the late nineteenth century that the average country potter was able to provide suitable power, usually steam, to be able to operate one successfully. The vaned blunger consisted of a deep tub in which a number of rapidly rotating paddles agitated the clay until it was completely dissolved in the water, after which it was run off to be sieved and evaporated.

Another technique copied from the industrial potters at this time was the use of artificial heat to dry the clay in the sun-pan. Long flues were laid beneath the pan and heat passed through them from a specially constructed fireplace, or from the kiln if it was a down-draught type. More clay could be prepared more quickly by this method, and the claypan could be roofed over, thus freeing the potter from his dependence on the English summer weather.

The Pug Mill

When the clay had been purified, and lay in a soft mass in the claypan, it still had to be brought to a state of maximum plasticity before being formed into pottery. The first step was to take a quantity of clay from the pan and pile it on the clayhouse floor. Here it was 'tempered' by being trampled underfoot, the potters of northern England wearing heavy clogs for this operation, while others, such as those of Buckley, worked the clay with their bare feet. Slowly more and more clay was added to the heap and trampled, until a large 'dess' of clay, up to 4yd square and 2ft deep was built up. The potter then used this stock of clay as he required, digging out a lump, kneading or wedging it on his bench to remove any air pockets or hard lumps that might remain, and finally weighing it into balls ready for throwing. This trampling process continued to be used in some potteries up to the 1950s, but in other potteries, particularly in the South of England, it was mechanised by the introduction of the pug mill early in the eighteenth century.

The first pug mill had an iron-bound wooden tub, down the centre of which ran a heavy iron spindle, turned by means of a long beam hauled round by the pottery horse (see p 93). A number of long knives protruded horizontally from the central spindle, and they were set at a slight angle so that the clay from the claypan would be slowly sliced and pressed downwards to issue as a long extruded strip of uniform clay from the base of the mill. Fishley Holland, commenting on the pug at Fremington Pottery in the early 1900s, tells us that when the old horse driver died, he was detailed to the job 'and so learnt to mix the various clays for the different kinds of pots; as dug, for small pots and pitchers; some fine Bideford grit for large pots and pitchers, and more grit for the cooking pots. The clay was wet down, chopped and slapped before being put through the pugmill twice . . . It was stiff work, and "Jumbo" [the pottery horse] knew that after six rounds he was entitled to a rest'.

These machines were often made by one of the local craftsmen, usually the cooper, and not by any specialist manufacturer. At William Smith's pottery at Farnborough, for example, the

The pug mill, from Pyne's *Costume of Great Britain* 1808

pug mill was made in the mid-nineteenth century by Mr Sturt of Farnham, the local wheelwright.

The horse-operated pug mill fell out of use towards 1900 and was replaced by the cast-iron mill powered by steam, which can be seen in all the country potteries still working today. Even with the introduction of these labour-saving devices, however, the potter's traditional methods died hard, and potters such as Mr Sims of Verwood were still trampling their clay well into the 1940s.

Each particular pot required a known weight or volume of clay. In most potteries the shape of the ball was directly related to the shape of the finished vessel, but in some regions the potters always started to make their pots by using a ball of a particular shape : in North Devon they preferred a flat cheese-shaped ball and in Staffordshire a taller conical ball.

Note for this chapter is on page 160.

Chapter Seven

Potting

The methods used by the country potter to convert his clay into useful wares can be divided into three categories—throwing, pressing, and forming. In the first method the potter takes a lump of clay, throws it on to the potter's wheel, and swiftly shapes it by hand as it revolves; in the second he presses the clay into prepared moulds; and in the third he uses his bare hands and feet to work the clay into its final shape.

Throwing

The essential piece of equipment required for throwing is, of course, the wheel. Wheels of varying types have been used in England from the late Saxon period up to the present day, but unfortunately we have no information on their construction before the mid-late eighteenth century. The wheels in use then were so crude, however, that they were probably little different from those used during the preceding 2-300 years.

The simplest form of wheel used in England and on the Continent was the disc-wheel, shown on p 96. This wheel had a vertical shaft with the potter's wheel itself at the top, and a simple bearing at the base. Just above the bearing a large stone flywheel was mounted horizontally in such a position that the potter could kick it round with a fair degree of ease, thus powering his wheel. When Warner made his visit to the Buckley potteries shortly before 1798 he found that this was still the only type of wheel in use, and the same wheel was illustrated by Pyne in his *Microcosm*

95

The disc-wheel, from Pyne's *Microcosm* of 1806. This wheel was powered
by the thrower, who swung his legs with a running action

The crank-wheel, from Pyne's *Costume of Great Britain* 1808. This type of
wheel is still in use at the Farnham pottery

of 1806. From this time on the disc-wheel fell rapidly out of use, and by the mid-nineteenth century was completely obsolete except for chimney-pot making, where a low wheel-head was necessary.

By the late 1790s at least, the crank-wheel (opposite) had developed from the archaic disc-wheel. In this new machine the large stone flywheel was discarded, and the motion supplied instead by a crank-and-rod arrangement powered by a labourer. Although requiring two men to operate it, this wheel had the great advantage of allowing the thrower to concentrate his whole mind and energy on shaping the pots, and thus the output was much increased. The potters of southern England in particular found the crank-wheel highly suitable for making their larger wares, where a comparatively slow speed was required. At Verwood this wheel was still being used as late as the 1950s, while at the Farnham Potteries a single example is still in regular use at the present time.

Once the crank-wheel had become established it was a relatively easy matter to convert the crank and rod into a crank and foot-pedal, so producing the kick-wheel. Kick-wheels were installed in many potteries throughout England during the second half of the nineteenth century, but they were not popular with the professional throwers. They were a convenient wheel for coarse work, or for the apprentice to practise on, but they provided no competition for the power-wheels described below. During the present century this situation has been reversed, for the potters can no longer employ a man to turn their wheels, and now, next to the electric-wheel, they are the most popular potter's wheels in use.

During the early eighteenth century a new type of wheel was introduced to the pottery: the great-wheel. One example of this type, that used by Josiah Wedgwood, can still be seen in the City Museum, Hanley, Stoke-on-Trent. The wheel is powered by means of a large pulley wheel about 6ft in diameter, from which a cord passes beneath a set of rollers to a pulley on the shaft of the wheel itself (see p 98). The technique is very similar to that used by wheelwrights for operating their lathes, and it is possible that this form of transmission was adapted from the lathe. In use, the large wheel was slowly turned by the turner, who was usually a labourer specifically employed for the job, though an

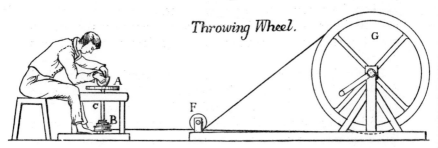

Throwing Wheel.

The great-wheel, from Chambers' *Cyclopedia* 1834

apprentice often undertook the work, as it gave him a good opportunity to study throwing techniques. For making a large pot, the wheel would be required to turn at a range of speeds: fast for centring, medium for raising, and slow for finishing off. The thrower would call out the speed he required to the turner, but with practice this was unnecessary, and the turner automatically varied the speed himself. For small wares, however, the wheel was turned continuously at a steady pace, the thrower rapidly throwing the pots, removing them by a deft flick of his right thumb, catching them with his left hand, and finally placing them on a board to dry. To the present-day potter this kind of throwing sounds almost impossible, but to the skilled potter of the nineteenth century, equipped with a five-year apprenticeship and a thousand-year-old tradition, it was just everyday work. The great-wheel was widely used in England, and continued in all but the smallest works until replaced by the steam power-wheel.

When steam power was introduced in the late nineteenth century many potteries used it for throwing, and installed heavy cast-iron framed wheels. Two distinct speed controls were employed. In the most common type two cones were placed head to tail in such a way that the alteration of the angle of one determined the point of contact, and therefore the speed, of the other. The second variety received its power from a small driving wheel that was able to slide from the centre to the edge of a large horizontal disc on the main shaft of the wheel. For slow speeds the driving wheel engaged the perimeter of the disc, the speed gradually increasing as the driving wheel moved inwards towards the shaft. Both the above wheels were fitted with foot pedals with which the potter could vary the speed just as he wished.

Over the last two decades the remaining country potters have all dismantled their steam engines because of the rising cost of fuel and the inconvenience of having to raise steam for a greatly reduced staff. In most cases, however, a petrol engine or electric motor has taken the place of the steam engine, and the formerly steam-operated plants still remain in use.

To prepare the wheel for throwing, the potter first makes sure that he has all his tools and a supply of water readily to hand, and then starts to prepare the wheel-head. If he is a bigware potter, working in the south of England, he will do this by slightly damping the wheel, sticking a pad of soft clay on it, levelling this pad, and banging a circular board, or bat, on top of it to form a false wheel-head on which to throw. Once the pot has been completed he will lever the bat off its clay support and lift it clear, pot and all. The potter on p 96 (below) is throwing in this way, and his stock of bats can be seen stacked at his side on the shelf above the wheel. In the North this technique would be used for nothing but extra large pots, perhaps over 2ft in diameter, all other vessels being thrown as normal on the bare wheel-head, sliced free with a dry wire, and lifted clear by hand. Mr Curtis of Littlethorpe, the last bigware potter in the country, has no difficulty in removing such items as a 30in pancheon from the wheel, his technique being to free the pot from the wheel with a dry wire and lift it directly upwards by encircling it with his arms, occasionally joining his hands behind it with a length of broad lath for additional support.

To make a pot the thrower first takes his ball of clay and smacks it firmly into place on the centre of his wheel. Then, spinning his wheel rapidly anti-clockwise, he lubricates his hands with water and proceeds to 'centre' the clay, pressing it with both hands until it is perfectly concentric. This task, though seemingly simple, needs considerable experience. Once the clay has been centred the shaping of the pot begins.

In Staffordshire it was customary to start by centring a tall conical ball, hollowing it out at the top with the thumbs, and pulling the upper rim to its final size. The left fist, led by the crooked forefinger, was then plunged down into the centre of the clay until it rested a short distance above the wheel, when it was pushed outwards to form the bottom of the pot to its final size.

99

Mr Curtis knuckling up on his double-cone drive wheel at Littlethorpe, 1967

In these operations the sides of the pot had been forced to rise upwards, so, as the top and bottom were finished, it only remained to straighten up the sides, and the pot was shaped.

Other areas used a simpler technique in which a rather flat ball was centred and then hollowed by the use of the thumbs and the left hand. By these means a thick-walled cylinder of clay was produced, and to bring this up to its finished shape a number of 'knuckling up' movements or 'draughts' were made. These consisted of pulling up the clay between the knuckles, the right hand pressing outwards and upwards from inside the pot, while a similar inwards motion was performed by the left hand from outside (opposite). After two or three draughts the pot had reached its full height and needed only a little adjustment to perfect it.

For particularly small work, such as 2in plant-pots, many potters used a single-handed throwing technique. Once the clay had been centred by the clasp of the right hand, the right thumb was inserted, forming a cylinder, and one or two draughts between thumb and fingers brought the pot to its final form. Often a potter doing such repetitive work would be assisted by a 'passer' or 'taker-off' whose job was to keep a stock of balls handy, remove the pots from the wheel, and place them on the boards on which they were to be dried.

The usual limitations on the size of a pot were the diameter of the potter's wheel and the length of the potter's arm, it being necessary for him to reach the bottom of the pot to knuckle up. These limitations could be overcome, however, in two ways. If a particularly tall pot, such as a 6ft chimney-pot, was required the potter would throw a number of smaller pots and join them end to end to make up the full height of the cylinder. If skilfully done, it was impossible to see the joints. Extremely broad pots, however, such as the tree-pots 3ft high by 3ft across that A. E. Kitson made at Littlethorpe for the park at Newby Hall, needed a different technique. First, a large circular board was mounted on either the wheel-head or on a turntable at ground level. A thick slab of clay was placed on the board to act as the base for the pot, and the walls were slowly built up by coiling long rolls of clay upwards from the base. When the walls were a few inches high the board was slowly rotated by hand while the potter smoothed them, just as if he was throwing a pot as usual on the

wheel. Once this section was smooth and concentric another
section was coiled on above it, the board rotated, and the walls
smoothed yet again. In this way a pot of any size could be made,
but care had to be taken that the walls at the base were thick
enough and hard enough to support the clay above it.

The potter might use a height gauge to help him produce an
identical range of wares. Usually this was, and still is, quite a
crude device, such as a rod with one end stuck into a lump of
clay at the side of the wheel and the other pointing forward to
touch the lip of the finished pot. Some potters prefer a more
sophisticated version with a strut and a steel pointer.

Another type of throwing aid used by potters were the templates of wood, metal, or pottery, with which the pot was shaped
and smoothed down to a predetermined form. These tools were
used from the fifteenth century at least[1], and were called 'ribs'
or 'spoons'. Using a rib cut to the silhouette of a vessel made it
possible to produce a number of highly finished identical pots
very quickly, and small ribs were also used to complete minor
throwing details, such as the edge of a plate rim, etc. At some
potteries the ribs were extremely well made and long-lasting,
that illustrated on p 106, for example, having been made by a
Sunderland potter in 1835 and still in everyday use today at the
Weatheriggs pottery.

The roulette was also used to finish and decorate the pots before they were removed from the wheel. This tool consisted of a
small roller into which a number of notches or a pattern was cut,
and was impressed into the pot as it revolved, leaving behind it
an ornamental border in low relief.

When the pot had been brought to the required finish on the
wheel it was cut free with a taut wire, which some potters
lubricated with water, and removed to another section of the
pottery to dry. For most coarsewares, such as plant-pots, this was
the last stage of their manufacture before firing, but other types
of vessel required further attention.

From the mid-seventeenth century onwards any good-quality
item, such as a blackware mug or a fine jug, might have the wire
marks where it had been severed from the wheel carefully removed, and its base levelled—by taking the pot when it had
dried to a leather-hard state, mounting it upside down on the
wheel on soft clay, and shaving its base with a broad chisel-edged

Page 103 (above) Westmorland slipwares which are still being made today; (below) Farnham greenwares, typical 'Art' wares of the late nineteenth century (see notes on page 165)

Page 104 (above) Nattes' drawing of the Silkstone Pottery of 1806 shows a large multi-flued kiln in operation; (below) a similar kiln firing very similar wares was used at the Littlethorpe Pottery, the staff of which were photographed in about 1913 (see notes on page 165)

tool to a smooth flat surface. This process was confined to particularly fine pieces, since it took time and added to the expense.

Often plates and shallow bowls had a rough area of surplus
clay round the base where the wire had cut them free from the
wheel-head, for it was difficult to throw cleanly in this area,
which was half-covered by the projecting rim of the pot. In
these cases the trimming was usually carried out with a sharp
knife, giving a fairly smooth, yet quick and cheap, finish to
the base. This practice dates from the post-medieval period and
is still occasionally used today.

When the pots were firm enough to hold, but not dry enough
to be brittle (ie leather hard), the handles were affixed. The potter
started to make his handles by first preparing a foot long cone-
shaped lump of wedged clay, which he gripped in his left hand.
Then, wetting his right hand, he proceeded to stroke the point
of the cone down to a suitable handle section, slowly extruding
the clay between his thumb and forefinger. By this means he
could pull numerous handles from the same cone of clay, each
one being nipped off when drawn out to the correct length.

With mugs, jugs, or jars, the wide end of the handle from
nearest the cone, was stuck on to the pot near its rim, and
thumbed securely in place. The handle was then curved into a
smooth loop and the lower end thumbed down on to the body
of the pot. This was 'bowing' or 'stouking', to use the traditional
terms, at its simplest. As each potter had his own particular
methods, there are an infinite number of handle forms to be
found on the vessels made in England over the last 500 years.
Perhaps the most intricate handles are those to be seen on the
Staffordshire and Wrotham tygs and posset pots of the seventeenth century, which have double loops, applied spirals of red
and white clays, finials, and slip-trailed ornament down their
edges; but most of the country potter's handles were extremely
well designed in a practical and functional manner.

Handles for bread-crocks, stewpots, or cream-pots, which lay
alongside the body of the pot, were pulled and placed in position
in the same way as before. The handle was then stroked to a
smooth curve with the thumb and crooked forefinger of the
right hand, and joined to the pot by the same action. A final
slicing or pressing action was then made with the thumb at each
end of the curve, and the handle was completed.

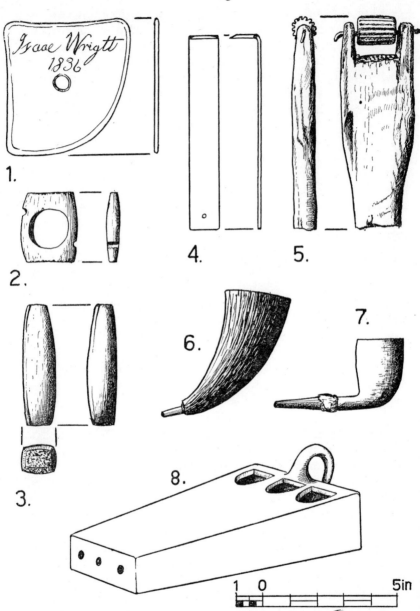

The potter's hand tools: 1, a pottery rib; 2 & 3, wooden ribs; 4, a turning tool; 5, a wooden roulette; 6, a cow-horn slip trailer; 7, a Halifax 'quill stringer'; 8, a multi-spouted trailer from Sussex

Two other forms of handle were thrown on the wheel, and joined to the pots when they too were leather hard. The more common of these was the tubular variety (seen on pipkins, bedpans, etc), which appears to have become popular during the period of Dutch influence on English pottery in the late sixteenth century, and has been used ever since. The second type of thrown handle was constructed from a small thrown bowl that had been divided longitudinally, each half bowl forming a strong handle when joined to the pot.

For some varieties of vessel, throwing is only the first of a number of forming operations. Details of the main varieties are now given.

BATHS AND TROUGHS

To make a long pottery bath or trough, such as the author saw being made at Littlethorpe in 1967, the potter first threw two identical pots some $2\frac{1}{2}$ft in diameter, and 18in high. These were placed about 18in apart on a long board, the inward-facing sides slit vertically from top to bottom, and the sides of each pot opened out to a U-shaped plan. The cut sides were then joined to those of the opposite pot to form a single long trough with semicircular ends. The hole remaining between the two bases was then filled in with extra clay, and the body of the pot thus completed. For a bath it was customary to pull a broad handle for each end.

FISH DISHES

During the seventeenth and eighteenth centuries a number of oval fish dishes were made by first throwing shallow pans of about 15in diameter and 2-3in deep, and after slicing them from the wheel and allowing them to dry a little, cutting a long leaf-shaped panel of clay from the centre of the base of the pans; the sides were then pushed into an oval form, so that the hole in the centre was sealed by the remaining clay. In this way the round pan was given the oval form required. Once a pouring lip had been nipped into one or both ends, and a handle fixed half-way down one of the long sides, the fish dish was completed.

HAM PANS AND SALTERS

These pans were used for salting down meat in the eighteenth, nineteenth, and early twentieth centuries, and were regional variations of the same vessel. Both had a flat base and vertical sides up to a foot deep, but the northern ham pan was pear-shaped to receive a full ham, while the southern salter was oval. To start making either of these pans a large bottomless pot of the required depth was thrown on the wheel and cut free with a wire. The potters then lifted off the complete wheel-head, including the pot, and placed it at ground level by the side of a previously prepared ham pan or salter base. From this position the pot was lifted free of the wheel-head, placed in position on the base, and pulled to the correct shape. Once the base and the pot had been securely joined together by thumbing, the pan was complete, except that pulled handles might be attached to each end.

DUTCH OVENS

Dutch ovens, such as were produced at Donyatt and Yearsley in the eighteenth century, were formed from large thrown pots perhaps 2ft in diameter and 1ft in depth. These were cut vertically into two equal halves, each half forming one oven. Once the cut edges of each half-pot had been smoothed down, a horizontal shelf was thumbed round its interior wall to act as a support for the food to be cooked and also to prevent the back of the oven warping when in the kiln. Now it only remained to fix two handles, either thrown knobs or the pulled variety, to the back of the oven, and it was ready to be fired.

PUZZLE JUGS

Puzzle jugs were trick drinking vessels made from the seventeenth century up to the early 1960s. At first sight it seemed impossible to drink from them, the puzzle being to find the correct method without being drenched in the process. When the jug body came from the wheel it looked just like an ordinary vase with a rather broad rim, but this rim was hollow, and concealed a narrow tube which had been carefully thrown into it. Taking the pot in this state, the potter first cut out a fretted design through the upper section of the jug's wall to render any kind of pouring action impossible. The next stage was to make the handle, which had to be hollow to enable the liquid from the bottom of the jug to be sucked up through it, into the hollow rim, and so to the mouth via a series of ornamental mouthpieces.

The tubular handle was made of a rod of clay about $\frac{1}{2}$in in diameter and 8-9in long, cut out of a solid block of clay by means of a stiff wire loop of the correct diameter. A deep groove was made down the length of the rod, giving it a U-section into which a length of thick damp string was inserted. The open ends of the U were then sealed together enclosing the string, and the whole handle hung up to dry. When the handle was dry enough to hold its shape, but was still flexible, it was taken down, the string pulled free, and the handle bent to shape, and fitted to the jug. Great care was required at this stage, as it was essential that the tube running up the handle from inside the base to the rim was kept perfectly clear. Having fitted the handle, it only remained to fix three mouthpieces round the rim, each disguised as an ornamental boss, and the jug was complete. To drink from the jug any two of the mouthpieces had to be blocked with the fingers, so that the liquid could be sucked up through the third. Some jugs, however, had an extra hole pierced into the tube just under the top of the handle, thus making the puzzle even more complex.

SALT KITS

Salt kits, made in the North of England from the late eighteenth century, were thrown in two sections which were later joined together. The main section of the kit, the body, was thrown first as a tall cylinder, and then 'collared in' until the top of the cylinder was completely domed over, and finished off with a knob finial. In this state it was taken from the wheel and allowed to become leather hard before having a large circular hole cut into its shoulder. The second section of the kit, the projecting hood, was thrown as a small round-bodied bowl whose top half was cut off at a slight angle with a wire, and fitted into the hole in the salt kit body. Once the two sections had been smoothed together and a small loop hanger thumbed on to the back, the kit was complete except for any slip decoration which might be added.

Pressing

Clay, being a soft and plastic material takes the impression of any object into which it is pressed. This is an extremely useful property, for once a mould has been made, any number of identical clay pressings can be made from it.

The earliest examples of English press-moulding are the fine yellow and green wares made in the mid-late sixteenth century in the London area. These stove-tiles, cisterns, and plates are usually decorated with the Elizabethan royal coat-of-arms, royalist symbols such as Tudor roses and crowns, and architectural devices in a well developed Renaissance style. The quality of both the design and the modelling is of such a high standard that it appears unlikely that they were the work of a native English potter, and as they are similar to contemporary Continental wares, it is suggested that they were made by either a Dutch or Flemish artist working in this country. To produce such pieces an intaglio (ie negative or female) mould of wood, or, perhaps more likely, unglazed clay, would be made, into which a slab of clay could be pressed. The clay picked up all the details of the mould and a completely decorated surface resulted from this single operation. The tiles made and decorated by this technique usually had a flange modelled round their back edges, so that they could easily be cemented into place on the side of stoves, and also to check any tendency to warp during firing. The cistern panels, meanwhile, were made up into full cisterns by the addition of three more sides and a base, while the plates were all thrown in the normal way, and had their bases pressed over a seal-like mould to decorate their interiors.

By the early seventeenth century press-moulding had become an established method of plate-making. The moulds were dome-shaped slabs of unglazed fired clay, made by the potters themselves. One late example, now in the British Museum (see p 52) has the inscription 'William Bird made this mould in the year of our Lord 1751' scratched on its underside, but most moulds were undated and anonymous.

The plate-making technique was to roll out an even sheet of clay about $\frac{1}{4}$ to $\frac{3}{8}$in thick, lay it over the mould, then pat and push it down to the shape of the mould, and trim off any surplus clay from the edges with a sharp knife. Then the mould and plate were turned over on to a thick coil of clay, placed to prevent the edges of the plate sagging, and the mould lifted free. A notched edge was rouletted round the rim of the plate, which, after drying, was ready for the kiln.

It was quickly realised that if a pattern were impressed into the mould, a raised pattern would result on the surface of the plate; so by the mid-seventeenth century, it became the usual practice to stamp or grave a pattern into the mould before it was fired. It had been thought that pressed plates of this type were only introduced in the late seventeenth century, but sections of highly developed pressed slipware plates were found by Mr K. J. Barton in a deposit exactly dated between 1652 and 1656 at St Nicholas Almshouses, Bristol[2], proving that decorated pressed plates must have been made from the early seventeenth century, and that by the 1650s a very high standard of both workmanship and design had been achieved. Pressed plates with moulded decoration continued to be made up to the mid-late eighteenth century (see William Bird above); these later examples often had their decoration traced on to the mould by a narrow toothed roulette rather than a graver, and may be distinguished by the raised milled edges of their designs. From the 1750s, however, plates with press-moulded decoration became less popular, and slowly fell out of production, but the other forms of pressed plate, particularly those with simple slip decoration or feathered 'Welsh Ware' patterns, continued to be made up to the early 1960s, when Henry Watson's Wattisfield pottery finally ceased to produce them.

Plates were not the only articles to be made by the pressing technique, for loaf-pots, pie-plates, meat dishes, jelly-moulds, and other utilitarian wares were all quickly produced in this way in many potteries throughout the eighteenth and nineteenth centuries. Press-moulding was also found useful for making ornamental garden urns, etc, in the 1890s and 1900s. In potteries at Burton-in-Lonsdale, Fremington, and Farnham, these were made by pressing thick slabs of clay into detailed moulds, using an old sock stuffed with sand or rags as a beater. The moulds were often commercially made of either plaster-of-Paris or unglazed earthenware, and were sectional, so that different parts of the pot could be moulded separately, and then joined together by hand when leather hard—necessary when a complicated three-dimensional object was being made, as any form of undercutting would prevent the impressed clay from being extracted from the mould.

Forming

In the previous sections some form of artificial aid to potting was required—the potter's wheel, the mould, etc—but other wares were made just by the potter's hands and feet, perhaps aided by a rolling-pin or knife.

Perhaps the most interesting of these formed wares were the large West Country bread ovens, made at Fremington up to the late 1920s. The potter first prepared his clay by mixing into it a high proportion of Barnstaple grit to improve its refractory properties and render it easier to work, and then had it trodden out on a wooden floor until it was about $\frac{3}{4}$in thick, about 2ft wide, and horse-shoe shaped in plan, an iron frame being used as a template. A further panel of clay was then trodden out on a board to form the back of the oven, and propped in position, while yet another panel was similarly prepared to form the front. The next operation consisted of joining the front, the back, and the base into one, carefully smoothing together the joints, pulling and beating the clay into the form of a miniature igloo. When the top had been carefully domed over, perhaps with the addition of extra coils of clay, the oven was allowed to harden a little. A square panel of clay was then cut out of the front, fitted with a handle, and replaced to form the oven door. With a little more drying the oven was firm enough to be rested door-uppermost on its back to dry with the minimum of warping and cracking, and so be ready for the kiln.

These ovens were made in various sizes between two and twelve pecks, and were used mainly for baking bread or meat. A wood fire was first lit inside, and the temperature built up until the top of the oven would produce sparks from any stick rubbed over it. The ashes were then taken out, the inside rapidly mopped clean, the food inserted, and finally the door sealed in position with wet clay. After a certain time, determined by experiment, the door was removed and the fully cooked food taken out.

Another method of forming, used mainly in the North during the seventeenth to the twentieth centuries, was slab-building. This involved rolling out slabs of clay to about $\frac{1}{4}$in thick, allowing them to become firm enough to handle, cutting out pieces of the desired shape, and sticking them together with slip. A few truly useful articles were produced in this way, such as the Halifax knife-trays, but the majority of the slab-built wares were for ornaments—including beautifully made chests-of-drawers, rocking chairs, and miniature cradles (Plate, p 86), the latter being given as fertility symbols at weddings and christenings from the late seventeenth century onwards.

Drying

Regardless of the manner of making, the pottery had to be carefully dried before being placed in the kiln. If this was not carried out successfully the water inside the fabric would rapidly expand as the temperature increased within the kiln and cause the pot to shatter, destroying itself and ruining many of the surrounding pieces. One of the simplest techniques was to rest the pots outside in the open air to be dried by the sun and the wind, but this could be rather chancy. Mr S. Shuttleworth of Haworth has told the writer of the great fun he had as a boy when, with his friends, he visited the local potteries, standing behind a nearby wall and hurling stones at the neatly stacked pancheons, which shattered with the regularity of clay pigeons. There was also the inclemency of the weather to be considered. A foggy day or a sudden downpour of rain could easily wet the raw pots down once more, and a hard frost would cause them to shatter. From the mid-seventeenth century at the latest the potters of Staffordshire were using a somewhat improved method of drying when the weather was bad, as described by Dr Plot in 1686 : 'When the *potter* has wrought the clay either into *hollow* or *flat ware*, they are set abroad to dry in fine weather, but by the fire in foule, turning them as they see occasion, which they call *whaving*.' An identical method was used in the North Devon potteries, as recorded by Mr Fishley Holland of Fremington. On being removed from the wheel the pots were taken to the drying room. This was a room specially designed for the purpose, having a number of strong upright poles round the walls, each pole having a series of holes bored horizontally into it throughout its height to take a series of stout 15in pegs on which the long planks carrying the pottery could be rested. This convenient racking system was open enough to allow the pottery to dry out naturally in fine weather, but in poor weather artificial heat had to be used. A faggot of furze was first split up, scattered about the drying-room floor, and covered with a layer of 'glows' as the furze and bramble kiln-embers were locally called. The glows were then wet down to prevent flaming, and the whole left to smoulder away until next morning, when the pots would be almost dry. If frost was likely a rather more potent method of heating was employed in the form of a 'devil', which consisted of a mixture of small coal and wet clay formed into the size and shape of a goose egg. A number of these were placed in a small pile on the drying house floor and lit, a sheet of iron being placed over them to prevent their burning too rapidly but yet allowing them to produce sufficient heat and smoke to counter the frost.

In the North of England the climate was generally colder and damper than in the South, and in consequence many of the northern potters built permanent drying racks, for year-long use if necessary. One of these still remains in use to this day at the Weatheriggs Pottery, Westmorland. It consists of a table-high stone-topped bench running down the inside of the workshop wall beneath the pottery racks, with a firebox arranged at one end of it so that a current of air can pass down through the hot coals, under the bench or 'hob' as it is known, and out through a chimney built at the opposite end. In this way the pottery in the racks above is subjected to a gentle convected heat that dries the ware quite quickly but with little risk of cracking. A similar device is also used at the Littlethorpe Pottery near Ripon in Yorkshire.

Notes for this chapter are on pages 160-61.

Chapter Eight

Decorating

The country potter's decorative techniques were extremely simple, nothing but local materials and a few primitive tools being used. This did not inhibit him in any way, for, as the majority of his decorative ware shows, he possessed a combination of skill, vitality, and freedom of design that enabled him to produce unrivalled examples of ceramic peasant art. From the mid-nineteenth century the growing interest in 'art' and the subsequent demand for 'artistic' wares led many potters into adopting new decorative techniques, but these only succeeded in debasing the traditional craft standards. Where the potter had previously made his wares honestly, as he knew they should be made, he now pandered to the new demand for medieval or rustic designs copied either from original examples, book illustrations, provided sketches, or directly from nature. The new trade in 'art' wares soon became extremely popular, as it provided an alternative to the traditional market for domestic wares, now rapidly dwindling in the face of competition from the Staffordshire factories. The production of most of the highly ornamental wares ceased during, or shortly after, the First World War because of a change in public taste and the shortage of money for purely ornamental items. Since then the potter has tended to return to his more utilitarian products, leaving the decorative wares to the college-trained studio potter.

The majority of the decoration was carried out when the pottery was in a leather-hard state, the clay being firm enough to handle but still soft enough to have extra clay or slips applied to it.

Slip Decoration

Slip, which is clay watered down to the consistency of thick cream and sieved to remove any coarse particles, was by far the most common decorative medium. It could be obtained in a variety of colours, as described in the previous chapter, and could be applied in three ways—by dipping, by painting, or by being trailed on to the wares through a fine nozzle.

The practice of slip dipping was late-medieval in origin, being largely restricted to the South-west of England, and little used in the rest of the country up to the latter end of the sixteenth century. As most potteries had plentiful supplies of red firing clay but only small deposits of the white, the production of solid white-fabric wares was a time-consuming and therefore expensive business; so most of the white-fabric wares of the sixteenth and seventeenth centuries were luxury items—chalices, sweetmeat dishes, chafing dishes, etc—as illustrated by Paul Woodfield's *Yellow-glazed wares of the Seventeenth Century*, 1966. Although the northern potteries, situated on the edge of the coal-measures, were able to use the local fireclays to make wares with a pale buff fabric, many potteries found it more convenient to make their pottery in the more common red fabric and cover it with a disguising coat of white slip. Thus, from the middle of the seventeenth century up to the present day, slip dipping by various techniques has been a fairly common practice in many potteries throughout the country.

For a small item, such as a jug, it was simply a matter of dipping the item into a tub of slip. In Devon and Cornwall only the topmost inch or two of a jug would be dipped, to give the characteristic white rim and spout, but in other areas the whole vessel might be dipped. Salt kits, with their complicated domed shape, were dipped by inserting the right hand, opening the fingers wide to support the pot, and sliding it base-first into the slip until only the rim of the hood remained above the surface (thus keeping the interior completely dry). Pancheons, being rather large, were impossible to slip in the normal way, so a specialised method was required. The potter first poured a quantity of slip into the pancheon, and then lifted it up in his arms. Standing in a hunched position, with legs apart and elbows supported on hips, the potter proceeded to spin the pot rapidly about its own axis, tilting it at the same time until the rim was almost vertical and facing away from him. In this way the slip was distributed evenly round the interior of the pancheon by a combination of gravity and centrifugal force, any excess slip being spun off the edge of the rim. To finish the operation the potter ceased his spinning, catching the base of the pot in his left hand, returning it to its normal position, and quickly running his right forefinger round the underside of the rim to remove the surplus slip before setting the slipped pancheon down on the floor to dry.

Some of the earliest post-medieval examples of slip dipping are the jugs housed in the County Museum at Truro. Dating from the early sixteenth century, they show that dipping was often restricted to a small bib or frontal portion, the remainder of the vessel remaining its true dark-red colour. The bib was not used throughout the South-west, however, as other contemporary examples are seen to have been dipped entirely, and further decorated by having portions of the slip scratched away to reveal the darker fabric beneath, a technique now known by the Italian term 'sgraffito'. A good sixteenth-century example of this technique, discovered in a lead mine at Priddy in Somerset, is illustrated in *The Connoisseur* of September, 1906. From these early sgraffito wares there grew a wide range of plates and bowls, some of which were found in deposits dated between 1652 and 1656 at St Nicholas' Almshouses, Bristol[1]. These have a red body, white slip, and yellow glaze, the sgraffito being restricted to a number of simple rim decorations in trellis, zig-zag, or recurring S-shaped motifs. Although some high-quality sgraffito wares were made in potteries like that at Wrotham in Kent, the main development of English sgraffito took place in the latter half of the seventeenth century in the potteries of Donyatt in Somerset, and Barnstaple and Bideford in North Devon. Using the now traditional methods and materials a range of plates, harvest jugs, tygs, and candlesticks were produced bearing a great variety of surface decoration. Donyatt used largely semi-natural geometric motifs for decoration, and also commemorative designs—such as plates showing the celebrated Siamese twins, Aquilla and Priscilla, born at nearby Il-Browers in Somerset on 19 May 1680.

At the North Devon potteries a great variety of subjects were used, particularly on harvest jugs. Ships, compasses, lions and unicorns, the Royal arms, deer, flowers and birds were all scratched through the white slip, along with suitable harvest rhymes like—

> Harvis is cam all Bissey,
> Now in mackin of your
> Barley mow when men do
> Laber hard and swet good
> Ale is better far than meet.
> Bideford   April 28
> 1775   M.W.

Harvest jugs, all fairly similar in shape and decoration, continued to be made in the same red fabric and white slip until about 1900, when they finally went out of production.

One other characteristic form of sgraffito ware was made in Staffordshire in the early-mid eighteenth century. It consisted of a range of finely thrown mugs and jugs in a cream fabric and a near-black slip, and carried lively drawings of deer, lions, and foliage.

In the rest of England, however, sgraffito appears to have been used rarely until the late nineteenth century, when it became popular on the more exotic art wares. Some potters, such as Absalom Harris of Farnham Pottery and Isaac Button of Soil Hill, Halifax, found that many people now wished to decorate pottery for a hobby; so they produced a range of 'artistic' shapes in a red fabric with a white slip, which were bought by the would-be artists to take home and decorate by the sgraffito technique, the pieces being returned afterwards to the pottery for a free glazing and firing. As a bone-dry pot is an extremely brittle article, the number of pots completed in this way was rather small.

Perhaps the latest use of sgraffito as a commercial technique was in the potteries of Devon and Cornwall throughout the first half of the present century. Most of these wares retained the familiar dark red-brown fabric and white slip, but were now made in the form of scent-bottles, ash-trays and the like, the decoration being restricted to simple patterned borders and mottoes such as 'A Present from . . .' or 'Real Devon Violets'.

SLIP TRAILING

The most popular form of slip decoration was undoubtably that in which the coloured slips were piped on to the wares through a fine quill. This was slip trailing, a technique introduced into England from the Netherlands during the late sixteenth and early seventeenth centuries, and rapidly adopted by our native potters. Dr Plot, in his *Natural History of Staffordshire* of 1686 tells us how the potters of that county

> then *slip* or paint them [the pots] with their severall sorts of *slip*, according as they design their *work*, when the first *slip* is dry, laying on the *others* at their leisure, the *orange slip* makeing the ground, and the *white* and *red*, the *paint*; which two colours they break with a wire *brush*, much after the manner they doe when they *marble* paper, and then *cloud* them with a *pensil* when they are pretty dry.

By far the commonest form of slip trailer, as the combined quill and reservoir was called, was the cow-horn (see p 106), consisting of the topmost 3-4in of the horn with a hollow goose-quill nozzle inserted into a narrow hole bored concentrically through its tip. In use the junction between the horn and the nozzle was first caulked with clay to render it slip-proof. The trailer was then held horizontally and the slip poured into the open end of the horn until it rose up within the semi-transparent quill at the tip. When filled in this manner the potter could use it just like a fountain pen, tilting it forward to run the slip out on to the ware, merely raising the nozzle again to stop the flow. This form of trailer was used in the North Devon, Buckley, and Penrith potteries, and many others[2].

The Halifax potteries used a somewhat cruder device, comprising the bowl of a clay pipe with a section of goose-quill stuck over its broken stem (see p 106). This 'quill-stringer', as it was known, could be used in the same way as the cow-horn trailer; or it could be held in the clenched fist, the thumb sealing the top of the bowl and the stem protruding between the first and second fingers, and the slip allowed to ooze out on to the ware when the thumb was removed. One major disadvantage of this form of trailer was its small capacity, which accounts for the relatively short runs of trailing in the Halifax wares.

The present-day slip trailer with its rubber bag and wooden or plastic nozzle was never used by the country potter, as the rate of flow depended entirely on the pressure of the hand on the bag. By comparison with the traditional gravity-fed trailers this is a slow and troublesome tool, ideal for the painstaking work of the amateur, but worthless for the confident strokes of the master potter.

In the earliest examples of English trailed slipware one can see that the slip was trailed directly on to the damp fabric of the pot itself. It was quickly realised, however, that the slips would adhere far more firmly to the pot if they were trailed on to a freshly slipped surface. A preliminary coating of slip also had the effect of smoothing over the throwing marks, besides which it prevented any impurities in the basic fabric from staining the lead glazes. For these reasons it soon became common practice in most potteries to slip the wares prior to trailing on the decoration. Although only plain trailing has been considered here, other forms, such as marbled, feathered, or jewelled slipware, were also produced from the mid-seventeenth century on, as discussed under Staffordshire in Chapter three.

COMBING

The process of combing (not to be confused with *feathering*) consisted of dipping a pot in a slip of a contrasting colour, and then simply running a blunt-toothed comb through it to reveal the colour of the fabric beneath. This type of decoration was in use at Donyatt in Somerset from the mid-seventeenth century at the latest, and it tended to remain a predominantly West of England technique. Perhaps the last combed wares to be made by a country potter in England were the baking dishes produced at Fremington during the opening years of the present century, though the simple comb had been superseded by a tool made of four whalebone prongs tipped with the teats from babies' bottles —which produced excellent results.

Inlaying

Inlaying was only adopted by the post-medieval potter during the mid-late eighteenth century, though the technique was simple enough. All the potter had to do was to scratch the required design into the fabric of his leather-hard pot, fill the incisions so made with a clay of a contrasting colour, and finally smooth over the surface, to produce an extremely well defined pattern. By the early-mid nineteenth century most of the urban potteries were decorating at least some of their wares in this manner, but it was in Sussex that the finest examples of inlay were made. At potteries such as Brede, Dicker and Rye, numerous harvest barrels and bottles, money boxes and jars were made, often bearing the date, the name of the owner or the potter, or a suitable inscription in beautifully clear and well proportioned characters. This degree of perfection was achieved by the use of printer's type to make the initial impressions, a typical Sussex feature.

Applied Decoration

The use of applied clays to embellish plainly thrown vessels was medieval in origin, but only survived into the post-medieval period within the northern reduced greenware tradition. Large cisterns and ovens made in the greenware potteries of Yearsley and York were still having broad rolls of clay robustly thumbed round their rims, handle joints, and spigot-holes in a thoroughly medieval manner as late as the 1840s. This survival of a medieval technique was exceptional, however, as most of the applied decoration carried out in the post-medieval period appears to have been freshly conceived and relatively free from external influence.

A somewhat finer variety of applied decoration was used on the Cistercian wares (see p 20), particularly during the second quarter of the sixteenth century. Here the colour of the applied clay contrasted sharply with that of the pot itself, usually being white on red or, very occasionally, red on white, these colours appearing dark brown and yellow respectively beneath a yellowish lead glaze. Great care had to be taken when using two different clays together in this manner, for if one should contract slightly more than the other in the kiln it would cause the decoration to break away, ruining the pot. The actual form taken by the decoration varied from one pot to another and also from pottery to pottery. Some Cistercian ware types had their own characteristic patterns, while others were usually left completely plain. For pots of Type 1 the design shown on p 20 was most common—fine rolls of clay of about $\frac{1}{16}$in diameter placed carefully in position and then pressed flat against the walls of the pot by means of a narrow roulette some $\frac{1}{2}$ or $\frac{5}{8}$in wide. Other designs used on the Type 1 pots included vine or plant-like borders in an identical technique, trefoils, plain pellets arranged in small clusters or pellets overstamped with a cartwheel, face masks, or ear of corn designs. For the last mentioned the potters made their own intaglio seals of fired clay, being careful to leave a register mark on the back so that each impression was correctly orientated. Type 3 pots usually bore a single stag or goat head, or a quatrefoil, whose edges were either smoothed down or hatched with a pointed instrument to ensure good adhesion; whereas Type 2 pots, together with the remainder of the Cistercian ware type series, were rarely decorated in any of the designs so far mentioned, more often being left quite plain.

The practice of rouletting or stamping relief patterns over patches of applied clay was greatly developed during the seventeenth century, particularly in Staffordshire and in the potteries of the South. Staffordshire examples, which also include the so-called 'Hughson' wares and those usually attributed to Fareham (for no apparent reason), usually took the form of bulbous jugs or mugs decorated in pellets stamped with cartwheel designs and ornamental strips rouletted with an X- or lozenge-shaped repeat. In the South of England, particularly at Wrotham and in South Wiltshire, the overstamping tended to be much less geometric in character and somewhat freer in its choice of motifs, as described at the end of Chapter three.

The use of applied decoration declined greatly during the late seventeenth and early eighteenth centuries, probably as a result of the increasing popularity of the colourful Staffordshire slipwares; but this decline was only temporary, for by the early nineteenth century, with the development of the trade in decorated horticultural wares (and the slightly later art wares), the advantages of using applied and stamped decoration to produce ornate products quickly and cheaply were soon recognised once more. Throughout the country potters began to apply leaves, knotty tendrils and other 'rustic' details to their ornamental pieces, which thus became far more saleable. Up to the 1850s the decoration was usually executed in a fairly simple and straight-forward style, but from this time on potters tended to aim at higher and higher standards of technical achievement.

One of the new methods adopted in the urban potteries at this period was 'sprigging', in which a quantity of soft clay was pressed into a shallow intaglio mould, the surplus clay scraped away, and the resultant finely detailed sharp-edged clay 'sprig' carefully applied to the ware. This was certainly an improvement over the older method of overstamping a crudely shaped pellet of clay already stuck on to the ware, but the results obtained by sprigging tended to look rather mechanical and certainly lacked the confident spontaneity of the older pieces.

Sprigging, stamping, and hand modelling continued to be widely used until decorated wares themselves disappeared from the market in the late 1920s and early 1930s.

Agate Ware

Unlike the techniques discussed so far, agate ware was not a surface decoration, but relied solely on the colour of its integral fabric for its effect. The potter first prepared equal quantities of the red and white clays, wedging each one carefully to remove all air bubbles and to bring them both to the same consistency. He then took a piece of (say) the red clay and rolled it out to a thin slab, a treated piece of white clay in the same way, rolling that on top of the red, and continued the process until a large layered block of contrasting clays was built up. If the wares were to be formed on the wheel the mixture was left in this state and thrown directly, but if a slab-building technique was to be used, further preparation was necessary. Having sliced the layered block into a number of small cubes by means of a taut wire, the potter then proceeded to re-form it, thumbing one cube upon another in a variety of directions so as to produce a consistent marble-like fabric. When the block had been re-formed in this way it was a simple matter to slice off slabs of the required thickness, each side displaying the rich red and white agate-ware finish. It should be noted that the slabs were produced by *slicing* and not by *rolling*, as the latter gave the fabric a smudged and patchy appearance. The outer surfaces of both wheel-thrown or slab-built wares were always inclined to become slightly blurred in the finished article, and so they were usually turned or scraped down when almost bone dry to show the fabric to its greatest advantage.

Although the occasional piece of agate ware was made during earlier periods, the technique only became popular in the urban potteries of the late eighteenth and early nineteenth centuries. Its actual title, and the forms of its products, varied greatly from one area to another. In Westmorland, for example, it is called 'grained ware', and is still being used to make ornamental plant-pots, whereas in Yorkshire it was called 'snail-horn ware', and was used to make money boxes, chests-of-drawers, cradles, etc.

Painted Decoration

It is not generally realised that pottery was often given its final decoration in ordinary oil paints during the eighteenth and nine-teenth centuries. Those painted pots which have managed to survive the misguided cleaning of the collector or the curator usually show a lively use of colour and brushwork typical of un-restrained peasant art. The chosen topics are usually quite popular, and include nativity scenes, birds, flowers, heraldic beasts, or the Royal coat-of-arms.

Notes for this chapter are on page 161.

Chapter Nine

Glazing

The process of glazing consisted of covering the ware with a chemical coating, which, under the heat of the kiln, produced the hard glass-like surface we normally associate with pottery. From early medieval times the English earthenware potters had used lead glazes to render their products more attractive, easier to clean, and rather less porous than before, and glazes of this type remained in constant use to within living memory.

Of the various lead-based glazing materials available, galena was by far the simplest to prepare, and as it gave particularly good results it was widely used. Galena emerged from the mines of Derbyshire, the Mendips, or the Yorkshire dales, in hard black lumps of a compact semi-crystalline material that consisted mainly of lead sulphide. At the pottery this was, as Dr Plot described in 1686: 'beaten into dust, finely sifted, and strewed upon them [the pots] which gives them the *gloss*, but not the colour; all the *colours* being chiefly given by the variety of *slips*'. This crude technique of sprinkling the powdered galena over the pottery had one major disadvantage; only the upper surfaces of each pot were glazed, the others being left completely raw. If, for example, a spherical bottle was to be glazed in this way the upper half of the exterior would bear a heavy coating of glaze, as would the interior of the base immediately below the mouth, but all the other surfaces would be bare, as the glaze would have fallen past them. This patchiness makes it quite easy to tell if a pot has been glazed in this way, and so, by examining excavated examples, it can be seen that most post-medieval wares made before c 1650 were in fact powdered with a galena glaze.

The retention of such a crude technique up to this rather late date was no doubt due to the difficulty of finding any other. It was impossible to mix the galena with water to form a slip-like dipping solution, for the ore was completely insoluble and, being particularly heavy, sank rapidly to the bottom of its container even after the most vigorous agitation. It was only after repeated experiments that a satisfactory method was discovered : the addition of a quantity of slip to the glaze mixture. This not only enabled the glaze to be applied by dipping, but also tended to stabilise the glaze in the kiln, producing superior results. From the late seventeenth century at least, and particularly with the rise of the urban potteries, this improved glaze mixture became extremely popular, though different potteries used slightly different methods of preparation. At the Fremington Pottery it had been customary to pound up the dry galena in a large iron trough, but as the toxic dust gave the men 'bellyache', which they considered to be colic, a wet-grinding technique was developed late in the nineteenth century. A double-stoned mill, such as is used for grinding flour, ground up the glaze in water, thus greatly reducing the risk of lead poisoning. The actual glaze recipe was as follows:

> 12 dippers of slip from River Taw clay
> 12 lb galena, ground to crystals
> $\frac{1}{2}$ lb ground flint

This gave a good treacle-brown glaze, the colour resulting from iron impurities in the galena and from the iron nodules occurring naturally in the river clays. The Halifax potters, on the other hand, ground their galena by a technique introduced into the area from Buckley in Flintshire by Jonathan Catherall in the mid-late eighteenth century. Lumps of ore were placed in a large circular masonry trough, covered with water, and pounded into a smooth paste by the action of two large stones dragged round on the ends of chains by horses. The resulting mixture was then mixed with a quantity of white slip, and was ready for use.

One of the disadvantages of using galena-based glazes was sulphuration. If the wares were fired in an open kiln the sulphur content of the galena (ie lead sulphide) was quickly carried off by way of the hot gases rushing through the firing chamber; but if the wares were fired in an unventilated space, such as a closed saggar, it was almost impossible for the sulphur to be removed, and so it remained in the glaze, staining it an unpleasant sulphur-yellow colour. To avoid this staining, which made the pot worthless, holes were pierced through the saggar walls, thus allowing the sulphur to escape freely as the temperature increased.

To avoid any chance of sulphuration and also to give a higher gloss to the glaze, the galena was eventually replaced by litharge, or lead oxide. Dr Plot described how the Staffordshire potters—

> when they have a mind to shew the utmost of their *skill* in giving their wares a fairer *gloss* than ordinary, they *lead* them with lead *calcined* to a powder, which they also sift fine and strew upon them as before, which not only gives them a higher *gloss* but goes much further too in their work than *lead ore* [galena] would have done.[1]

Litharge continued to be made and used in many potteries as late as the 1920s and 1930s. Messrs Arthur and Reginald Harris of the Farnham Potteries used to take scrap lead and convert it into litharge in a small furnace specially built for the purpose in one corner of their glazing room. Once the lead had melted it was continuously stirred until it had completely lost its metallic appearance and resembled a dirty silver-grey powder. This powder, or litharge, was then mixed with a quantity of finely sieved sand and sufficient water to form a paste stiff enough to be brushed directly on to the raw wares. The glazes applied in this way were surprisingly even in their density and surface, and were it not for the occasional slip of the brush, they might easily be mistaken for the more common dip-glazes.

During the second half of the nineteenth century a number of new glazing materials became generally available through developments within the chemical industry and the emergence of the wholesale pottery supplier. For the first time small potteries were able to buy prepared ingredients like ground flint, china clay, red and white lead, all of which had previously been used in the factory potteries alone. Taking advantage of these products, many potters developed their own glaze recipes to suit both their individual clays and the demands of their customers. Some extremely good glazes were developed by trial-and-error

and intuition, but the legislation of the 1920s and 30s, which pro-
hibited the use of free lead and its oxides in the potteries and in
the glazes, virtually forced the potters to buy their glazes ready-
made from the wholesaler. Most of the potters working today use
one of the low-solubility lead glazes supplied ready-ground, but
the results obtained with these tend to be rather uniform and
uninteresting in comparison with the rich and characterful glazes
they replaced.

In addition to the unstained glazes detailed above a number of
coloured glazes were also widely used, the brilliant copper-green
glaze being perhaps the earliest. The medieval English potters,
probably adopting an existing French technique, discovered that
the addition of copper filings to an ordinary glaze mixture would
produce a bright green glaze enlivened by a fine mottling where
the copper was unevenly distributed. This glaze gave the Tudor
greenwares their characteristic colouring from the early fourteenth century to the time, the early seventeenth century, when
green pottery lost its popularity. Copper greens enjoyed quite a
considerable revival, however, during the latter half of the nineteenth century, particularly with Harris's 'Farnham Greenwares'
—whose green was made by heating a quantity of scrap copper
gauze in a furnace until it was converted to copper oxide, grinding this to a fine powder in a pestle and mortar, and adding it
to the normal glaze mixture. The glazes made in this way were
particularly good, having an even dark green colour, a rich glossy
surface, and an unusually vivid iridescence. Most other potteries
bought their copper oxide in a prepared form from a supplier,
but some, such as Messrs Mitchell of the Cadborough Pottery,
Rye, still preferred to use cuprous filings in the form of 'pin dust',
the by-product of the brass pin industry.

The addition of iron to the glaze gave a range of golden
yellows, browns, and blacks, the actual tone depending on the
percentage of iron in the mixture. One of the difficulties experienced in tracing the history of iron-stained glazes is the fact
that iron occurs naturally in most clays and is readily absorbed
by the normal galena or litharge glazes, which means that a good
black iron glaze can be achieved by using a plain glaze over a
naturally iron-rich clay, the results being indistinguishable from
any glaze purposely stained with iron.

The decorated Cistercian wares illustrate this action quite

clearly. If a cup of this ware is studied in detail it will be seen that the glaze covering the white iron-free clays has retained its normal pale yellow colour, but that which covers the red iron-rich clays has stained itself to a black or dark brown by absorbing some of the iron present in the clay. So the iron staining was largely due to absorption at this period. By the third quarter of the seventeenth century at the latest most potters had discovered that superior black glazes could be obtained by deliberately adding iron oxide to their glaze mixtures, and this is verified by the large percentage of iron to be found in such glazes—far in excess of any which could be absorbed from the clay of the pot alone. Black iron-glazed wares have been fairly popular from the time of the Cistercian wares up to the present century, particularly during the Midlands blackwares period, and later with the rise of the urban potteries.

A second metal used to give a range of browns and blacks, this time with a rather purple hue, was manganese. In Staffordshire, Dr Plot tells us, 'the *Motley colour* . . . is procured by blending the *lead* with the *manganese*, by the *workmen* call'd *Magnus*'. The 'motley colour' this produced often retained the basic yellowish colour of the lead glaze but had numerous specks of manganese mixed into it, and each speck gave forth a dark purple-brown stain. The later manganese glazes tended to be overloaded with the metal, producing very rich, dark, and often semi-metallic results.

Glazes of this type are first found on the South Wiltshire wares of the seventeenth century described in Chapter 3, which are very like the Avignon wares of the late sixteenth century, and it is possible that they resulted from contemporary French influence. A second group of manganese-glazed wares was produced in the potteries of Staffordshire and Derbyshire in the late seventeenth and early eighteenth centuries, chiefly in the form of extremely attractive and well thrown mugs and jugs.

Whichever glaze had been used, the raw wares were allowed to dry out thoroughly before being packed or 'placed' in the kiln. This was a particularly skilled operation, for unless a carefully devised system of stacking and separating was used the molten glaze would glue the pottery together into one mass.

Placing

If unglazed wares were being placed in the kiln, it was simply necessary to stack them one on top of another in such a way as to ensure an even firing throughout the stack. It did not matter if they touched each other, for, being dry, they would not stick together during the firing.

During the medieval period the potter had fired his jugs in short stacks, the glazed rim of one resting against the unglazed base of the next. By this rather crude method the pots tended to stick to one another where they touched, but unless the glaze was particularly tenacious they could be chipped apart fairly easily. A slightly improved method was to place three or four parting sherds (ie small pieces of broken pottery) between the glazed surfaces, thus quite simply reducing the scarring to a minimum. Both techniques sound crude, but they represent the normal practice for placing large jugs, cisterns, bread, or brewing pots in the kiln up to the early years of this century at least. As these wares were always strongly made and coarsely finished the occasional scar at the rim was hardly noticeable, but such methods were totally unsuited to the placing of the finer wares.

The cups and mugs introduced into this country in the late fifteenth and early sixteenth centuries demanded a much more sophisticated treatment, for their fine walls and delicate rims could not withstand either the weight of vertical stacking or the chipping off of the parting sherds. The alternative system developed or adopted by the cup-makers of this period involved the use of saggars—coarsely thrown cylindrical pots large enough to hold a single piece of fine ware each: a cup was placed on the floor of the kiln and a saggar inverted over the top of it, a second cup was then placed on top of the saggar and a second saggar placed over it, the process continuing until a tall stack of full saggers had been built up. Dr Plot in his 1686 *Natural History of Staffordshire* described how the pots

> if they be *leaded hollow wares*, they [the potters] doe not expose them to the *naked* fire, but put them in *shraggers*, that is, in coarse metall'd pots, made of *marle* (not *clay*) of divers forms according as their *wares* require . . . they put them in the *shragers* to keep them from sticking

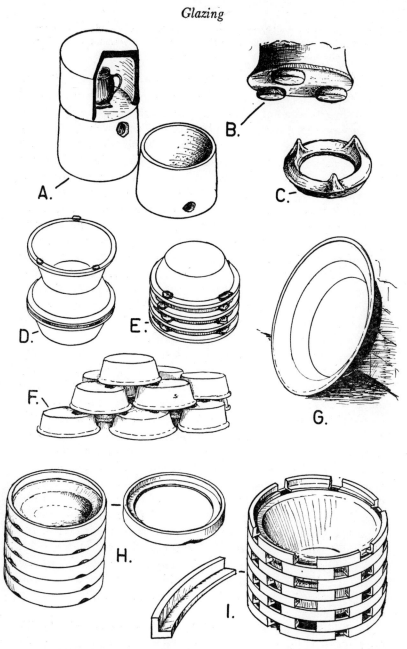

Methods of 'placing' or stacking glazed wares in the kiln

to one another (which they would certainly otherwise doe by reason of the *leading*) and to preserve them from the vehemence of the *fire*, which else would *melt* them doune, or at least warp them.

Saggars continued to be used in the country potteries as long as fine wares were made, but quite a number of potters managed to substitute large unfired pots for the saggars, this being a much cheaper process if only a few pieces of fine ware were being fired.

The use of saggars did not dispense with the necessity of parting sherds and other propping devices, for without these the pottery would have glazed itself permanently on to the top of its supporting saggar. When placing the Cistercian wares in the saggars it was normal practice to wedge a small parting sherd under one side of the cup's base so that it rested at an angle of 5-10°. This meant that any glaze that might trickle down the side of the cup would flow round the base and down on to the saggar at the single point where the cup and saggar met. After firing, the cup could easily be extracted, for it was only held at this single point, but had the parting sherd been omitted the cup would have been gripped about the entire circumference of its base, and so have been virtually irremovable.

By the third quarter of the seventeenth century the Midlands blackware potters had developed their glazing and firing techniques to such an extent that the parting-sherd method was no longer necessary. The glaze was now much more controlled, and so the risk of trickling was much less. Even so, precautions still had to be taken, the most common employing three 'bobs', circular pellets of clay about ½in across (see p 131, B). The Staffordshire potters, according to Dr Plot, 'put commonly three pieces of clay called *Bobbs* for the ware to stand on, to keep it from sticking to the shragers'. If no trickling occurred, the unglazed bases of the pots could be lifted from their supporting bobs, leaving no scars or deformities whatsoever, but even if the glaze did run, it only involved the chipping off of the bobs, which only left minimal scars. The use of bobs was apparently a characteristic feature of Midlands blackware, but pottery was still being fired occasionally by this method during the early twentieth century.

In the Tudor greenware tradition of Surrey a completely different form of prop was used from the late fifteenth century on. It took the shape of a thrown ring of clay from ¼ to ½in thick and from 1 to 4in across. At regular intervals round the ring's circumference three sharply pointed spikes were pinched up to give each pot a secure tripod support (see p 131, C). These props were very convenient, for they were quickly made, easy to use, and left little scarring on the pot's base. For these reasons the ring-props have continued to be used, and they are still to be seen in the kilns of the Farnham pottery today.

Plates, bowls, and other flatwares were always fired in the open kiln, as described once more by Dr Plot. Unglazed wares, he says, 'are exposed to the *naked* fire, and so is all their *flat ware* though it be leaded, haveing only *parting shards* i.e. thin bits of old pots put between them to keep them from *sticking* together'. For wares of an average size, say up to 12in diameter, the potter built up tall stacks of 'bungs' of bowls, etc, in the kiln by one of the three following methods: commonest, to judge from the writer's excavations at the Potovens potteries, was to place one bowl rim uppermost on the kiln floor, place three or more parting sherds on top of its rim, and then lower a second bowl base uppermost on top, the process continuing until a sufficient height had been attained (see p 131, D); the second method was to place a bowl rim downwards on three or more parting sherds, place more sherds round the upper surface of the rim, and lower a second inverted bowl into position directly above the first, thus forming a very compact stack (see p 131, E); and the final method, which gave a very open stack, was to cover the kiln floor with a single layer of inverted bowls, each one supported on sherds and lying almost rim to rim with its neighbour, then adding a second layer, each bowl resting on the upturned bases of three of the first layer, plus further layers in a similar manner until the kiln was full (see p 131, F). Larger flatwares, such as the huge slipware plates by the Tofts, Simpsons, etc, were never stacked within the kiln, presumably because they were only made in relatively small numbers, and also because they would tend to warp excessively if fired in any of the normal stacking positions. From a detailed examination of the plates themselves, noting the angle of the 'bleeding' from the iron rich slips and the slight warping of the rims, it would appear that they were fired in a vertical position, probably leaning against one of the kiln walls (see p 131, G).

Most of the techniques mentioned above remained in occa-

sional use up to the present day, but they were generally superseded by newer techniques developed in the urban potteries of
the late eighteenth and early nineteenth centuries. One of the
most important of these was the introduction of 'cupboards',
which were open-fronted shelf structures built round the kiln's
interior to support the finer wares, thus dispensing with the
space- and time-consuming saggers. There were two methods of
building the cupboards. The older method, used in the coal-
measure regions of the West Riding from the mid-eighteenth
century at least, built its shelves from slabs of Elland Flag, this
being a particularly heat-resistant sandstone quarried only in the
Halifax region. The slabs, or 'quarries' as the potters called them,
were about 2ft square by about 1½in thick, and were supported
at regular intervals round the kiln's perimeter by vertical walls of
brick or stone bound in position with the local fireclay. The more
recent method employed a similar structural arrangement, but
replaced the quarries with 'bats', stout firebrick slabs some 12 by
3in in section and of varying lengths, the shortest being 26in. From
the mid-nineteenth century a number of stoneware potteries began
to produce bats specially for the coarse earthenware kilns, the
most prominent being the Leeds Fireclay Co and Enos Morton
& Sons of Huddersfield. When using a kiln with cupboards (see
p 142), the potter had only to place his glazed wares side by side
on each shelf, where they would be perfectly fired, while the
central area of the kiln was left free to receive either stacks of
unglazed pottery or stacks of large baking bowls or pancheons in
their 'rings'.

Ring-firing had first been practised in the late seventeenth
century Staffordshire kilns, where each bowl had been supported
beneath its rim by a ring-saggar—a saggar having no base but
only a heavy flange running around its interior (see p 131, H).
As the size of bowls and pancheons increased throughout the
eighteenth century, so the size of the ring-saggars increased; but
it was soon realised that the continuous ring was too brittle and
unwieldy to be convenient, and so the sectional ring-saggar, or
'ring', was introduced. Each ring, or segment, consisted of an L-
sectioned strip of clay curved laterally to the radius of the bowls
to be fired. In use a circle of rings of the correct diameter was
formed on the kiln floor and further rings added until they
reached the same height as an unfired bowl. A single bowl was

then lowered into the circle of rings, the underside of its rim resting on the upper surface of the rings' flanges (see p 131, I). A further circle of rings was then added and a second bowl, the process continuing until a tall stack had been formed. If the bowls had been well thrown little difficulty was to be expected in the firing, but should they have been thrown too finely disaster was certain. When Nicholas Taylor, the Halifax fineware thrower moved to the Littlethorpe Pottery where only coarsewares were made, he inevitably threw his pancheons and bowls far too lightly, with the result that the body of each vessel fell away from its supporting rim during the firing and crashed on to the vessel beneath, which reacted in a similar manner. When the stack was opened it was often found to contain a series of perfect hoop-like rims still supported in the rings, while beneath lay a large mass of fused and shattered bodies.

The stacking of wares in any of these particularly economical ways demanded a particularly high standard of accuracy in the throwing and also a strict standardisation in both shapes and dimensions. At first sight a coarse earthenware bowl appears to have an uninteresting and somewhat functionless form, but when considered in detail it proves to be extremely well designed. The rim, for example, has been thrown thicker than the walls to give additional strength, and has usually been specifically shaped to throw off with a neat edge any slips or glazes applied to its interior, and also to hang securely on the rings during firing. The walls are normally conical in section, and thus able to bear immense loads in the stacking. These facts are amply borne out by a demonstration repeated for the writer by Mr Curtis of Littlethorpe Pottery. Some years ago Mr Curtis applied for a grant to rebuild his kiln, supplying sketches of the structure he proposed to erect. Shortly afterwards he received a visit from the head of one of the leading Staffordshire pottery companies, to whom the sketches had been sent for approval, who informed Mr Curtis that his proposals were ridiculous, as no kiln furniture was specified, and it was impossible for any pot to withstand a direct load of half a hundredweight during the firing. In answer Mr Curtis picked two 8in plant-pots at random from a stack of his dry but unfired wares, and placed them rim to rim in a vertical position on the drying-room floor. A short plank was then laid across the topmost pot and loaded with two 56lb weights. Surprisingly the two pots stood firm, even though their walls were only about $\frac{1}{4}$in thick. Imagine the astonishment of the Staffordshire man when Mr Curtis, then approaching 18 stone (252 lb) in weight, suddenly turned round and sat on top of the stack, raised his feet from the ground, bounced, and, with his pots still standing firm beneath him, cried, 'Now, lad, I've done it with mine, let's try some of yours!' Needless to say, Mr Curtis soon got his new kiln.

Note for this chapter is on page 161.

Chapter Ten

Firing

The process of firing was perhaps the most important single act in the whole course of pottery-making, for it converted the soluble and porous clay into the hard and virtually indestructible material we know as pottery. To carry out this conversion successfully required a tremendous amount of skill and experience for the dangers associated with firing were many: if the temperature rose too quickly the combined water within the ware expanded and caused the vessels to shatter; if the final temperature was too high the pottery would warp or even fuse completely, while if it was too low the ware would emerge in a soft and friable condition with the glaze still not melted; and if a cold draught entered the kiln at any time it would shatter the wares through thermal shock. So a carefully designed and well constructed kiln was essential for the production of sound wares.

The study of post-medieval kilns and firing techniques is still very much in its infancy, for very few kiln-structures have yet been excavated and documentary research into the subject is virtually non-existent. Even so, the meagre evidence so far obtained is sufficient to confirm two general statements: firstly, the kilns of the post-medieval period were the direct descendants of the medieval, and, secondly, the design of any kiln was dependent on the type of fuel available. Fuels were either mineral, in the form of coal or peat, or vegetable, in the form of wood or furze, and the difference between them was one of flame length and speed. When the mineral fuels were being burnt in the firemouth all the incoming air was forced to pass slowly through a mass of glowing ashes, where it was evenly heated before entering the kiln. When vegetable fuels were being used, however, the incoming air rushed through the loosely packed fuel to enter the kiln as an uneven mixture of long hot flames and relatively cool draughts. If this mixture played directly on the raw wares they responded to the strong thermal shocks by instantly shattering, and so experience proved it necessary to build a separate combustion area into the kiln to enable the incoming air to reach a uniform temperature before entering the actual firing chamber. We have, therefore, two distinct traditions of kiln-building, one designed specifically for coal and peat, the short-flame fuels, and the other for the long-flame fuels such as wood and furze.

Coal and Peat Burning Kilns

THE CLAMP KILN

One of the simplest types of kiln was the clamp, which was conpletely without structure. The method of clamp-firing consisted of stacking the wares in open stacks or in saggars on a flat bed of hard earth, clay, or stone. Narrow spaces were purposely left between each stack to act as flues, each one being loosely filled with a supply of dry fuel. The stacks were covered by a temporary insulating skin of clay, broken saggers, turves, etc, holes being left round the sides to act as firemouths and in the top to act as flues, and then the 'kiln' was lit and fired in the conventional manner. The whole process sounds crude and impracticable, but experimental firings made in Leeds in 1967 proved the efficiency of these kilns, even glazed wares emerging with an outstanding gloss.

It is only in recent years that such kilns have been recognised, for excavators have usually expected to find solid buildings on old pottery sites, and overlooked the disappointing 'layer of burnt earth' that could easily have been the base of a clamp kiln. Clamp kiln bases of the late fifteenth and mid-seventeenth centuries have been excavated at Silcoates and Potovens near Wakefield, Yorkshire, where a documentary source suggests their use as late as 1702. In his diary for 16 March of that year[1] Ralph Thoresby, the Leeds antiquary, described how he travelled to 'Pott Ovens [Little London in the dialect of the poor people], where I staid a little to observe not only the manner of forming their Earthen-ware . . . but to observe the manner of building their furnaces, their size and materials, which are small and upon the surface of the ground'. The suggestion that the small kilns were actually in the process of being built '*upon the surface of the ground*' can refer to clamp kilns only, the surface presumably being of burnt clay in this particular village. It is unlikely that clamp-firings continued to be practised into the mid or late eighteenth century for pottery, but the technique remained popular for coarse brick production up to some 40 years ago.

THE CIRCULAR MULTIFLUE

Given the burning properties of coal and peat, the most obvi-ous form of permanent kiln to build was a hollow circular struc-ture with a number of small firemouths equally spaced about the perimeter of the firing chamber. A kiln of this type could be fired with a fair degree of ease, for the heat was evenly dis-tributed round it, and extra heat could be directed to any parti-cular section merely by stoking at the appropriate firemouths. A circular multiflued kiln of this variety was already working at Sneyd Green in Hanley, Staffordshire, by the early thirteenth century[2], and by the late fifteenth and early sixteenth centuries further multiflued kilns were working at Holme on Spalding Moor, West Cowick, Follifoot, Potterton, and Potovens in York-shire, at Old Bolingbroke and Toynton in Lincolnshire, and at Chilvers Coton near Nuneaton in Warwickshire[3]. It is possible that future research may confirm the location of such kilns near supplies of mineral fuel—Chilvers Coton, Sneyd Green, Potter-ton, and Potovens were each fired with local coal, and the re-mainder all lay close to plentiful beds of peat and turves[4].

The structure of these kilns has posed many problems for the archaeologist, for the only remains have been walls, which have never stood more than 2ft in height. Excavations have always shown a flat burnt-clay firing-chamber floor some 8-10ft in dia-meter surrounded by a truncated kiln wall, usually made of burnt clay but on rare occasions built of stone. Through these walls have been cut four to six firemouths, each carefully arched over and showing the effects of intense heat. For some time it was thought that the domed clay superstructure with its presumed central vent was built over the stacked ware every time the kiln

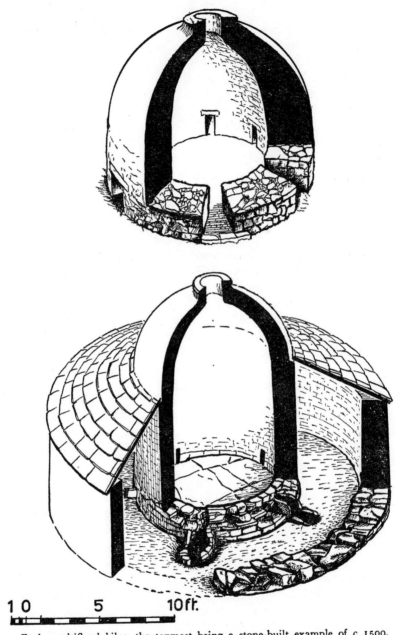

1 0   5   10ft.

Early multiflued kilns, the topmost being a stone-built example of c 1500, from Potovens, near Wakefield, while the lower is from Halifax and dates from the late seventeenth century

was to be fired. In 1967, however, the students of Leeds University's extra-mural course in advanced archaeology built a full-sized replica of the West Cowick kiln and conducted a series of experimental firings within it. As a result of this work it was realised that the building of such a large solid clay dome for every single firing would have been too great an effort, so it is now thought that the dome was a permanent feature. This proposition was recently given considerable support by the finding of a complete fired-clay vent-opening, which could *only* have come from a permanently domed kiln superstructure[5].

If there was a permanent dome, the question arises as to how the kiln was loaded or unloaded; but recent excavations, particularly those carried out at Chilvers Coton, have answered this question, demonstrating that either one firemouth was built wide enough to allow access for the potter and his wares, or else there was a specially designed walk-in entrance or porthole that could be temporarily blocked up while the firing was in progress. A tentative reconstruction of the late fifteenth-century Potovens kiln 2, embodying these suggestions, is given on p 140.

The circular multiflued kilns were still being used in the late seventeenth century, but only two of this period have been excavated—one at Hanley, Stoke-on-Trent and another at Puel Hill, Halifax, Yorkshire[6]. The Hanley kiln, now re-erected at the City of Stoke-on-Trent Museum, is a well built stone structure with seven firemouths, a single walk-in entrance, and a 7ft diameter firing chamber. Dr Plot has described such kilns as being 'ordinarily above eight foot high, and about six foot wide, of a round copped forme, where they [the pots] are placed one upon another from the bottom to the top . . . In 24 hours an *oven* of *pots* will be burnt, then they let the *fire* go out by degrees which in 10 hours will be perfectly done, and then they draw them for *sale*'. The only marked technical improvement between this kiln and its fifteenth- and sixteenth-century predecessors was the addition of a masonry baffle at the inner end of each firemouth by means of which the fierce initial blast of heat was distributed more evenly throughout the wares. The Puel Hill kiln had no such baffles, and probably relied on experience and careful stacking alone to prevent the wares nearest the firemouths being 'bloated' or 'dunted' by the excessive incoming heat. In most other respects this kiln was very similar to that at Hanley,

The potteries at Burton-in-Lonsdale, c 1870, showing the multiflued kilns with their surrounding hovels

142

having thick stone walls, five firemouths, and a 9ft diameter firing chamber. Its construction differed in one important respect, however, for it had a second masonry wall some 1ft 6in thick running round the outside of the kiln to form a sheltered 5ft wide passage (see p 140). The situation of this kiln is particularly exposed—just below the 1,000ft contour on the summit of a high Pennine pass—and such a protective wall would have been essential to keep the firemouths under control and shelter the potter from the perpetual gales of the area. Presumably this circular passage was roofed, for the remaining foundations are certainly heavy enough to have supported a wall 6-8ft high, in which case we can see here an early version of the later 'hovels' or kiln-houses such as those shown in the plate on p 104 and the drawing opposite.

Unfortunately not one eighteenth-century kiln of this type has yet been excavated, though this implies lack of research rather than a decline in their popularity in the coal-producing areas. In fact, all the Northern urban potteries of the nineteenth century used the circular multiflued kilns exclusively. Some of them are still standing today, and by measuring them and talking to the few remaining potters who fired them, it is possible to build up quite a good picture of the later developments in their construction and use.

One of the minor defects of the earlier kilns had been the tendency for the incoming heat to flow up the sides of the firing chamber to leave a rather cold conical area in the centre of the chamber floor. Careful stacking could reduce the extent of this cold spot, but never very satisfactorily, so it is not surprising to see that specially constructed flues were built under the floors of the later kilns, such as that at the Weatheriggs Pottery, Penrith, built in 1855 (p 144), or that at the Littlethorpe Pottery, Ripon, probably erected in the 1840s.

The Weatheriggs kiln, in regular use until 1959, illustrates the final form of the circular multiflued kiln. Around the wide base are spaced eight large firemouths, which taper to slits 28in high by 4in wide where they cut through the kiln wall. The flames thus concentrated did not strike directly on to the ware but were split in two, one half being contained within the triangular flues running up between the square cupboards, and the other half passing under the kiln floor to rise up through the central vent.

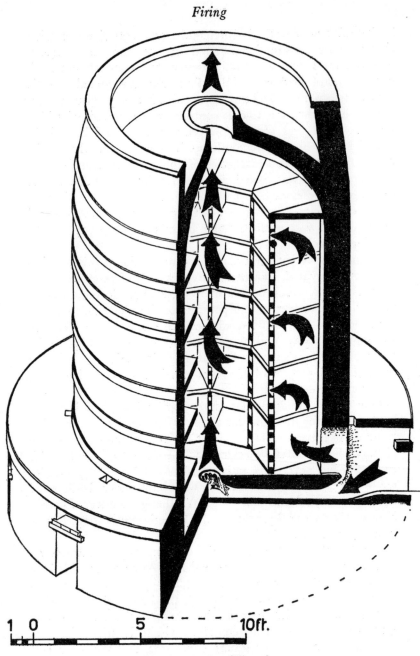

The Weatheriggs Kiln, 1855

144

This caused an even heat distribution, as shown on p 144. This particular kiln needed 5-6 tons of coal to bring it to the 1100°C required to mature the local clay, the actual firing taking some 30-36 hours, and another 2-3 days being allowed for cooling.

The kiln at Littlethorpe, demolished in 1968, was of identical construction to that at Weatheriggs. Mr Curtis, the present potter, remembers well how the kiln used to be fired until its replacement by one of the Newcastle type in the 1950s. Once the ware had been placed or 'set' in position, a task for which only one day was allowed, the doorway was bricked up and a low fire lit in each of the seven fireplaces to dry the ware out. During the course of the next 24 hours the temperature was gradually raised to 400°C, the small vents above each fireplace (see p 142) being left open to allow a certain amount of cool air into the fires to reduce the total heat intake. Firing then continued at a moderate rate for 12 hours, after which the small vents were blocked with bricks and the fires stoked to their fiercest heat until the required temperature was reached a further 12 hours later. Test pieces were then withdrawn from the kiln on the end of long iron poles, and if they had matured satisfactorily the fireplaces were quickly bricked up and the whole kiln left to cool for 3 more days before being opened. On the morning of the 4th day the load was withdrawn (a 5 hour task), the entire process of firing having taken a total of $5\frac{1}{2}$ days to complete, and 5 tons of high-grade low sulphur content coal having been burnt.

The decline of the large coal-fired multiflue kiln within the last few decades has been entirely due to fuel problems. A coal-fired kiln of this type requires constant attention to bring about a gradual rise in its temperature and an even distribution of heat. It is impossible for one or even two men to fire such a kiln successfully through the long period of stoking, and so, with the declining numbers of potters, the kilns have fallen out of use one by one. A second problem has been the continuing rise in the price of coal, making the kilns uneconomical to run. Fortunately those potters who still work on today have found an excellent replacement in the form of smaller electric kilns, which can be fired automatically to a predetermined temperature and are much cheaper to use.

Wood-burning Kilns

The history and development of the post-medieval wood-burning kiln is still obscure, for the scanty remains of only seven have been excavated throughout England. So it is only possible to review the present state of our knowledge and record the working techniques used in the later wood-firing kilns by those few potters who are still alive today.

Despite their many differences, the kilns excavated to date do appear to have two points in common[7]; firstly, a circular or slightly oval firing chamber having some form of raised floor structure, and secondly, either one or two firemouths, in contrast to the greater numbers found in the multiflued kilns. The raised floor structures were necessary because of the nature of the fuel, for, as has been explained, the uneven heat caused by long flames and cool draughts passing in from the firemouths needed to be converted to an even heat before coming into contact with the wares. Each kiln excavated has produced a completely different form of floor structure, presumably reflecting each potter's individual answer to the problems of firing.

The two seventeenth-century kilns at Potterspury in Northamptonshire, for example, each had two D-shaped pedestals built up some 6 in from the flat kiln floor to form a continuous flue 6-10in wide round the kiln's walls, with a similar flue running diametrically from one firemouth to the other. The flames entering the kiln would tend to follow the lines of these flues and then rise evenly through the wares stacked above, so avoiding a great concentration of heat just inside the firemouth passages.

At Crockerton in Wiltshire it was found that the late sixteenth-century kiln was divided into two distinct sections, the lower for distributing and mixing the incoming flames and the upper section containing the actual ware. This type of kiln, with its single firemouth, central sandstone pedestal, and radiating firebars (p 147) has an almost continuous history in England from Roman times and (though Wales lies outside the scope of this study) it was still in use at Ewenny in Glamorgan early in the present century.

The kiln excavated at Boresford in Herefordshire was presumably of a mid-seventeenth century date and showed no signs of

any internal structure whatsoever, but the excavator concluded
that a raised platform of stone bats would have been erected a

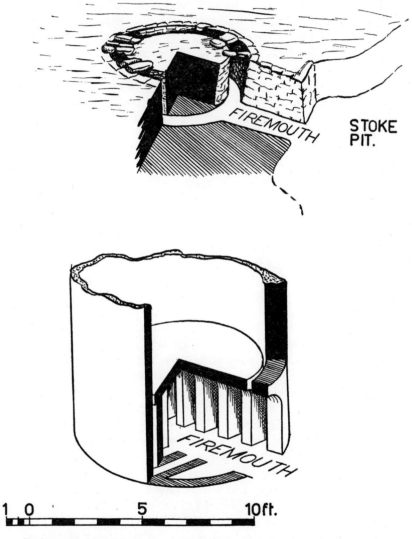

STOKE
PIT.

FIREMOUTH

FIREMOUTH

1 0   5   10ft.

Early wood-firing kilns, the upper being a late sixteenth-century example
from Crockerton, Dorset, while the other, dating from c 1800, was excavated
at Charles Hill, near Farnham, Surrey

few inches above the clay floor. With the exception of three other wood-burning kilns, the remains of which were too slight to be meaningful, these four kilns represent our total knowledge of kiln-building between the early sixteenth and the early nineteenth centuries. It is impossible to draw any definite conclusions from such poor evidence, but it is suggested that it does at least show that post-medieval kiln designs were directly descended from those of the medieval period.

Having thus exhausted the scant archaeological evidence we must now turn to those structures still standing today and to the potters who fired them to trace the later developments in kiln design and firing practice.

Probably the most primitive form of wood-burning kiln to be used in modern times was that at Verwood, on the perimeter of the New Forest in Dorest. The kiln used here up to the early 1950s consisted of a tall open-topped brick cylinder of about 15ft internal diameter surrounded by a high bank of waster sherds and soil. The base of the cylinder had a single firemouth, whose flames passed beneath a raised floor structure, up through the stacked wares, and so on to emerge from the top of the kiln. The potters loaded the kiln by carrying their wares up the side of the soil bank and passing them down a ladder into the firing chamber to be placed in position. Once the kiln had received its full load of pans and pitchers, a temporary dome was constructed from waster sherds, and the kiln lit. For the next 3 days the wood fire burnt continuously, the temperature gradually rising until flames began to emerge from the top. As soon as the flames reached the height of 6-8ft the kiln was flashed, gorse and faggots being used to give a final burst of heat to flux the glaze. The firemouth was then quickly sealed and the load allowed to cool for a further 3 days before the dome was removed, and the wares lifted out.

Mr Fishley Holland remembers that a very similar method used to be followed by the potters at the Fremington Pottery, North Devon, though its wares were passed into the kiln at floor level through a temporary side door that was bricked up during the firing period. The top of the kiln was left open, as at Verwood, but instead of patching the top with a layer of waster sherds, the potters built a temporary dome from specially shaped clay slabs, which were carefully secured by means of iron chains. By the time Mr Holland had entered the pottery in 1900 the kilns were all permanently domed in brick and were burning coal, but, even so, the old firing techniques still remained in use. When the kiln was almost at maximum temperature the hot coals and their supporting firebars were raked out and a number of faggots of furze and bramble used to flash the glaze. After this the samples were withdrawn and the firemouths sealed if the results had proved successful. Three days then elapsed before the kiln was cool enough for the wares to be withdrawn.

A second group of wood-fired kilns, which developed in a slightly different way, still exists at Farnham in Surrey. In October 1966 H. G. A. Booth of the Wilmer House Museum, Farnham, excavated the base of a kiln at Charles Hill, Elstead. From a study of local records it was known that this kiln had been built at some time during the late eighteenth or early nineteenth centuries, and had last been used in the period 1860-66 by Absalom Harris. The kiln (see p 147) remained intact up to floor level, and had a circular outer wall of brick with an internal diameter of 8ft. Across the kiln ran seven parallel brick walls, which supported the kiln-floor itself and also formed a series of narrow parallel flues. At right-angles to these ran the long central firemouth, formed by piercing an arch 3ft high by 2ft wide through the centre of each wall. The kiln was most probably loaded through a side door, the door sealed, and a fire of bavins and perhaps a little coal lit in the firemouth. Bavins, or bush bavins as they are occasionally known, are large faggots of light timber averaging about 1ft in diameter by about 8ft in length. From the firemouth the flames would pass beneath the kiln-floor, into and through the series of cross-flues, upwards into the kiln, and so on to the wares. From the size of the kiln the present Farnham potters estimate that a firing period of 3 days would be necessary to fire this kiln to the temperature at which the local clays matured.

In 1873 Absalom Harris built himself a series of larger kilns at his new pottery at Wrecclesham, near Farnham. Being much larger than his old Charles Hill kiln, they required much more heat, and so he built four firemouths into them, two to fire one half and two to fire the other (p 150). Even with this enlarged structure, he still retained a regular series of cross-flues beneath the kiln-floor, but these he now linked with a circular bag wall built a few inches inside the true kiln wall. By these means he

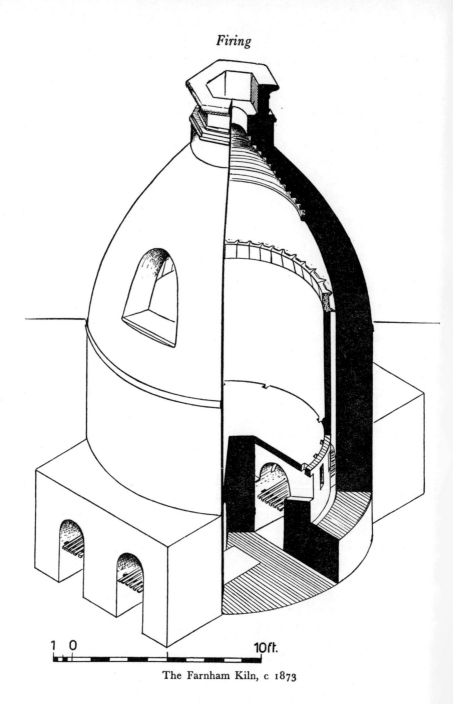

The Farnham Kiln, c 1873

distributed the heat evenly throughout the kiln, eliminating the risk of any particular section being overfired. When these kilns had been stacked with the ware the side door to the kiln, now at first-floor level, was bricked up, and slow fires started in each of the four firemouths.

For the next 48 hours the firing continued, about 4 tons of coal and 100 bavins being consumed in the process. As the kiln heated up, the stacks of ware inside reacted to the changing conditions by alternately expanding and contracting, the extent of the movement being observed through a spy-hole left in the blocking of the doorway. During the initial heating, perhaps for the first 400°C, the ware contracted as the water was driven off. As the temperature rose still further the wares expanded with the heat, but then began to contract once more when the pottery began to mature at about 1,000°C. The degree of final shrinking was carefully noted by comparing the height of the topmost pot with the projecting bands of brickwork at the far side of the kiln. When the stack had shrunk the depth of one brick experience showed that the wares were perfectly fired, and so the firemouths were instantly sealed; 4 days later the kiln was cool enough to be drawn, the whole firing having taken 6 days. The Farnham kilns are still being fired in this way, but since 1967 oil has replaced coal and bavins, which were proving prohibitively expensive. One oil burner is fixed in each firemouth, giving the same results more easily and cheaply.

Notes for this chapter are on pages 161-2.

Notes in the Text

1   Developments from the Medieval Tradition (Pages 13-39)

1   Chaffers, W. *Marks and Monograms on European and Con-tinental Pottery*, 9th Ed (1903), 41.
2   Emmison, F. *Tudor Food & Pastimes* (1964).
3   Inderwick, F. A. *A Calendar of the Inner Temple Records*, (Vol 1 1896).
4   'York Civic Records (II)', fol 136b, 26 May 1495, *Yorkshire Record Series CIII*.
5   Jarrett, M. G. & Edwards, B. J. N. 'Excavations at Tullie House, Carlisle; Report on the Medieval Pottery Nos 18-20', *Trans Cumberland & Westmorland Antiq & Archaeol Soc,* Vol LXIV (1964).
6   Richardson, K. M., & Le Patourel, J. 'Excavations in Hungate, York', Fig 25, no 3, *The Archaeol Jnl*, Vol CXVI, (1959).
7   Jarrett, M. G., & Edwards, B. J. N. 'Medieval Pottery from Finchdale Priory', *Archaeologia Aeliana*, Vol XXXIX, (1961), 229.
8   As note 7, no 129, and also Cruden, S. H. 'Melrose', *Proc of the Soc of Antiquaries of Scotland*, Vol LXXXVII (1952-3), 161
9   As note 7, no 125.
10   As note 6.
11   The earliest sherd of Cistercian ware excavated to date was discovered beneath the tiled refectory floor at Kirkstall Abbey, Yorks, which must therefore date to the late fifteenth century or earlier.
12   Examples have been published from: Finchdale (see note 7); Melrose (see note 8); Potterton (see Mayes, P., Pirie, E., & Le Patourel, J. 'A Cistercian Ware Kiln of the Early Six-teenth Century at Potterton, Yorks', *The Antiquaries Jnl,*

XLVI [1966] 255-76); Potovens (see Brears, P. C. D. 'Excavations at Potovens', Fig 6, *Post Medieval Archaeology*, I [1967] 3-43); Pontefract (see Bellamy, C. V., & Le Patourel, J. 'Excavations at Pontefract Priory', Figs 38-9, *Proc of the Thoresby Soc*, XLIX [1962-4], 116-19); Rockley (see Crossley, D. 'Excavations at Rockley Smithies', Fig 11, *Post Medieval Archaeology*, II [1968], 39); and York (see note 6, and also Brears, P. C. D. *Catalogue of English Country Pottery housed in the Yorkshire Museum, York*, [1968] 5).

13 Examples have been published from Kirkstall Abbey (see Le Patourel, J. in forthcoming Leeds Museum Report); Potterton (see note 12); Potovens (see note 12); and Worcester (see Barton, K. J. 'An early post-medieval group from Nudix Court, Worcester', *Post-medieval Ceramics Research Group Broadsheet*, 3 (1965), 18.

14 Examples have been published from Pontefract, Potovens, Rockley (see note 12 for all three), and Ticknall (see Solon, M. L. 'On some fragments of English Earthenware', *Derbyshire Archaeol & Nat Hist Soc*, IX [1887], 179).

15 Examples have been published from Finchdale (see note 7); Pontefract, Potterton, Potovens, Rockley, York (see note 12); Kirkstall (see note 13); Ticknall (see note 14); Ormskirk (see Steane, J. M., & Kelsall, A. F. *Trans of the Lancs & Ches Hist Soc*, CXIV, [1962], 86); and Newcastle (see Jarrett, M. G. & Edwards, B. J. N. 'Medieval Pottery in the possession of the Society of Antiquaries of Newcastle upon Tyne, *Archaeologia Aeliana*, [4th series], Vol XLI, [1963]).

16 Examples have been published from Pontefract, Potovens, Rockley (see note 12 for all three).

17 Examples have been published from Yearsley (see Brooke, S. 'A Late Medieval Pottery Site at Yearsley', *The Yorks Archaeol Jnl*, XXXVII [1951]).

18 Examples have been published from Pontefract and Potterton (see note 12); and York, Hungate (see note 6).

19-21 Examples have been published from Silcoates (in Potovens, see note 12).

22 Examples have been published from Kirkstall (see note 13) and Potovens (see note 12).

23 Examples have been published from Kirkstall (see note 13), Newcastle (see note 15), and Potterton (see note 12).

24 Examples have been published from Potterton (see note 12) and Silcoates (in Potovens, see note 12).

25 An example has been published from Potovens (see note 12).

26 An example has been published from Potterton (see note 12).

27 Examples have been published from Potovens, Potterton, Rockley, and York (see note 12); Coventry (see Woodfield, P. 'Yellow Glazed Wares of the Seventeenth Century', *Trans Birmingham Archaeol Soc*, 81 [1966]); Basing House (see Moorhouse, S. 'Basing House', *Post Medieval Archaeology*, 4 [1970]); and London (see Mathews, L. G., & Green, H. J. M. 'Post-Medieval Pottery of the Inns of Court', *Post Medieval Archaeology*, 3 [1969]).

28 Examples have been excavated from Potovens; Rockley (?) (see note 12); and Coventry (?) (see note 27).

29 Although only two examples have been published from York (note 12) and Ticknall (Jewitt, L. *The Ceramic Art of Great Britain* [1883]), other examples have been excavated from London (British Museum), Sandal (Wakefield City Museum), and Cardiff (National Museum of Wales).

30 For a full discussion of Tudor Green, and further sources, see Hurst, J. G. 'Tudor Green Ware' in *Winchester Excavations, 1949-60*, Winchester (1964).

31 See Mathews, L. G., & Green, H. J. M. 'Post-Medieval Pottery of the Inns of Court', *Post Medieval Archaeology*, 3 (1969). Southampton—excavations still in progress, report forthcoming.
Oxford, see *Oxoniensia*, VI (1948) 88.
Also Hurst, J. G. 'Tudor Green Ware', *Winchester Excavations 1949-60*, Winchester (1964), 140; and Barton, K. J. 'An early Post-Medieval Group from Nudix Court, Worcester', *Post-Medieval Ceramics Research Group Broadsheet*, 3 (1965), 18.

32 Examples have been published from London (the Inns of Court, note 31, nos 5-18; Rackham, B. 'Farnham Pottery of the Sixteenth Century', *Surrey Archaeol Collections*, LII [1952], pl VI; Jarrett, M. G., & Edwards, B. J. N. 'Medieval Pottery in the Possession of the Society of Antiquaries of Newcastle upon Tyne', *Archaeologia Aeliana* [4th series], XLI [1963], nos 41 & 42); and Farnborough Hill (Holling, F. 'Excavations at Farnborough Hill', Typescript [1969]).

33 Examples have been published from London (the Inns of Court, note 31, nos 28-35; and Hobson, R. L. *Catalogue of the Collection of English Pottery in the British Museum* [1903], nos B239-40); and Farnborough Hill (see note 32).

34 Examples have been published from London (the Inns of Court, note 31, no 36); and Farnborough Hill (see note 32).

35 Examples have been published from Winchester (see Cunliffe, B. *Winchester Excavations 1949-60*, Winchester [1964], Fig 17, nos 1 & 2).

36 Examples have been published from Winchester (see note 35, Fig 27, no 8); Farnham (see Rackham, B. 'Farnham Pottery of the Sixteenth Century', *Surrey Archaeol Collections*, LII [1952], Fig 2 & pl VII); and Worcester (see note 31).

37 Examples have been excavated from London (Victoria & Albert Museum Collection); Farnborough Hill (see note 32).

38 Examples have been published from Farnborough Hill (see note 32); and London (the Inns of Court, note 31, nos 37 & 38; and the Treasury, see interim report by Green, H. J. M., & Curnow, P. E. in 'The Palace of Whitehall & After', *Illustrated London News*, 6 July 1963, 14).

39 Examples have been published from London (the Inns of Court, note 31, no 39; the British Museum Collection, note 33, nos B245 & B246; and *The Catalogue of the Collection of London Antiquities in the Guildhall Museum*, London [1908], no 339 & Pl XCIV no 7); Sussex (see *Sussex Archaeol Collections*, CII [1964], 127); Winchester (see note 35, Fig 27, no 4); and Lincoln (see *Lincolnshire History & Archaeology*, I [1966], 41).

40 Examples have been published from London (the Inns of Court, note 31, Fig 27, no 6); Nonsuch (see Biddle, M. 'Nonsuch Palace 1959-60—An Interim Report', *Surrey Archaeol Collections*, LVIII [1961], Fig 6, no 14); and Winchester (see note 35, Fig 27, no 6).

41 Examples have been published from London (the Inns of Court, note 31, nos 40 & 41).

42 Examples have been published from Ash (see Holling, F. 'Pottery from Ash, Surrey', *Post Medieval Archaeology*, 3 [1969], Fig 6 F4); Farnborough Hill (see note 32); London (British Museum Collection, note 33, nos B181-5).

43 See Blake, B. P., Hurst, J. G., & Gant, H. L. 'Medieval and Later Pottery from Stockwell Street, Colchester', *Trans of the Essex Archaeol Soc*, I, Part I (1961), Fig 23; and Mayes, P. 'Kilns at Potterspury, Northamptonshire', *Post Medieval Archaeology*, 2 (1968) Fig 30, no 18.

44 See note 57.

45 Examples have been published from Potterspury (see note 43, Fig 29, no 8); Nonsuch (see note 40, Fig 7, no 17); Taunton (see Ralegh Radford, C. A., & Hallam, A. D. 'History of

Taunton Castle', *Somerset Archaeol Soc Proc* [1953], Fig 9, no 1); and Winchester (see note 35, Fig 43, no 10, and Fig 27, no 11 [?]).

46 For an account of these wares see the article by J. G. Hurst in the Stockwell Street Report (see note 43, p 45).

47 An example has been published from Potovens (see note 12, Fig 11, no 6).

48 Examples have been published from Basing House (see note 27), Coventry (see note 27, no Gg), and Potterspury (see note 43, Fig 30, no 11).

49 Examples have been published from Farnborough Hill (see note 32, no 2), Potterspury (see note 43, Fig 30, no 8), and Oxford (see Jope, E. M. 'Pottery from a seventeeth century well filling', *Oxoniensia*, XV [1950] 61).

50 Examples have been published from Basing House (see note 27), and Coventry (see note 27, no Le).

51 Examples have been published from Ash (see note 42, Fig 7, no H), Coventry (see note 27, nos Aa-c), Farnborough Hill (see note 32), London (the Inns of Court, note 31, Fig 3, no 47), and Taunton (see note 45, Fig 9, no 8).

52 Examples have been published from Basing House (see note 27), London (the Inns of Court, note 31, Fig 3, no 42), and Nottingham (in the York Catalogue, see note 12, Fig 2, no 34/a).

53 Eg, compare 44/a in the York Catalogue (see note 12) with Fig 2, no 25 in 'London Tin-glazed Pottery-2' by B. Bloice and J. Thorn in *The London Archaeologist*, I, no 4 [1969].

54 See Barton, K. J. 'Excavation of a Medieval Bastion at St. Nicholas's Almshouses, King Street, Bristol', *Medieval Archaeology*, VIII (1964).

55 Examples have been published from Coventry (see note 27, no Ad), Nottingham (in the York Catalogue, see note 12, no 40/c), Potovens (see note 12, Fig 11, no 19), Taunton (see note 45, Fig 9, no 6), York (see note 12, Types 40-41), and York, Hungate (see note 6, Fig 25, no 6). Also, compare the above with the Netherlands Majolica pot decorated with orange and blue brushwork, published in the Hungate report (see note 6), which is probably pre-1570 in date.

56 Examples have been published from Colchester (see note 43, Fig 1, no 2); London (the Treasury, note 38, and the Inns of Court, note 31, nos 25-7); and Potterton (see note 12, Fig 7, no 24).

57 Examples have been published from Basing House (see note

27), Coventry (see note 27, no Ja), Potterspury (see note 43, Fig 32, no 10), and York, Hungate (see note 6, Fig 25, no 5).

58 Examples have been published from Coventry (see note 27, no Ha), Basing House (see note 27), and Potovens (see note 12, Fig 12, no 4).

59 Examples have been published from London (see the *York Catalogue*, note 12, no 21/a; the *British Museum Catalogue*, note 33, C 4-6; and Rackham, B. *Catalogue of the Glaisher Collection*, no 20); Oxford (see *Oxoniensia*, IV [1939] 132-46, Pl XIV); Potterspury (see note 43, Fig 30, no 20); Potovens (see note 12, Fig 11, no 3); and Walton (see the *York Catalogue*, note 12, no 21/b).

60 Examples have been published from Birmingham (see Rackham, B. *Catalogue of the Glaisher Collection*, no 32); Gravesend (see *Archaeologia Cantiana*, [1962] 197); Harlow (see *Trans of the Essex Archaeol Soc*, XXV, part III [1960] 358-77); and Nonsuch (see note 40).

61 Examples have been published from London (?) (see under Newcastle in note 15, no 58; Southwark and Potters Bar in *Blackware Mugs*, dyeline by J. H. Ashdowne [1967]; and Potterspury [see note 43, Fig 28, no 7]).

62 Examples have been published from London (see note 61, *Blackware Mugs*), and 'Cambridge (see *Cambridge Antiq Soc*, XI [1906], 425-45, no 40).

63 Examples have been published from Cambridge (see note 61, *Blackware Mugs*), Harlow (see note 60), Oxford (see note 59), and Waltham Abbey (see Huggins, P. J. 'Excavations at Sewardstone Street, Waltham Abbey', *Post Medieval Archaeology*, 3 [1969], Fig 28, nos 16-17).

64 Examples have been published from Dover (see Mynard, D. 'An early Post-Medieval Group from Dover Castle', *Post Medieval Archaeology*, 3 [1969], Fig 13, no 37), Gravesend (see note 60), London (see the *York Catalogue*, note 12, no 22/a), Nottingham (see the *York Catalogue*, note 12, no 22/b), and Wrotham (see note 61, *Blackware Mugs*).

65 Examples have been published from Nottingham (see Rackham, B. *Catalogue of the Glaisher Collection*, no 22), Potovens (see note 12, Fig 11, no 4), and York (see note 12, no 23/b).

66 Examples have been published from Potterspury (see note 43, Fig 30, no 19), Potovens (see note 12, Fig 12, no 6), and York (see note 12, nos 28/a-n, 29/a-m).

67 Examples have been published from Dover (see note 64, Fig 14, no 2), Potterspury (see note 43, Fig 28, no 8), Waltham

Abbey (see note 63, Fig 27, no 6), and Wrotham (see note 61, *Blackware Mugs*).

2 *The Effects of Trade* (Pages 40-54)

1 Will of Robert Morris of Halifax, Potseller, dated 13 January 1679, and now in the Borthwick Institute, St Anthony's Hall, York.
2 'Collections towards a History of Derbyshire' by Philip Kinder, manuscript now housed in Bodleian Library, Oxford.
3 When Solon found the Chirk plates clamped on to the walls of the Chirk dairy he tried to discover how the collection had come into being, but no one could remember. It is the writer's belief that the collection was already very old and its collector long forgotten. Other authorities, however, believe that Solon's irritable character alienated the inhabitants of Chirk, who would tell him nothing, and not that the collection was of seventeenth- or even early eighteenth-century date.
4 See Barton, K. J. 'The Excavation of a Medieval Bastion at St Nicholas's Almshouses, King Street, Bristol', *Medieval Archaeology*, 8 (1964), 202-7; and Ralegh Radford, C. A., & Hallam, A. D. 'The History of Taunton Castle', *Proc of Somerset Archaeol Soc*, 98 (1953), 81-8.

3 *The Urban Potteries* (Pages 55-71)

1 Chaffers, W. *Marks & Monograms on Pottery & Porcelain*, 3rd ed (1870), 643.
2 Phillipson, J. 'Whiskey Smuggling on the Border', *Archaeologia Aeliana*, 39 (1961), 154.
3 See North Devon in the Gazetteer (p 175).

4 *Art Wares* (Pages 72-6)

1 For example, such vessels as the tall blackware mug dated 1599, as mentioned in Chapter 1.

Notes in the Text

2 The following Guilds were set up about this period (see Pevsner, N. *Pioneers of Modern Design*, Pelican ed, [1960], 54): Century Guild, 1882; Art Workers Guild, 1884; Home Arts & Industries Association, 1884; Guild & School of Handicraft, 1888; Arts & Crafts Exhibition Society, 1888.

3 Following the Arts & Crafts movement a great number of 'Art Potteries' were set up round the country, usually by gentlemen of private means (such as Lord Elton at Clevedon Court), or designers (such as Cristopher Dresser at Linthorpe) who wished to propagate their own range of designs. The products of their potteries were usually quite exotic, and are not within the scope of this volume.

4 Brears, P. C. D. *The Farnham Potteries*, Farnham (1970).

5 Letter dated 19 August 1594, from the Treasurer of the Inn, Julius Caesar, to Sir William More, one of the controllers of the Bishop of Winchester's park at Farnham during the vacancy of the see. It was first published in *The Losely Manuscripts* (1835) by A. J. Kempe, and later in *The Seventh Report of the Royal Commission on Historical Manuscripts*, Part 1, Appendix (1879), 652. The most accurate transcription is that published by Bernard Rackham in 'Farnham Pottery of the Sixteenth Century', *Surrey Archaeol Collections*, 52 (1950-1), 50.

5 *The Decline of the Potteries* (Pages 77-82)

1 Burnett, J. *Plenty & Want*, Pelican ed (1968), 20.
2 Levi, L. 'Wages & Earnings of the Working Classes', Report to Sir Arthur Bliss, MP (1885), 30.

6 *Clay Preparation* (Pages 83-94)

1 British Museum Additional Manuscripts 26.732.

7 *Potting* (Pages 95-114)

1 Only templates or ribs could have produced the finely thrown

rims and mouldings found on Cistercian and Tudor greenwares of this period.

2 Chapter 2, note 4.

8 *Decorating* (Pages 115-24)

1 Chapter 2, note 4.
2 See Kleyn, J. de. *Volksaardewerk in Nederland* (1965).

9 *Glazing* (Pages 125-36)

1 This identical technique was used by William Smith of Farnborough, Hants, until the 1850s. The crude hand-sprinkling
crippled his hands.

10 *Firing* (Pages 137-51)

1 Diary of Ralph Thoresby. Manuscript in the Yorkshire
Archaeological Society's Library, Leeds.
2 Bemrose, G. J. V. '13th Century Pottery Kilns at Sneyd Green',
The North Staffordshire Field Club Trans, 91 (1956-7), 86.
3 See Mayes P. 'A late Medieval Kiln at Holme on Spalding
Moor', *Hull Museum Publications*, 216, and 'A Cistercian
Ware Kiln of the Early Sixteenth Century at Potterton,
Yorks', *The Antiquaries Jnl*, 46 (1966), 255-76; Le Patourel,
H. E. J. 'Note on the Folifoot kiln', *Medieval Archaeology*,
9 (1965), 218; Brears, P. C. D. 'Excavations at Potovens near
Wakefield', *Post Medieval Archaeology*, 1 (1967), 3-43;
Mayes, P. & Thomson, R. 'Note on the Chilvers Coton kilns',
Medieval Archaeology, 12 (1968) 208; and Barley, M. W. &
Rudkin, E. H. Notes on the Toynton kilns, *Medieval
Archaeology*, 4 (1960) 163, 8 (1964) 296, and 3 (1959) 235.
4 For an excellent discussion of the fuels used in this region in
the medieval period see H. E. J. Le Patourel. 'Documentary
Evidence and the Medieval Pottery Industry', *Medieval
Archaeology*, 12 (1968) 101-26.
5 Excavated by K. Bartlett at Potovens near Wakefield.

6   See Kelley, J. H. Note on the Hanley Kiln, *Post Medieval Archaeology* 1 (1967) 116 and 2 (1968) 187; and Bryant, G. Note on the Puel Hill kiln, *Post Medieval Archaeology*, 1 (1967) 116-18.

7   See Mayes, P. 'A Seventeenth Century Kiln Site at Potterspury Northants', *Post Medieval Archaeology*, 2 (1968), 55-82; Algar, D. Note on the Crockerton kiln, *Post Medieval Archaeology*, 1 (1967) 116 and 2 (1968) 187-8; Newton, E. F. & Bibbings, S. E. 'Seventeenth Century Pottery Sites at Harlow, Essex', *Trans of the Essex Archaeol Soc*, 25, part 3 (1960), 358-77; 'Lake's Pottery, Truro', Note in *Post Medieval Archaeology*, 3 (1969), 198; and Holling, F. Note on the kiln at Hawley, Hants, in *Post Medieval Archaeology*, 2 (1968), 185.

Notes on the Plates

Cistercian Wares (Page 33)

The vessels illustrated here are both housed in the collection of the Yorkshire Museum, York. The tall Type 3 cup on the left (no 3/j) has a red fabric with applied white decoration beneath a dull yellow lead glaze. It was excavated from Lord Mayor's Walk, York. H 7in. The Type 4 vessel on the right (no 4B/b) has a red fabric covered in a dark brown glaze, and was found during the erection of the new markets in York. H 3¾in.

Tudor Greenwares (Page 33)

These Type 2 vessels are all from the British Museum Collection and have an off-white fabric with a mottled green glaze. They are, left to right: No B237 Franks Collection (on a silver mount about the rim is the inscription 'Found in a Vault under the Stewards Office Lincoln's Inn, 1788'—H 4.7in); No 242 Franks Collection, 1896, found in Liverpool Street, London, in 1874—H 4.3in); No B240 Roach Smith Collection—H 4.6in.

Midlands Blackwares (Page 34)

From the Yorkshire Museum Collection. The Type 6 cup on the left (no 22/a), 5in high, was found 'in a house in Wood Street, London, 14th November, 1878', while the Type 7 cup on the right (no 23/a), 2¾ high, is unprovenanced. Both have a red fabric and a very dark lead glaze.

Midlands Yellow-wares (Page 34)

From the Yorkshire Museum collection. The Type 8 candlestick

163

(no 33/a), 5½in high, and the Type I cup (no 25/a), 2⅞in high, both have a very pale buff fabric and a yellow lead glaze, and were found in Nottingham in 1883.

Plate by Thomas Toft (Page 51)

From the British Museum Collection. This plate (no 1916.5-61), 22in in diameter, is decorated with dark brown, light brown, and white slips over a white slip base.

Pressed-ware Plate (Page 52)

From the Thomas Greg Collection of Manchester City Art Gallery. This plate (no 1923-196), 16⅜in in diameter, was made from the mould below, and decorated with dark and light brown slips over a buff fabric.

Pressed-ware Plate Mould (Page 52)

Given by Mr Harland to the British Museum in 1914 (no 1914, 4.1, 1), 13.7in in diameter, this mould is made of buff clay and has the following inscription incised on its inside surface : 'William Bird/made this mould/In the year of/Our Lord/1751'.

Wrotham Tyg (Page 85)

From the British Museum Willett Collection (no D 13). H 6.7in. This pot is decorated with stamped pads of white clay bearing a crown, a fleur-de-lis, an angel, a rose, the initials 'I.E.' and the date 1697, besides a certain amount of white slip trailing over its red fabric.

North Devon Sgraffito Jug (Page 85)

From the British Museum Willett Collection (no D 115). H 13.1in. This red fabric jug has a design cut through its white slip which includes flowers and fruit, birds, a lion and a unicorn, and a youth and a maid with a heart between them inscribed '1708 It is cupids dart wounded my hart'. Around the neck the inscription reads

'Lo i unto your house am sent as a token from a frind
When your harvest folks are dry then I will them attend. 1708'.

Notes on the Plates

Sussex Harvest Barrel (Page 86)
From the Victoria & Albert Museum Collection (No C853/1922), 4½in in diameter. The inlaid inscription on this red-fabric barrel reads 'H. F. Foster Dec th 23 1865 East Grinstead'.

Halifax Wedding Cradle (Page 86)
Halifax Museum Collection, H 7⅜in. This cradle, probably made at the Soil Hill Pottery, has a red fabric decorated with applied and trailed white slip. The inscription runs 'F.R.B 1835'.

Penrith Slipwares (Page 103)
These were made for the writer H. Thorburn at the Weatheriggs Pottery, Penrith, in 1969. They have a red fabric with white slip decoration trailed on with the cow-horn trailer. Heights 8.5in and 4in respectively.

Farnham Greenwares (Page 103)
These pieces were both made by William Freemantle Harris in 'Farnham Greenware', c 1900, and have a red fabric, white slip, and an iridescent dark green lead glaze. They are still at the Wrecclesham Pottery, Farnham.

The Silkstone Pottery (Page 104)
This view, taken from Nattes' *Views from Nature of* c 1806 and now preserved at Cannon Hall Museum and Art Gallery, Cawthorne, Barnsley, is probably the most complete illustration of an urban pottery in operation. In the foreground the workman can be seen crating the wares, while in the background, from left to right, is the clay-preparation area, the workshop itself, and the tall multiflued kiln with its surrounding hovel.

The Littlethorpe Pottery Staff, c 1913 (Page 104)
In this staff photograph the workmen are seen standing behind a selection of wares set in front of the throwing room door. They are, from left to right, George Curtis, Jackson, Hutchinson, Albert E. Kitson (with dog), Wharton, Mr Richardson (seated, the owner),

165

Lofthouse, Simpson, Hymas, Limbert, and Huller. Of these the most notable is certainly Albert Kitson, who was probably the greatest thrower in the country. He was responsible for the 36in high by 36in diameter tree-pots used at nearby Newby Hall. His apprentice, George Curtis, took over Littlethorpe in 1926, and still continues to make 'bigware' as before.

Gazetteer

In this section an attempt has been made to gather together all the available information on the numerous country potteries working in England during the post-medieval period. It will be noted that the standard of documentation is poor compared to that of other industries, the references often being restricted to chance entries in court rolls, directories, or parish registers. The reasons for this dearth of material are twofold : firstly, there has been little original research into the subject, no body of theses, surveys, or monographs beyond the arts-biased tomes of last century and a brief half-dozen kiln-excavation reports published within the last five years; secondly, the country pottery was a trifling industrial concern when compared with most of those dealt with by the economic historian. Throughout its history it has been little better than a cottage in-dustry requiring only simple plant and moderate finances. This has meant that virtually no records or accounts have been kept by the potters themselves, and only a few descriptions of their works have been made by contemporary writers.

The gazetteer is arranged by counties, individual potteries being placed in alphabetical order under their county heading. Where a number of individual potteries form one distinct community, as at Halifax, Yorkshire, or Fareham, Hampshire, the potteries are arranged alphabetically under their communal title. Each pottery is also indexed on a national basis in the general index.

In most of the following descriptions the sources employed have been quoted, but where a date-range of working has been given without a source, eg 'Richard Kiln, Wallington Pottery, 1850s-70s', the information has been taken from local county directories.

The *Victoria County Histories* are abbreviated to *VCH*.

BEDFORDSHIRE

AMPTHILL. Sole evidence for pottery comes from Bedfordshire County Records Office lease deposited in 1619 in which Agnes Smyth of Ampthill, widow of Hugh Smyth, potter, leases from Robert Harrold of Cainhoe, Yeoman, a 'messuage [being the corner house] wherein the said Agnes dwells, in the High Street in Ampthill, abuting on the Market Place, towards the cross on the south'.

RISELEY. Industry first mentioned in 1567 when William Lord of Riseley, potter, made will (in Bedfordshire County Records Office). Although Lord family remained in village up to nineteenth century at least, no further evidence that they made pottery beyond sixteenth century. Second potter, John Bulmer of Ryseley, known from his will of 1654, entered in Prerogative Court of Canterbury. This is last known mention of the industry in Riseley, but pottery probably made in numerous brick-kilns of the area up to early twentieth century.

BERKSHIRE

BRACKNELL. The Bracknell Brick, Tile, & Pottery Company (manager : Thomas Seaward) made bricks, tiles, drain-pipes, chimneypots, garden requisites and coarse redware from 1870s to early twentieth century.

COLEY & GROVELANDS. Samuel and Edward Collier opened brickworks and pottery at Coley in mid-nineteenth century, but removed to Grovelands between Reading and Tilehurst in 1877 when clay supplies ran out.

INKPEN. Coarseware pottery opened in late 1840s by C. Buckridge, whose family continued it until closure in 1880s.

PINKNEYSGREEN. Pinkneysgreen works founded by Charles Cooper in 1825 for making bricks, tiles, drain-pipes, terracotta, and coarse red earthenwares. During 1860s passed to John Kinghorn Cooper & Co, who expanded and improved works. Over 100 men employed by 1870s, when steam replaced horse-power, enabling company to survive well into twentieth century.

READING. Kelly's *Directory of Berkshire*, 1847, records J. Barker of Coley Street, and T. Barr of Bucklebury, Reading, as earthenware manufacturers, but as no potteries are mentioned in 1842 or 1863 directories, they probably only worked for short period.

BUCKINGHAMSHIRE

AKELEY. Pottery worked here 1870s and 1880s by Robert Watts.

AMERSHAM. A number of potteries worked in Amersham area during nineteenth century, main ones being:

W. Carter	Penn Street,	Amersham	1850s-60s
E. Pratty	Coleshill,	Amersham	1850s
Allan Redding	Coleshill,	Amersham	1870s-80s
Henry Redrup	Coleshill,	Amersham	1860s
Thomas Saunders	Coleshill,	Amersham	1870s-80s
James Slade	Coleshill,	Amersham	1840s

BRILL. Large pottery industry at Brill during medieval period, probably continuing into post-medieval, though no documentary continuity established. When Barwood, Brill, was disaforrested in early seventeenth century there were 'many artificers of Brill having received employment by making brick, tyle, lyme, and potts out of the soyle of Brill Hills' (see Pottery section, *VCH of Buckinghamshire*). This industry continued into eighteenth century, for *VCH* records redware jug inscribed 'John Shepherde, Poter Brill, Bux.' on base and 'M.M.1764' on side. As in other areas, main expansion of the industry took place in early nineteenth century, with seven potteries in full production, employing thirty-five men (1831 census). A little later the industry declined through the rising costs of fuel and carriage and competition from Staffordshire, and by 1863 only Henry Hubbocks' pottery remained, specialising in flower-pots, large pans, and jugs, but this closed on proprietor's death c 1877. Kelly's 1883 *Directory of Buckinghamshire* records that Thomas Home was making drain-pipes and tiles at Crossroads, Brill, but he appears to have gone out of production within next decade.

BUCKLAND. Pottery's existence evidenced by number of similar jugs with red fabric and dark brown glaze, two at Chequers, country home of Prime Minister, being dated 1701 and 1759 and latter inscribed 'Thomas Brackley, Potter'. Further vessel, No 44 in Glaisher Collection, inscribed 'Buckland Common, 1793' and 'T.B.1793'. Thus it would appear that Buckland Common pottery in eighteenth century was worked by Brackley family.

CHALFONT ST PETER. According to *VCH of Buckinghamshire* a pottery was established in 1805 by William Wellins, but bought shortly after by John Swallow, who was responsible for its major development in early nineteenth century. Throughout 1870s and 80s pottery was worked by Robert Swallow; in 1908 Messrs Saunders & Sons were leasing it (now called 'Beaconsfield Pottery'), and producing flower-pots, stands, chimney-pots, pipes, and other small wares; about time of Second World War it closed.

HIGH WYCOMBE. In 1870s Samuel Sears worked small pottery here, at Lane End.

SLOUGH. Charles West operated pottery here in 1880s.

CAMBRIDGESHIRE
CAMBRIDGE. *VCH of Cambridgeshire* records that a pottery working Gault clays of Cambridge, operated by Robert Subey, closed in 1863.

ELY. LUCAS' POTTERY. Pottery of Jabez Lucas, beside the Ouse, worked from late eighteenth century to c 1840, and was presumably 'pottery for coarse ware' mentioned in county Report to Board of Agriculture of 1811. Glaisher Collection contains two pieces from this pottery: No 45, redware jug inlayed 'J.L.1796'; and No 46, second jug, inscribed 'Henry Paton [?] Ely, July [?] 18, 1836' and 'M. Lucas [Jabez's widow] Ely'.

ELY. SIBLEY POTTERY. Situated behind house in Broad Street and worked by Robert Sibley from early nineteenth century to c 1861. Redware barrel, No 47 in Glaisher Collection is inscribed 'His Majesty's Barrel, 1861'.

CHESHIRE
MATLEY. John Olerenshaw Mottram is listed as coarse earthenware manufacturer of Matley in Pigot & Co's *National Commercial Directory* of 1822. Matley lies 8 miles west of Manchester on narrow belt of coal-measure deposits.

NANTWICH. Pottery worked by Mrs Hannah Borton during 1870s and 80s.

RUNCORN. Two potteries at the Old Quay operated respectively by

John Cliffe and Thomas Norman during second half of nineteenth century.

CORNWALL

PENZANCE. According to Chaffer, Mounts Bay Pottery was founded by a Mr Collier, with clay imported from Bideford. From c 1856 worked by Charles Sloman, but 'Scarcely worthy of the name of a manufactury' in 1905 edition of Chaffer's *Marks & Monograms*.

ST GERMAN'S. Will of Walter Prince, of St German's, entered at Consistory Court of Canterbury, 1618, indicates that a pottery was then working.

TRURO. LAKE'S POTTERY (SW 810450). In March 1968, workmen cutting foundations for new kiln at Lake's Pottery, Chapel Hill, discovered remains of late seventeenth-century brick-lined kiln having walls of 2ft 6in thick and total diameter of 10ft, and sherds glazed green, black, yellow, and all shades of brown. Pottery worked by Edward Tucker, brown earthenware manufacturer, according to Kelly's 1856 *Directory*, but passed to Lake family later in century. Products then included salters, pans, bussas, pitchers, and cloam ovens, the last continuing in production up to opening years of this century. Some traditional wares still made, but pottery now concentrates on tourist wares.

Pigot's 1830 National Commercial Directory also records Blacker & Co (pottery & pipes), Back Quay Pottery; and Simpson & Long, Back Quay Pottery.

CUMBERLAND

LITTLE BROUGHTON. Earliest evidence comes from entries in registers of Bridekirk Parish Church, about 3 miles from site:

> April 23rd, 1637, Henry, son of Thomas Foorth, Potter, baptised.
> August 21st, 1727, Rowland, son of Timothy Malkin of Little Broughton, Potter, baptised.
> January 31st, 1773, Mary, d. of Jas. Touncety of Little Broughton, Potter, baptised.
> December 25th, 1790, John, son of John Coulthard of Little Broughton, Potter, baptised.

According to early nineteenth-century *Cockermouth Guide*, however, Little Broughton Pottery was 'situated about two miles beyond the village towards Dereham [where] we see, 4 fields beyond, a low dark-looking building-Whistling Syke, built by the grandfather of Josiah Wedgewood in 1708'. Apparently pottery worked throughout eighteenth century, making yellow-ware dishes, puzzle jugs, etc, with chocolate-coloured ornamentation; and closed in the early nineteenth century, for there was no mention of it in earliest county trade directories.

GLASSON. Mentioned in White & Parsons' *Directory*, 1822, and Pigot's *National Commercial Directory*, 1834, as owned by Daniel Brough, manufacturer of coarse black and brown earthenwares and firebricks.

PENRITH. Apparently a pottery worked here during late eighteenth century, from following entries in registers of Penrith Parish Church:

Nov. 20. 1774 Samuel, son of John Dixon, Potter, baptised.
June 19th, 1776, Mary, daughter of Joseph Miller, Potter, baptised.
Dec. 10, 1772, George Stewart, Potter, aged 59, buried.
Jan 29, 1777, William Stewart, Potter, aged 24, buried.
July 18 1780, Elizabeth, Wife of Henry Steward, Potter, aged 38, buried.
Dec. 4, 1790 Mary, Wife of Henry Steward, Potter, aged 37, buried.

The better-known local pottery was Weatheriggs Pottery at Clifton, 3 miles south of Penrith, in Westmorland.

WHITEHAVEN. As Whitehaven lay on good clay and coal deposits, and had good transport facilities (first road, then rail), pottery industry flourished. It had the following potteries in nineteenth century: John Kitchen, brownware potter, Ginns, 1830s-40s; E. Lewis, Preston Street, 1850s; Frederick Patman & Co, Ginns Pottery, 1850s-1900s; Jonathan Richardson, brown & blackware potter, Ginns, 1820s; John Trousdall, blackware pottery, Ginns, 1820s-30s; John Wilkinson, Whitehaven Pottery, 1850s.

WIGTON. Wigton, some 10 miles WNW of Carlisle, supported pottery industry during late eighteenth century, as following entries in Wigton Parish Registers illustrate. Note the recurrence of Steward family, previously mentioned at Penrith.

Feb 22, 1789, George, son of Charles Steward, Potter, Wigton, Baptised.

Sept 5, 1790, George, son of Charles Steward, Potter, Wigton, Baptised.

April 1, 1792, Jane daughter of James Lowther, Potter, Hazlehead, baptised.

Dec 19, 1794, John, son of Tolson Lowther, Potter, Hazlehead, baptised.

March 8, 1795, Eleanor & Thomas, children of Thomas Williamson, Potter, Wigton, bapt.

Feb 21, 1796, Sarah, daughter of James Young, Potter, Wigton baptised.

DERBYSHIRE

BOLSOVER. Pottery near Market Place worked throughout early eighteenth century by Thomas and William Robinson, together with Thomas Robinson Jr. In 1749 Samuel Brailfford, who had property nearby, complained of foul smoke emitted from kilns during firing periods, whereupon four local tradesmen 'bound themselves under a sum of £20 payable to Brailfford to obtain the consent of the potters to stop the nuisance' (Downman, *History of Bolsover*, 1895). The potters agreed 'to remove or pull down the pot-work or pot-works, smoking house or smoking houses' on or before 24 June 1749, or to cease working them, under sum of £40. Thus pottery closed, and Robinsons left to start new pottery at Brampton, according to a local tradition. In late nineteenth century a site near Market Place in Bolsover was rebuilt, and large quantity of local pottery recovered. The sherds consisted of highly glazed redware, with some incised slip decoration (now in the British, Nottingham, and Derby Museums).

BRAMPTON. Earliest mention in 1636, when 'Kiln Flats' were recorded on Brampton Moor (see *Derbyshire Porcelain & Pottery*, Matlock, 1965). Industry expanded in late eighteenth to early nineteenth centuries and Bagshaw's *Directory* of 1846 says Brampton was 'Noted for its extensive brown earthenware and stone bottle manufacture', seven potteries then being in operation. At this time Brampton produced mostly stoneware, but earthenwares were made in the following works: Mrs Blake's Pottery, 1820s-30s; William Briddon's Pottery, 1820s-60s; Oldfield Pottery, at junction of Walton Road and Chatsworth Road, 1820s-80s; Charles Silcock's pottery, 1840s; Wheatbridge Pottery, Wheatbridge Road (proprietor, Edward Walton Wright) 1820s-80s.

CHURCH GRESLEY. Pottery established for production of coarse wash-pans, etc, by Mr Leedham in 1790, but converted to cane-wares in 1816 (Jewitt). During first half of century product was mainly coarse red and yellow wares, but from about late 1860s potteries made large quantities of 'Bargee' wares, including huge bargee teapots, still in production during early twentieth century. Coarse-ware potteries included: Nehemiah Banks' Pottery, 1880s-c 1920; Thomas Collins' Pottery, 1830s-40s; John Cooper's Pottery 1820s-60s; Cooper & Massey's Pottery, 1830s-40s; Thomas Cooper's Pottery, 1850s-60s; John Eardly's Pottery, 1820s-30s; Aaron, Edward, Thomas, & Mrs Jones' Pottery, 1840s-c 1900; William Mason's Pottery, 1870s (became Mason, Cash, & Co, c 1900); Mathew Sankey's Pottery, 1850s-60s; William Simpson's Pottery, 1820s-30s; Tell & Gough's Pottery, 1880s; Witeman & Co's Pottery, 1850s-60s.

CRICH. G. Smith's article on Crich ware (*Derbyshire Arch and Nat Hist Soc Transactions*, Vol 29), records transfer of plot of land at Crich from Lady Mary Dixie to Thomas Morley, of Nottingham, potter, in 1666. Morley probably founded Crich pottery at this time, making earthenwares with buff body and streaky brown glaze (see *The Connoisseur*, 9 October 1905). From early eighteenth century at latest Crich probably produced nothing but stone wares. Pottery must have closed before early nineteenth century, as it is not recorded in early trade directories, though 'the Pothouse' in Crich parish listed as farm in 1829.

ECKINGTON. According to Jewitt, two coarseware potteries worked here in 1789, but they cannot have lasted long, for *General View of the Agriculture of Derbyshire*, 1811, records them working 'formerly'.

HARTSHORN. Pottery mentioned in *General View of the Agriculture of Derbyshire*, 1811, but not subsequently.

ILKESTON. Pottery started at Canal Bridge in 1801 by George Evans, who made stonewares until death in 1832. His son, Richard, carried on until late nineteenth century, producing redware chimney-pots, pipes, and garden pots (Jewitt), and also retailing beer throughout the 1850s. Second pottery, also near Canal Bridge, worked by William Hanshaw, who made coarse redware, 1820s to 40s.

NEWBOLD AND SMALLEY COMMON. Both sites listed as potteries in 1811 *General View of the Agriculture of Derbyshire*, but little else known of them.

TICKNALL. In mid-nineteenth century Miss Lovell of Calke Abbey conducted a series of excavations in Abbey grounds on site of sixteenth-century Ticknall potteries. Remains covered large area, sherds of Cistercian-ware cups, costrels, and figurines being found throughout two-mile long site. Miss Lovell gave number almost complete specimens to Jermyn Street Museum, where they long represented almost the only production-site Cistercian wares in England, and caused nearly every sherd of Cistercian ware from North to be mistakenly attributed to Ticknall. The pottery continued to work throughout seventeenth century, successfully resisting Staffordshire competition. Philip Kinder in his collections towards a history of Derbyshire, c 1650 (Bodleian Library), writes of 'earthen vessels, potts, and pancions at Tychnall, and carried all East England through'. Pilkington's *View of Derbyshire*, 1803, records the industry's decline : 'Formerly a large quantity of earthenware was manufactured at this place, but lately the business has very much declined. It is said, that, since the land in the neighbourhood has been enclosed it has been difficult to meet with proper clay'. Even so, '2 potteries for redware' were still working in 1811 (*General View of the Agriculture of Derbyshire*), and last pottery here, Thomas Charville's, lasted until late 1880s.

DEVON

THE NORTH DEVON POTTERIES. Potters established themselves round estuaries of Rivers Taw and Torridge from late sixteenth century on. This area was suitable geologically and geographically, as *Gentleman's Magazine* (Vol 25, 445 & 564) of 1755 pointed out : 'In the parish of Fremington are great quantities of reddish potter's clay, which are brought and manufactured at Biddeford . . . Just above the bridge [over the River Torridge at Bideford] is a little ridge of gravel of a peculiar quality, without which the potters could not make their ware. There are many other ridges of gravel within the bar, but this only is proper for their use . . . Great quantities of Potters ware are made and exported to Wales, Ireland, and Bristol'. Export sustained these potteries, as described in Malcolm Watkins' *North Devon Pottery and its Export to North America in the 17th Century*, 1960, and Eric Talbot's *Welsh*

Gazetteer

Ceramics (SPMA, 1967). By use of Port Books deposited in Public Records Office both writers have investigated wide trade between North Devon Potteries and Irish ports of Coleraine, Cork, Dublin, Galway, Kinsale, Limerick, Youghal, Waterford and Wexford, and Welsh ports of Aberthaw, Cardigan, Swansea, and Neath, throughout seventeenth century:

North Devon to Ireland		North Devon to Cardigan	
1601	100 dozen Earthen Pottes	1609	40 dozen Earthen Vessels
1617	290 ,,	1616	80 dozen earthenware
1620	508 ,,	1681	120 ,, ,,
1632	260 ,,	1682	160 ,, ,,
1639	480 ,,	1683	150 ,, ,,
1694	50,400 parcels earthenware	1691	150 dozen Barnstaple Earthenwares

Eighteenth century trade has been little investigated, but Report to Board of Agriculture for Devon, 1808, records (p 386) that 'The potteries of Barnstaple, which consist of coarse ware for dairy and kitchen use, are said to be considerably increasing'. In same year Capper's *Topographical Dictionary* noted that 'large quantities of earthenwares are constantly manufactured here [at Bideford] and sent to Wales, in exchange for provisions'. As in other areas, increase in trade in early nineteenth century probably arose from rise in population.

BIDEFORD. Following potters listed in Pigot's 1830 *Directory*: Thomas Anthony, Path; James Bale, Potter's Lane; John Bird, Potter's Lane; Edward Petherick, East-the-Water; John Swaine, East-the-Water; John Tucker, East-the-Water. Last three were still working in 1906 (M. Watkins, *North Devon Pottery and its export to America in the Seventeenth Century*).

BRANNAM'S POTTERY. Founded in second quarter of nineteenth century at Barnstaple, and at first made normal range of local wares, including 'cloam' ovens (C. H. Brannam exhibited one at Great Exhibition of 1851, and they continued to be made until 1890s. During late nineteenth and early twentieth centuries made variety of art wares, often stamped 'C.H.Brannam/Barum/N.Devon'.

CROCKER'S POTTERY. Reputed established at Bideford in 1668, and made full range of North Devon wares until closure in 1896. According to Llewelyn Jewitt rebuilt in 1870, when products included flower-pots, seakale-pots, rhubarb-pots, chimney-pots, and ovens stamped 'W.H.Crocker,Bideford'. Last North Devon sgraffito ware jugs were also made here by Henry Phillips, who died in 1894 (Bemrose).

FREMINGTON. According to family tradition, first Fremington Pottery was on present site of Muddlebridge House, but in the late eighteenth century, when the owner wished to build there, was removed to its later position. Potter who carried out move, George Fishley (b 1771), was responsible for number of delightfully modelled groups, including watchstands with birds, grapes, figures of Napoleon, figures of John Wesley, spaniels, and cats with mice (*Catalogue of the Glaisher Collection*, nos 86-8, 92, & 94-6). Later, pottery passed to Edmund Fishley (d 1861) and then Edwin Beer Fishley (d 1911), and closed in 1912. See Fishley Holland's *50 Years a Potter*, 1958.

HOLLAMORE'S. Jug inscribed 'Made at Samuel Hollamores Barnstaple 1764' sold at Sotheby's on 6 July 1933, appears to be only recorded example of Hollamore ware.

HONITON. Pottery worked here in early nineteenth century making pans, pitchers, pancheons, etc (see Jewitt).

PLYMOUTH. Jewitt recorded pottery making common brown and yellow earthenwares in late eighteenth century.

TORQUAY. The Royal Watcombe Pottery. Otherwise known as Watcombe Art Pottery (see Haggar, R. G. *English Country Pottery*, 1950), it was founded in 1869 and made multi-coloured slip and sgraffito wares inscribed 'Tak a dish o' Cream', etc, and terracotta figurines for the growing tourist trade. Now closed, but articles on it appeared in *The Times* for 29 May and 14 August, 1965; its wares are on show in Museum of the Torquay Natural History Society.

ALLER VALE POTTERY. At work in the opening years of the present century producing wares similar to Royal Watcombe Pottery, and examples also in museum at Torquay.

DORSET

BEAMINSTER. Report to the Board of Agriculture of 1812 records two coarseware potteries working. In 1830, Pigot's *National Commercial Directory* listed only one—George Hallet's in Hogshill

Street. This was still in production in 1867, when Kelly's *Directory* recorded 'A. Meech (Late B. Brinson), Beaminster Pottery', but appears to have closed later in the century.

BRANKSEA. Unsuccessful attempt to establish pottery on the Bagshot Beds of Branksea Island made in 1857. *Catalogue of British Pottery & Porcelain in the Museum of Practical Geology*, 1871, lists 'W4 Small Pitcher in brown earthenware, with a sample of the clay of Branksea Island, from which the ware was manufactured'.

GILLINGHAM. Gillingham Pottery, Brick, & Tile Co Ltd produced bricks, tiles, garden vases, rustic ferneries, rhubarb pots, seakale pots, and flower-pots from 1866 to opening decade of present century.

HOLNEST. Pottery worked Oxford Clays at Holnest, 4 miles south of Sherborne, during late sixteenth and early seventeenth centuries. Will of Thomas Vincent of Holnest, potter, entered at Consistory Court of Canterbury in 1617.

KINSON. On London Clays between Wimborne Minster and Bourne-mouth, had small coarseware pottery industry during late nineteenth century : The Bourne Valley Pottery Co (J. Davis, Manager) 1860s-70s; The Kinson Pottery Co (Prop, W. Carter) Hamworthy Junction, Newton, Kinson, 1880s-90s (also producing bricks & tiles).

VERWOOD. Main customers, large rural communities of Wiltshire, Dorset, and northern Hampshire; and main products, coarse yellow-ware jugs, cream settling pans, and well known 'Dorset pills' or costrels used by agricultural labourers to carry ale or cider into fields. Will of Elias Talbet, potter, of Horton, some 3 miles WSN of Verwood, entered at Prerogative Court of Canterbury, 1674; in 1710, according to Morley Hewitt, potter called Charles Henning worked at Aldersholt, near Verwood; and 1812 *View of the Agri-culture of Dorset* recorded 'a pottery for coarse earthenware' at nearby Cranborne. Five potteries—under Job Andrews, Sam Bailey, Frank Ferrett, Jas Shearing, and Robert Sims—listed in 1895 directory.

In recent paper (*The Wiltshire Archaeological and Natural History Magazine*, Vol 63, 1968) John Musty describes later history of Verwood, much of his information coming from Mrs Mesech Sims, wife of last Verwood potter. Clay was collected from Hotwell or Lytchett Minster and processed by soaking and trampling, the latter continuing even after introduction of mechanical pug-mills. After being thrown on a crank-wheel wares were dried naturally and then fired in large wood-burning kilns. The kiln at cross-roads pottery was used until early 1950s and another, which still stands at the rear of Purbeck House, Black Hill, was built by Mr Mesech Sims' father, c 1850, and used until c 1920. Good collection of Verwood wares in Red House Museum, Christchurch.

DURHAM

BARNARD CASTLE. Parish registers of Brough-under-Stanmore for 1 March 1804, recording burial of 'Jane, daughter of John Proctor, Barnard Castle, Potter', are only evidence for pottery.

SUNDERLAND

BURNSIDE'S POTTERY. Built in 1850 by William Batey Burnside in Pemberton's field near north end of Green Street, it made chimney-pots, tiles, etc, until closed in 1858 when Mr Burnside died.

DEPTFORD OR BALL'S POTTERY. Established in 1857 by William Ball, and continued after his death in 1884 by his two sons until 1918. Made lustred whitewares, canewares, coarse brown glazed wares, patent flower-pots, bread mugs, and seed boxes.

JERICHO OR BRIDGE END POTTERY. S. Moore & Co of the Wear Pottery built this pottery in late 1830s. About 1861 leased to Glaholm, Lisle, & Robinson, and in 1881 to John Patterson, former manager. From 1896 operated by C. E. Snowdon & Co (later Snowdon, Pollock, & Snowdon) until closure early in 1941. Products included brown glazed bread-mugs, stew-dishes, flower-pots, candlesticks, starch pans, cream-pots, dishes, trays, etc, some being exported to southern England and Denmark.

NEWBOTTLE. One of first potteries in Sunderland area, kilns being set up in Pottery Yard about 1720. On 10 August 1728, Houghton-le-Spring parish registers recorded death of Ralph Watson of Newbottle tilekilns, so tiles and other coarse earthenwares were probably the major products. About 1740 a flint-crushing mill was built at Newbottle, enabling the pottery to concentrate on whitewares for which area soon became famous. Second pottery at Newbottle, 'New Pottery', was used by George Harle to produce brown glazed wares 1850-60.

SILKSWORTH. 'Robert Markland of Silksworth, Potter', mentioned in trust deed of 1749, probably worked at pottery advertised in the *Newcastle Journal* of 12 January 1754: 'To be let at Silksworth, near Sunderland, a Pot House. Enquire of Mrs Ettrick at Sunderland'. Apparently pottery continued into later 1750s, for Bishopwearmouth parish registers record deaths of two sons of William Tyrer, potter, of Silksworth in 1758 and 1759.

SHEEPFOLDS OR RICKABY'S POTTERY. Founded by Thomas Rickaby in 1840, it produced brownware, Welsh trays, salt kits, etc, until December 1900, when business transferred to Snowdon & Co of Bridge End Pottery.

GATESHEAD. SHERIFF HILL POTTERY. Two miles south of Tyne bridge on the Durham road, it was worked by P. Jackson in the 1770s. In local *Chronicle* of 12 August 1775, 'P. Jackson, Pilgrim Street, Newcastle' advertised 'large Ware, as Milk, Cream, Butter, and Beef Pots and Washing Mugs, Hawkers from Northumberland and Cumberland may be supplied at his shop'. After Paul Jackson's death in 1789 his sons William and Collingwood Forster Jackson became joint owners, former dying in 1798 and latter probably selling out before 1811. Fordy & Patterson are recorded as owners in 1827, but pottery not mentioned in 1834 directory. Information on this and other Durham potteries is largely gathered from F. Buckley's 'The Potteries of the Tyne', *Archaeologia Aeliana*, vol IV, 1927.

ESSEX
By W. Davey

ARDLEIGH. Richard Lea, potter, of Ardleigh, 4 miles north-east of Colchester, named in county quarter-sessions records for 1616 (ref 215/94).

COGGESHALL. Pottery worked at Coggeshall, 6 miles east of Braintree, by G. & W. Bryan during 1850s.

EAST HORNDON. Will of John Pomfret Sr, potter, of East Horndon entered at Chelmsford in 1710.

GESTINGTHORPE. Number of interesting eighteenth-century pieces of Gestingthorpe ware are known, each of red fabric with dark brown glaze. Large three-handled spouted vessel, No 149 in Thomas Greg Collection at Manchester City Art Gallery is inscribed 'Thomas

Green Josuph Reppingel Guesting Thorpe Essex August 6 1767', and 'IR 1767' underneath. No 97, jug in Glaisher Collection, bears inscription 'Ritcherd Murrells, Juseph Reppingel 1770 Pot maker'. Pottery still made in Gestingthorpe during first half of nineteenth century, E. Rayner working pottery there to c 1860.

HARLOW AND LATTON. First written record is for 1254 when 'Cok le pottere de Pottershull' was mentioned in the Assize Roll. By 1473 Pottershull had become Potterstrate, little removed from present name of Potter Street. A well chosen site, it lay on Hanningfield Till, an excellent red-firing clay containing small pockets of white clay suitable for making white slip. In early seventeenth century new road from Epping to London passed close to Latton Street and Potter Street, stabilising industry in these centres. Recently area extensively redeveloped as part of Harlow New Town, and number of kiln sites discovered during earth-moving and building. See 'Seventeenth Century Pottery Sites at Harlow, Essex' by E. F. Newton & E. Bibbings in *Trans of the Essex Arch Soc*, 25, part 3 (1960), 358-77, and 'Potteries at Latton, Essex' by W. Davy in *Broadsheet of Post Medieval Ceramics Research Group*, 3 (1966), 4-9.

Site 1. Carters Mead

Kiln foundations discovered during road-making at Latton in 1952-3, probably of 'Pot House' shown on estate map of Edward Althem in 1616, tenant then being William Prentice. Prentice family had moved into area c 1600 and lived there until 1669 when their name was last recorded in Latton parish register. Family probably reduced by plague of 1660-64 and kiln unused at this time. Site itself produced pitchers, water-pots, large pancheons, fish-dishes, cups and mugs, together with plates of Metropolitan slipware from 6 to 15in across. Only bottom brick course of kiln remained in form of egg-shaped enclosure 12ft by 9ft, with walls 13in thick and narrow fire-mouth at each end.

Site 2. Latton Ridden

Site 2 lies south of estate, pottery here probably started by George Prentice, who married the tenant's daughter in 1629. On map of 1776 clay diggings are shown with 'Pot House', but these buildings had disappeared by 1840. During agricultural drain-digging fine brick-lined dess or clay-ain was discovered. It had flat floor some 7ft square with sides extending upwards at 45° to give effective height of 12in, and still contained its load of prepared ochre-coloured clay, ready for use. Site also produced fine bowl and fragments of Metropolitan slipware, some sherds bearing words 'the' and 'gift of' in white slip letters 1¼in high.

Site 3. Pinchions, Latton Common

This kiln was close to site of Bush Fair, where its wares could easily have been sold direct to the public. Kiln uncovered during levelling of land for new buildings and only briefest details were recorded. Blackware tygs, mugs, and chamber pots made up most of kiln's products, though some Metropolitan slipwares might have been made here.

Site 4. Longcroft

Discovered during road-building and site-levelling for Brays Grove C. S. School sportsfield. K. Marshall of Passmore Edwards Museum succeeded in rediscovering shape and ground-plan of kiln, whose foundations contained sherds of Metropolitan slipware, many having words or letters trailed upon them.

Site 5. Latton Farm, Second Avenue

Manorial documents showed that in 1616 John Wright, potter, held Kitchen Croft, John II taking over on his father's death in 1636. Site is on farm land, but small trench dug has revealed blackware, brownware, and a few Metropolitan sherds. Documentary research continues on history of further local sites and on movements of potters from one potting community to another. The following list with dates of documentation may help research on other sites :

Adams, Nathaniel	1723–1790	Francis, Thomas	1637–1655
Baker, George	1640–1647	Hill, Thomas	1576–1639
Barfote, Robert	1580	Hills, William	1576–1602
Bates, Henry	1684–1688	Hunt, Thomas	1630–1642
Boreham, Nathaniel	1675–1745	Hylles, Robert	1569–1592
Browne, John	1615–1627	Jocelin, Richard	1646
Browne, William	1606–1655	King, Thomas	1623–1660
Cattrowle, John	1615–1630	Lynitt, John	1625–1629
Cattrowle, William	1584–1632	Moyne, John	1561–1592
Clarke, John	1656	Parker, George	1576–1630
Clerke, Hugomo	1431	Poole, Thomas	1640–1679
Clerke, William	1428	Prentice, Edmund	1728–1779
Emmyng, Emanuell	1592–1619	Prentice, George	1635
Emmyng, Emanuell	1643	Prentice, Samuel	1759
Emynge, Francis	1607–1608	Prentice, William	1640–1666

Starkes, Francis	1620–1650	Wood, Thomas	1640–1681
Starkes, John	1609–1646	Wright, George	1593–1647
Starkes, William	1584–1650	Wright, John	1586–1638
Wanel, James	1624–1653	Wright, John	1623
Waylett, John	1608–1620	Wright, William	1640–1655
Wennell, Henry	1640		

CASTLE HEDINGHAM. This pottery rose to fame through the efforts of one man who wanted to produce high-quality ornamental wares. For a full and well illustrated history, see R. J. Bradley's *Castle Hedingham Pottery 1837-1905* (1968).

Edward Bingham senior moved from Blackheath to Gestingthorpe in 1834, thence in 1837 to Castle Hedingham where he founded Castle Hedingham Pottery, making coarse redwares. Here his son, Edward junior learned to pot, being particularly fond of making ornamental pieces. His father did not encourage him, however, knowing there was little living to be made from such wares alone, and apprenticed him to a bootmaker. In 1846 his apprenticeship ended, and he returned home to continue bootmaking independently but spent more and more of his time in the pottery. Influenced by seeing Great Exhibition of 1851 he turned to production of ornamental wares entirely, and opened shop for their sale in Queen Street, Castle Hedingham. He slowly built up collection of moulds and his business, but he had to open a school (from 1856 to 1864) and then work as sub-postmaster to earn enough to keep pottery working. Edward Bingham, sr, died in 1872, and son was able to take over his pottery. From this time on met with more success, gaining numerous orders after showing his wares in art exhibitions held in Hertford and Sudbury in 1874 and Chelmsford in 1875. For next twenty years pottery flourished, but by mid-90s trade fell off and Edward W. Bingham, Edward junior's son, persuaded his father in 1899 to hand pottery over to him. But Edward W. was no businessman, and had to sell out to Devon firm of Hexter Humpherson in 1901, pottery now being known as 'The Essex Art Pottery Company' and Edward W. remaining manager. Things now went from bad to worse, and pottery was forced to close in 1905. Edward W. emigrated to America with his family, but Edward himself, now 76, remained behind for year before joining his son.

The wares made at Castle Hedingham defy description for their variety, wealth of detail, colour, and scale. Read Mr Bradley's publication, and see collections at Colchester & Essex Museum, Chelmsford & Essex Museum, and Victoria & Albert Museum, London.

PURLEIGH. Will of Henry Moynes, Earthen Potter of Purleigh, 4 miles south of Maldon, entered at Chelmsford in 1646.

SOUTHMINSTER. Will of Jacob Simpson, potter, of Southminster, 3 miles north of Burnham-on-Crouch, entered at Chelmsford in 1719.

STIFFORD. Morant, in his 1768 *History of Essex* (Vol 1, 99) says, 'in Stifford Street a pottery is set up by Kenrick Graham Esq'.

STOCK, BUTTSBURY AND HANNINGFIELD. Potters already worked this rich clay area only 24 miles ENE of London in late fifteenth century, but main expansion came in sixteenth and seventeenth centuries. An order to Prentice, potter of Stocks, from Sir William Petre of Ingatestone Hall, 1550 (see *Tudor Food & Pastimes* by F. G. Emmison, 1964), lists wares made here during mid-sixteenth century: '4 pots for flowers 2d, a cream pot and a cheese pan 4d, a dozen cups for the butler 12d; 2 pots for herbs for the parlour 4d, 3 stone pots 18d, pottle glasses 12d, 8 quart glasses 16d, 4 stool pots 8d, 2 milk pans 2d, 2 stew pots 2d', and also a still with cups for it, and two watering-cans.

Mention of glasses and stone pots indicates that Prentice not only made pottery, but also undertook to supply to order goods from elsewhere. Later, potteries presumably went on to produce Metropolitan wares, but in late seventeenth century collapsed through new competition from Staffordshire and growing salt-glazed stoneware and tin-glazed earthenware industries. By 1768, when Morant wrote his *History of Essex* (Vol 2, 52), he was only able to say that Buttsbury near Stock had pot kiln at which strong but coarse earthenwares were made out of local clays.

Following table lists potters recorded as having worked at these potteries, with dates of their documentary mentions.

Allen, Thomas	1674	Frauncis, John	1610
Ascroft, Will	1745	Gwyatt, Rich,	1656
Bondocke, John	1606	Hankin, Edward	1599
Bondocke, Rich	1574	Hankin, Thos	1674
Bondocke, Robt	1674	Hankyn, Will	1640
Brewer, John	1616	Hawlie, Thos	1639
Bush, Thos	1653	Johnson, Rich	1575
Castell, Jas	1606	Palmar, John	1618
Charford, Thos	1627	Palmer, Humphrey	1588
Charvell, Math	1628	Palmer, John	1482
Charvell, Thos	1606	Pawlmer, Rich	1554

Perryn, Humph	1642	Stonard, John	1527
Seamer, Rich	1612	Tailor, Chris	1581
Spilman, John	1606	Wilson, Thos	1610
Starlinge, Will	1623		

Note : According to Dr Laver in *The Reliquary & Illustrated Archaeology* 11, Richard Youngs was also a potter at Stock, and reputed maker of Braintree Ringers jug with inscription 'Made at Stock, 1685, R.Y.'

WEATHERSFIELD. Pottery industry flourished here on London clay during sixteenth and early seventeenth centuries, following potter's wills being entered at Chelmsford : John Cleavland, 1598; Daniel Lyvermore, 1632; William Livermore, 1589; Thomas Walkyr Senr, 1535.

GLOUCESTERSHIRE

COLEFORD. *VCH of Gloucestershire* records pottery at Coleford—which lies on edge of Forest of Dean, 4 miles west of Monmouth—from mid-nineteenth century at latest. Wares included glazed and unglazed brownware, chimney-pots, tiles, and drain-pipes. Owners c 1900 were Wanklyn & Grindell of Dark Hill, Futterill, Coleford.

CRANHAM. Messrs Ritchling's two potteries at Cranham, 4 miles south-west of Gloucester, were reputed to occupy site of Roman pottery. During second half of nineteenth century produced flower-pots, drain-pipes, pans and rough jars in brownware, but in 1905 introduced green glazes and turned out much ornamental ware. Pottery is believed to have closed pre-1910, not being mentioned in later directories.

Second pottery producing similar wares was also worked here late last century by William Moulton.

WINCHCOMBE. Richard Allen Beckett is listed as owner of Greet potteries in 1883. He made similar coarsewares to other Gloucestershire potteries, and Winchcombe is best known for reviving English slipware tradition in 1920s and 30s (see Digby, G. W. *Work of the Modern Potter in England*, 1952). In 1926 Michael Cardew left Bernard Leach's studio at St Ives, Cornwall, to take over Winchcombe pottery, and up to outbreak of war in 1939 worked at reviving quickly disappearing techniques of slip-trailing and galena-glazing, often experimenting to rediscover practical aspects of their use. Winchcombe products of this period are not easily confused with works of country potters, however, for Cardew's aim was to revive English slipware as a useful product, not to make academic copies of earlier wares. Raymond Finch has worked the pottery from 1939, continuing to lead-glaze slipwares, etc, as before.

HAMPSHIRE

FAREHAM. On London clays between Portsmouth and Southampton and having a good harbour, Fareham provided ideal location for pottery industry. Some eighteenth-century posset pots, etc, bearing applied decoration have formerly been attributed to Fareham, but there is no evidence of potting in this area before mid-late eighteenth century, and so-called Fareham pieces were most probably Staffordshire.

Fareham potteries greatly expanded c 1820-70 due to efforts of Thomas Stares of Wallington Pottery. *Post-Office Directory* of 1867 states, 'Fareham owes its rise and progress in a great measure to Mr Thomas Stares of Wallington, who introduced the manufacture of coarse pottery, which has since been of great importance to the town and neighbourhood. The west and other parts of England, the Channel Isles, and a portion of the European Continent are supplied from this town with red pottery'. Contemporary advertisements tell us that pottery was shipped from Fareham Quay, where coal for potteries would presumably be unloaded.

Nineteenth-century products included pancheons, bread-crocks, paint-pots, rhubarb- and seakale-pots, milk pans, etc, plus full range of horticultural and architectural wares. One characteristic product was chimney-pot, often seen in Portsmouth, Southampton, Winchester, Alton, and Farnham on eighteenth- and nineteenth-century buildings. These were often made in complex forms with additional draught tubes and decorated with broad bands of white slip, scratched through in zig-zag design to reveal red fabric beneath. The white clay required for slipping chimney-pots and milk pans was carted from Farnham Park claypit until 1840s when it was probably found easier to ship white clays of Poole in Dorset directly to Fareham Quay.

In addition to Thomas Stares, following potters worked in Fareham during nineteenth century, but by early twentieth most had either closed or switched to brick production as their main activity:

James Aburrow, Shidfield, Droxford, operated redware pottery 1850-70.

186

Richard Kiln, Wallington Pottery, made bricks; tiles; red earthenware; fancy, garden, and ridge tiles; and drain-pipes, 1850s-70s.

James Marriner, Swanmore, Droxford, operated redware pottery 1850s-60s.

William Oliver, Fareham. Mentioned in 1847 *Directory* as a brick, tile, and earthenware manufacturer, but not mentioned in either the 1828 or 1857 *Directories*.

E. Pridgett, Cheriton, Beauworth, produced bricks and tiles according to 1877 *Directory*.

Charles Smith, Wickham Road, Fareham, made coarse earthenware, terracotta, ridge tiles and agricultural pipes, c 1860-70.

Thomas Watts, West Street, Fareham, made coarse earthenware according to 1828 directory, but not mentioned after that.

HEREFORDSHIRE

Potteries form interesting group, for during seventeenth century they developed distinct regional style of shapes and decoration which, though unique, owes much to Midlands blackware and West County sgraffito. In *Transactions of the Woolhope Field Club* (35, part 2 [1956] 133-8 & 32, part 1 [1946] 1-12) number of pottery sites have been described, but research is needed into history of industry.

DEERFOLD FOREST. Earliest recorded reference occurs in 1616, when action was taken against Thomas Turner of Layntworden, woodward of the king's forest of 'Dervol', for allowing kilns to be erected in the forest 'for the makeing of earthen pottes, Cupps, panns, and other earthen vessels there'. Apparently 50 acres of woodland had been dug up, ten kilns erected, and 900 loads of oak and ash, etc, burnt, for which Thomas had received £40 at least for himself. A number of pottery sites have been located in the forest, including—

Boresford

Shard-heaps first noted in 1924, but it was not until 1946 that John Griffiths discovered kiln, a three-flued structure of silicious sandstone with a 4ft diameter firing chamber. Wares made were extremely fine, including puzzle cups with overstamped pads of white clay bearing large birds with outspread wings, stars, acorn clusters, or the fesses nebulé of the Blount coat-of-arms. Jugs, mugs, handled bowls, and a chafing dish also produced.

Deerfold Farm

Hard baked-clay bases of seven kilns discovered in 1945, diameters ranging between 3ft 6in and 4ft, but no superstructures remained. Seventeenth- and eighteenth-century pottery recovered from site included mugs with stamped and applied decoration similar to that from Boresford, and other mugs decorated with areas of crushed quartz in imitation of contemporary stonewares from the Rhine-land.

Dickindale

Shard-heap located and excavated by John Griffiths of Lingen in 1945.

Grove Head, Lingen

First noted by Rev James Turner in 1874, when he exhibited at Church Stretton green and white bottle in which one Mathew Lowe had kept his tea. Lowe had said that bottle came from pottery at Grove Head which had worked 'in his grandfather's time, or before that' where 'they used to make pans and dishes and oaks were used to burn the pots'. Shard-heaps found at Grove Head in 1924, but no trace of kiln.

Shirley Farm

Site located by John Griffiths in 1945 near high point known as 'The Camp'.

UPTON BISHOP. Site located at Upton Bishop, 3 miles east of Ross on Wye, in late 1920s. Lying ¼ mile due east of Daubies Farm, it produced fragments of medieval tiles, plus tygs and coarsewares such as were made in seventeenth century.

WHITNEY ON WYE. Cartloads of seventeenth- and eighteenth-century sherds discovered at Kiln Ground Wood, Whitney, between 1876 and 1917. Samples of these and other Herefordshire pottery may be seen in Hereford Museum.

HERTFORDSHIRE

WOODSIDE. Potteries date from eleventh century at latest [see Derek Renn. *Potters & Kilns in Medieval Hertfordshire*, Hertford (1964)]. Earliest post-medieval references in Peterborough register of wills: Henry Beane was potter of Woodside in 1522; Richard Bene potted here in 1538; Henry Mannynge, potter, left his clay to an apprentice and his servant in 1551; and Robert Mannyinge bequeathed his wheel and stock in 1570. Mr Renn notes that three unnamed potters had licences in 1607, and that in 1612 inventory of William Potter of Wildenhill, Bishop's Hertford, 'potter make' included 'a working wheel and a walking stock and lumber belonging to the trade'.

In 1965 John Ashdown recovered from a Woodside site (TL 25250705) early seventeenth-century sherds including range of coarse redware jugs, shallow bowls, storage jars, cooking pots, and some blackware tygs (see article by John Ashdown in *Post Medieval Ceramics Research Group Broadsheet* 4 [1966], 10-11).

HUNTINGDONSHIRE
PETERBOROUGH. Dogsthorpe Pottery operated here from c 1880 by George Cursley—closed pre-1914.

KENT
ASHFORD. Pottery worked here in 1850s by T. Talbot of Marsh Street.

BILLINGTON. Will of William Hampton of Billington, Kent, entered in Prerogative Court of Canterbury in 1657.

CHISLEHURST. According to Jewitt 'West Kent Potteries' opened in 1820, making redware flower-pots, seakale-pots, building and paving bricks and tiles, roofing and ridge tiles, chimney-pots, etc. The potteries were being operated by J. Pascall in 1855, but appear to have closed little later in century.

GRAVESEND. G. Willis operated pottery in West Street during the 1850s.

GREENWICH. Area south of Thames from Deptford to Woolwich was excellent for potting only 6-7 miles from City of London by road or water, and lying on clay deposits of Woolwich beds. Wills of following seventeenth-century potters are deposited in Prerogative Court of Canterbury: William Deane, East Greenwich, 1656; George Lyon, Woolwich, 1680; John Walton, East Greenwich, 1681; John Hall, Deptford, 1691; Joseph Hall, East Greenwich, 1692.

Industry almost certainly continued here during eighteenth cen-

Gazetteer

tury, but research has been lacking. In 1855 T. Gee operated potteries in Greenwich Road and Blackheath Road.

HADLOW. Pottery working at Hadlow, some 4 miles north-east of Tonbridge, under G. Richardson in 1850s.

HIGH HALDEN. Pottery reputed to have been started in seventeenth century by Anthony Paul, probably Flemish refugee, and continued to work at least up to 1904, when Daniel Farrence was the potter. (See also Rackham, *Catalogue of the Glaisher Collection.*) Parish churchyard of High Halden has tombstone 'In memory of Henry Hyland, of this Parish, Potter, who died may ye 3, 1704, aged 33'.

MAIDSTONE. John Walker worked pottery at Nettlestead, Maidstone, in 1880s.

TUNBRIDGE WELLS. Small group of potteries founded here early in nineteenth century, following being listed in 1855 directory: J. Elliott, Garden Lane; J. Miller, London Road; W. Richardson, Dry Hill. Last named had moved to Shipborne Road, Tonbridge, by 1887.

WROTHAM. Potteries owe fame to elaborate commemorative slipwares made during seventeenth and early eighteenth centuries. The vessels, which often bear date, initials of potter, or name 'Wrotham' range from 1612 to 1739, and are subject of authoritative article by A. J. B. Kiddell of Ightham in *Trans of the English Ceramic Circle*, Vol III (1954), 105. Due largely to his research following potters have been identified:

'I.E.' Although some twenty-six examples of I.E.'s pottery are known from period 1687-1712, it is impossible as yet to name him with certainty.

'I.G.', who made three known pieces between 1676 and 1683, was 'John Green, potter', buried in parish church, 1686.

'N.H.' Nicholas Hubble, whose son, Nicholas II, was also potter, made nine known examples between 1649 and 1687. His will, dated 16 April 1689 and prove on 13 July 1689, listed '3 horses, 3 mares', presumably his transport for delivering wares.

'H.I.' The Ifields lived in Wingfield Borough of Manor of Wrotham

190

from sixteenth century to late seventeenth. Henry Ifield owned house with two fireplaces here in 1663-4, and was responsible for some eighteen known examples of slipware dated 1652 to 1669. He was buried, 18 August 1673.

'I.I.' John Ifield, who made two ornamental pots dated 1674 and 1676 respectively, is known from following entries in the parish registers : 'John Ifield (potter) married Katherine Eastland on 20th November, 1677'; 'Katherine, ye wife of John Ifield (potter) buried 12th November, 1707'; 'John Ifield (potter) and of late a pensioner buried 2nd September, 1716'.

'T.I.' Probably Thomas Ifield, made three known pieces dated between 1621 and 1654.

'I.L.' John Livermore, responsible for some nine known pieces dating from period 1612-1649, was first mentioned as being 'of Ightham, potter' in lease of 1631. In 1638 he married Mary Cooper, who survived him on his death on 9 September 1658.

'G.R.' George Richardson, who made twenty-one known pieces between 1642 and 1677, was buried at parish church on 9 July 1687. In his will, proved on 11 October 1687 he, 'George Richardson the elder of Wrotham, potter', made various bequests of money to his children, remainder passing to son George and son-in-law Nicholas Hubble.

'I.W.', who made five known pieces between 1666 and 1669, is as yet unidentified, but maybe he was predecessor of Richard Wells of Wrotham, potter, whose inventory is dated 13 January 1710-11.

LANCASHIRE

CLIVIGER. Small township in parish of Whalley, situated on western face of Pennines on good deposits of clay, coal, and lead. Pottery first mentioned in Bennett's *History of Burnley*, which says that in 1792 the Cliviger Pottery was controlled by Widow Smith, though ware was produced by William Ingham. Another pottery, at Robin Cross Hill, rated at £35 per annum, was then being worked by James Walmsley. Both potteries were working under original owners in 1825 when Edward Baines compiled his *County Palatine of Lancaster*, but must have closed by 1854, for no potteries are mentioned in Mannex & Co's directory of that year. These works made redware with deep yellow lead glaze, often decorated with slip-trailing and sgraffito, including domestic wares, puzzle jugs, cradles, loving cups, etc. Examples in Townley Hall Museum, Burnley.

LIVERPOOL. Most potters made tin-glazed earthenwares and similar fine products, but some made blackwares and industrial ceramics, as shown by following advertisement from *Liverpool Advertiser* of 18 June 1756 : 'The Proprietors of the Mould Works, near the Infirmary, Liverpool, aquaint the public that they continue to make all sorts of sugar moulds and drips, chimney moulds, large jars for water, black mugs of all sizes, crucibles and melting pots for silver smiths, founders etc. and sell them on the same terms as from Prescot, Sutton, and other places'.

PRESCOT. Edward Baines, 1825 : 'There have been for ages several manufactories of coarse earthenware for which the clay of the neighbourhood is particularly well adapted'. Not only the clay, but also large deposits of coal and ever-growing market in nearby Liverpool, made Prescot ideal pottery centre. Pottery was certainly made here in early eighteenth century, for several wills of Prescot 'clay-potters' were deposited at Chester in the 1730s and 40s (see *Lancs & Cheshire Record Society*, vols 18, 20, 25, and 37). Dr. Pococke visited town during his *Travels Through England* in mid-eighteenth century, noting that 'They have two or three houses for coarse earthenware, and one for the whitestone'; while the 'manufacture of coarse earthen mugs' was noticed by Pennant twenty years later. Prescot pottery industry expanded in early nineteenth century as elsewhere, and by 1825 there were six potteries working. But potteries slowly declined in competition with mass-produced Staffordshire whitewares. Following potteries worked during nineteenth century :

Working in 1825 (Baines' Directory)		*Working in 1854* (Mannex & Co's Directory)	
John Dale	Snig Lane	John Dale	Whiston
T. J. & W. Spencer	Moss Pottery		Pottery
The Acres Pottery		Spencer & Co	Moss Pottery
Company	Acres	Thomas Webster	Brook
Edward Birchall	Mill Pottery		Pottery
Edward Bradshaw	Eccleston	Joseph & Edward	
Webster Brothers	Fall Lane	Twist	New Road

LEICESTERSHIRE

ASHBY DE LA ZOUCH. John Farey's 1811 *General View of the Agriculture of Derbyshire* recorded potteries for white and yellow wares. Potteries continued until early twentieth century, major firm being Wilson Brothers of Coleorton Pottery.

DONNINGTON HALL (SK 423268). *The Leics Archaeol & Hist Soc Trans*, vol XXXIX (1963-4) 51, records excavation of sixteenth-century pottery kiln in grounds of Donnington Hall in early 1960s, but unfortunately the excavator died, leaving no notes or records. Collection of sherds from site now housed in Leicester Museums.

LINCOLNSHIRE

By Miss R. H. Healey & Mrs E. H. Rudkin

Evidence still incomplete, and much research remaining to be done. In the field, fabrics of probable local origin increasingly being identified, so it should eventually be possible to locate centres of production. Intensive documentary work will undoubtedly provide much more information. Some account of best known sites given below, but seventeenth- and eighteenth-century inventories of potters suggest further lines of research in Lincoln (Edward Bowler 1599-1601), Great Grimsby (Zachariah Godhelpe 1685), Stamford (Richard Hargrave 1720), and in one of the Manthorpes (William Becket 1722).

BOURNE. In Bourne, as in Toynton, pottery-making well established in fourteenth century. Potters' inventories survive for 1555 and 1615, but most significant reference appears in parish register: 'On the 25 of May 1637 a fearful fire happened in the Eagate', and William Marrat, in his *History of Lincolnshire*, Vol III, 18, notes that 'this fire destroyed the greater part of Potter Street, and did much damage to East-Street (or Easgate). The cause . . . happened through carelessness at the Potteries, which were destroyed with the street and never after rebuilt'. Wasters have been noted from Eastgate area since 1890s. Between 1966 and 1968 many medieval and post-medieval sherds were retrieved from a wide area. All post-medieval forms appear to be made in distinctive smooth pale red fabric, sometimes with paler slip. Clear glaze on this partly slipped surface produces attractive mottled effect varying from yellow to light green or brown. No pieces with copper colouring have been found in Bourne, but very similar fabric with copper specks beneath glaze occurs on many South Lincolnshire sites. Wares in smooth

Bourne fabric include storage jars with two handles and sometimes a bung-hole, jugs, pancheons, small dishes, water bottles, chafing dishes, and skillets. Distribution area—whole south of county, within radius of about 16 miles.

EAST KEAL. Three references to potters, premises, or both occur in *Lincoln, Rutland, and Stamford Mercury* of early nineteenth century. In one instance potting is combined with brick and tile making. East Keal lies between Toynton and Old Bolingbroke, so field work might very well find earlier potteries.

LOUTH. *Lincoln, Rutland, and Stamford Mercury* records death of Mr Harrison, potter, in 1822. Nearly twenty years later Thomas Rose established 'glazed pot manufacture' whose products were considered equal to any in Staffordshire. Rose had died by 1850 when brickyard and pottery were sold as going concern producing mainly bottles and jugs in deep red fabric glazed black on upper half, the thick glaze being finished off in a clean line and not left to dribble down sides of vessel.

OLD BOLINGBROKE. No medieval industry recognised here, but from potters' names they may have moved in from Toynton. Family names do not occur before 1600, and earliest reference is to burial of three members of Owesman family, all potters, between 1609 and 1615. Lebbens Walker of adjoining parish of Hareby, d 1611, left 'eight doson off pottes' in his kiln, worth 6s 8½d, and in 1691 Robert Stanney left £2 worth. Dishes with 'ROBERT ƧTANEY' impressed round inside rim by roulette are distributed for radius of some 15 miles, but none have yet been recovered from dated context connecting them or otherwise with this Robert Stanney. Bolingbroke kilns must have been well reputed in seventeenth century, for Houghton wrote in 1693 of 'the blue clay of Bolingbroke pottery in Lincolnshire' and describes it as 'Pure, that is, such as is soft like butter to the teeth, and has no greetiness in it'. Excavations in 1966 and 1967 took place at approximately TF 356648. Great deal of other post-medieval pottery found in gardens in all parts of village, much of it fully oxidised so that glaze has orange or dark brown appearance. By eighteenth century most Old Bolingbroke potters had fallen on hard times, and last recorded burial, of 'Samuel Langley, harmless potter', was in 1793. A life-long resident, who died in 1942, remembered some disused kilns being demolished in garden east of castle moat.

TOYNTON ALL SAINTS AND TOYNTON ST PETER. Industry here flourished in Middle Ages and continued into post-medieval period, with inventories extant for 1559 and 1562 and potter's burial recorded in 1629. Some fourteen sites have produced waster evidence and three kilns have been excavated. Latest of these, kiln 2, dated archaeomagnetically to c 1475-1525 (TF 395631). Brick-built with five flues, internal diameter 9ft 9in, it produced fairly solid utilitarian wares in firm red fabric, sometimes with olive green lead glaze : pancheons, jugs, chafing dishes with pointed knobs in French manner, skillets and two-handled bung-hole storage jars, etc. Only decoration finger impression on some jar necks and round bungholes. Both kiln and its wares are almost identical to part of kiln and its products excavated at Old Bolingbroke, some 3 miles northwest of Toynton in 1966 and 1967. Other post-medieval pottery from Toynton includes chafing dish with square cut top, rather like battlements, barrel-shaped jars, lobed cups, and large rectangular handled dish.

NORFOLK

EAST DEREHAM. Number of small potteries worked in middle and late nineteenth century, most producing coarse redware horticultural wares, drainage tiles, etc, such as William Fox, Swanton Novers, Dereham, 1870s-80s; William Hubbard, Hill House Works, Market St, Dereham, 1870s-c 1900; Benjamin Perowne, Dereham, 1870s-80s.

GAYTON THORPE. Bardell Bros worked on Gault clays of Gayton Thorpe, some 7 miles east of King's Lynn, during 1870s & 80s.

LITTLE PLUMSTEAD & WROXHAM. William Frederick Green operated coarseware potteries in these villages, both 5 miles north-east of Norwich, during late nineteenth and early twentieth centuries.

SHARRINGTON. Pottery industry presumably existed during late sixteenth century and early seventeenth, for will of Thomas Fasett of Sharington, potter, was entered at Prerogative Court of Canterbury in 1617.

NORTHAMPTONSHIRE

PLUMPTON. Morton, in his 1712 *Natural History of Northamptonshire* mentions that at Oakley Bank in parish of Plumpton, 'There

Gazetteer

were made mugs, drinking pots, dishes, and all the thinner and finer
sort of ware from a ductile yellow clay; the glaze lying well upon it.
A more friable yellow clay interspersed with blue flecks was used for
flower pots, panchions, cloughs to salt meat in, and similar coarse
wares; a soft marly clay, blue in colour, for tiles and ordinary garden
pots'. Thorough search of Plumpton records by Mrs D. Warren has
failed to reveal any other details of industry here, which presumably
closed in late seventeenth century due to competition of Staffordshire and Derbyshire.

POTTERSPURY. Few small potteries during medieval period, but main
development during early seventeenth century. John Morton gives
full account in his *Natural History of Northamptonshire*, published
1712, but probably written earlier :

> The earth of the potteries at Potters Perry is found in Cosgrove Field
> nigh Goldsbury Mill. In some places there it lies next under the soil
> and is sometimes turned up by the plough. The depth of the bed is
> uncertain; tis scarce above two feet at the most. It is a yellowish clay,
> dense and firm, and free from mixture. Yet notwithstanding its density,
> the ware made of it is of a brittler and less enduring nature than that
> of Ticknall in Derbyshire; tho equal care and skil have been used in the
> managing it; an effect, which we may therefore reasonably suspect,
> proceeds from some salt ebody'd in the clay. The garden pots made of
> it tho' never so well baked, are very apt to scale, and be broken in
> pieces by foul weather and frosts; but being sized, that is, laid in oil,
> will abide the weather as well as any whatsoever as the sellers of them
> say; but others who made that experiment have found it fail them.
> Nevertheless it is the largest as well as the oldest pottery in all these
> parts . . . Were our materials never so good, [it] is never likely to
> flourish very much with us because the way of living here is more
> expensive than in Derbyshire and Staffordshire, and the potters of
> those two counties who bring hither their wares upon little horses or
> asses, usually begging their victuals, do on that account afford their
> wares at such under-rates as our potters here cannot live so well upon
> the trade.

In 1965 single and double-flued kilns, both second half of seventeenth century, were excavated by P. Mayes (see *Post-Medieval
Archaeology*, Vol 2, 1968). These could have been used by either
the Bentons or the Stowes. Leonard Benton arrived Potterspury
about 1646, and in his will of 1664-5 left his grandson Leonard
Benton 'all material belonging to a potter of potash making'. Inventory accompanying will also mentioned 'pots sold and to sell'
(£3 10 0d), 'a parcel of ashes' (6s 8d), and wood (£7), total value
of estate amounting to £113. When the grandson made his will in
1681 his inventory totalled £690, but no mention was made of
pottery equipment, and he described himself as 'Yeoman'.

John Stowe lived in High Street, Potterspury, for some time before 1694, when he made his will, in which he requested his brother William to 'go on with my art of potting, and bring up my son John to it'. In 1702 John mortgaged his cottage for £15, married the following week, and soon disappeared from all record. Presumably pottery closed about this time, for his uncle William Stowe was buried in 1706.

YARDLEY GOBION. Registers of parish of Potterspury, which includes Yardley Gobion, record burial of John Hoare, Potter, in 1680. In 1749 Thomas Hoare was recorded as occupying a house in Yardley 'commonly known as the Potters'. Thomas was succeeded by Robert Hoare, whose daughter Abigail married Thomas Woodward, described as a potter in his will of 1756. Dark redware jug inscribed 'Robin Woodward, Yardley Gobion, 1761' suggests that pottery continued in later eighteenth century, but first comprehensive directories, compiled in early nineteenth century, mention none.

NORTHUMBERLAND

NEWBURN (NEWCASTLE). Newcastle *Journal*, 10 June 1749 : 'John Brougham in the Keyside, Newcastle, sells . . . china ware . . . and is now made at his Potwork at Newburn, all sorts of Flower Pots for Gardens, ornamental Pots for Summerhouses, Garden Walls or Court Walls, having just procured a professed Workman for that purpose'.

MORPETH. Newcastle *Journal*, 25 September 1756 : 'To be sold by George Ward & Co. at their Manufactory at Cottingwood nigh Morpeth, all sorts of Earthen Ware, glazed and unglazed'.

These advertisements appear to be sole evidence for coarse pottery industry in the county. Its northern areas were probably served by hawkers from Scottish potteries like those at Preston Pans.

NOTTINGHAMSHIRE

NOTTINGHAM. Pottery-producing centre throughout Middle Ages. Number of kilns excavated late nineteenth century, together with later potteries, discussed in *Trans Thoroton Soc*, Vol 36, 79. Most interesting post-medieval potter was Charles Morley of Barker Gate, brought to court in 1629 for 'diginge a clay pite in the fields wch is a hindrance to the burgesses Common, and danger overthroinge mens cattell' (*Trans Thoroton Soc*, 1924), but cleared by the tribunal which concluded 'ytt may be done'. Next appeared in court in 1637 for withholding his transport facilities from 'Common worke, 5 dayes, being lawfully summoned' and ordered to pay 25s fine. Morley made great variety of lead-glazed red and yellow-ware, some influenced by contemporary Delftwares. Numerous vessels, presumably his, found in nineteenth century in Civil War débris round city walls and ditches, and now housed in Castle Museum, Nottingham, and Yorkshire Museum at York. Later Morley, Thomas, founded pottery at Crich, Derbyshire, in 1666, Crich clay being used at Nottingham pottery from then on. Shortly before 1693 Charles Morley's son John started to produce stonewares in Nottingham for the first time, and in 1693 he was sued by John Dwight of Fulham for infringing his patent of 1684 (giving him sole right to manufacture stonewares in England). Dwight's action was ineffective, however, and for following century the plentiful supplies of fireclay and coal of Nottingham region were used to produce wide range of stonewares.

Although conversion to stonewares was almost entire, some earthenwares were apparently made in mid-eighteenth century, for descendants of William Woodward presented to the Nottingham Castle Museum salt-kit with inlaid inscription 'W.W. 1749', which he was reputed to have made.

SUTTON-IN-ASHFIELD. Pottery appears to have worked from mid-late eighteenth to early nineteenth centuries. Robert Lowe in his 1813 *Agriculture of Nottinghamshire* reported 'a considerable pottery of coarse red ware for garden pots, etc.', but there was no mention in 1829, when Pigot & Co's county directory was first published.

OXFORDSHIRE

BANBURY. Nathaniel Banbury's Pottery at 27, Middleton Road, Grimsbury, Banbury, produced coarse earthenwares during last quarter of nineteenth century.

BURFORD. Two potteries in this area, 4 miles north-west of Burford, in late nineteenth century—John Morris of Wychwood in 1870s and Philip Williams of Leafield in 1860s-80s. Today Chris Harries, Dishmaker of Coldstone Kiln, Ascot under Wychwood produces slipwares, etc.

MARSH BALDEN & NUNEHAM COURTNEY. Dr Plot in his 1677 *History of Oxfordshire* states 'I shall not mention the making of pots at

Marsh Balden and Nuneham Courtney . . . since these places are now deserted'. They are still deserted, as they were cleared in the mid-late seventeenth century and never reoccupied.

NETTLEBED. Old Nettlebed Pottery was worked for coarsewares by Thomas Hobbs from early 1840s at latest, but closed down before 1867.

STOKE ROW. Coarse redware pottery was worked at Stoke Row, 2 miles south-west of Nettlebed in 1870s-90s by George Hope.

SHROPSHIRE
BROSELEY. According to Chaffers, Benthall Pottery, Broseley, was established in 1772 by John Thursfield, who had just returned from Jackfield. Pottery was worked throughout late nineteenth century and on into opening decade of twentieth by William Allen, who produced yellow and other common wares. From c 1870 Allen also made sgraffito 'Art' wares, taking students from South Kensington and Coalbrookdale schools of art.

COALMOOR. Jewitt, writing in 1883, described a site 'at Coalmoor near Horsehay, [where] a pottery of common coarse ware formerly existed, the hovels are still standing, but converted to other purposes'.

HAYBROOK. According to *VCH of Shropshire* George Weld founded pottery here in early eighteenth century, being succeeded by tenant, John Thursfield, on death in 1748. It made brown and yellow wares trailed with a trailer made from mocha-ware bottle into which quill had been inserted, its range including baking dishes and small handle-less mugs.

JACKFIELD. Long famed for magnificent glossy black-glazed wares, pottery is supposed to have worked from mid-sixteenth century until (Chaffers says) about 1780.

LUDLOW. Pottery worked by Richard Glover at Clee Hill, Ludlow, during last quarter of nineteenth century.

SOMERSET
BRISTOL. Good accounts of earlier post-medieval wares of Bristol

published by K. J. Barton in 'Some Evidence for two types of Pottery Manufactured in Bristol in the early eighteenth century', *Trans of the Bristol & Gloucs Archaeol Soc*, 1961, and in 'The Excavation of a Medieval Bastion at St Nicholas's Almshouses, King St. Bristol', *Medieval Archaeology*, VIII, 1964. Later potteries recorded in Bristol are—

Wilder Street Pottery. Established, according to Jewitt, in 1820 by Mr Macken who made flower-pots, etc, before emigrating to America.

Sugar House Pottery. Jewitt says carried on by George Hart until 12 August 1775, when it passed to Stephen Fricker, potter, and publican of Fountain Tavern, High St, Bristol, who made sugar baker's moulds, flower-pots, chimney-pots, and pancheons.

DONYATT. Village near Ilminster and centre of thriving pottery industry from early seventeenth century at latest. Will of Hugh Harris, potter, of 'Doniate' proved at Prerogative Court of Canterbury on 13 October 1620. Although some examples of Donyatt ware dated between 1664 and 1813 are known, first description of village is in Collinson's 1791 *History & Antiquities of the County of Somerset*: 'In the hamlet of Crock Street [Donyatt,] are three potteries in which a considerable quantity of earthen ware is made'. These potteries were at Crock Street itself and at Whitney Bottom, Donyatt.

The Crock Street Pottery (ST 332135). Worked by three generations of potters called James Rogers up to closure in 1900. In 1968 the writer and R. Coleman-Smith visited site, discovering kiln-house still standing and that even though kiln itself had been removed and hovel converted into milking parlour, upper walls were still coated in thick black residue deposited by kiln's smoke. Excavations in nearby fields produced quantities of mid-eighteenth century wasters, including sgraffito, trailed, combed and rouletted wares in form of plates, mugs, jugs, and large storage jars.

Pit Pottery. Still working in 1910, when Dr Glaisher visited it under Caleb Arlidge, who made two money-boxes for Doctor, Nos 177 & 178 in Bernard Rackham's catalogue of his collection.

WESTON-SUPER-MARE. 'Royal Pottery' established 1836 by Charles Phillips as brick and tile works (see Jewitt), but in 1837 glazed wares introduced, pottery finally making architectural terracottas alone.

Gazetteer

STAFFORDSHIRE
by Miss D. Griffiths

Medieval potteries worked in Staffordshire as proven by both documentary evidence and also the excavation of a kiln at Sneyd Green. The major early post-medieval deposits of pottery from the county are a group of Cistercian wares from Hulton Abbey, and a group of early seventeenth century blackwares from the Marquis of Granby site in Burslem. The major development of 'The Potteries' took place here in the mid-seventeenth century, as has been described. This is not the place, however, to attempt to trace the full history of this complex industrial development, and therefore only brief historical notes of each area, with comprehensive lists of coarse earthenware potters working in them, are given.

The following sources have been consulted in this section:

1 Mankiwitz & Haggar. *Concise Encyclopedia of English Pottery & Porcelain*, 1968
2 Allbut, J. *The Staffordshire Pottery Directory*, 1802
3 White, W. *History, Gazeteer & Directory of Staffordshire*, 1834
4 White, W. *History, Gazeteer & Directory of Staffordshire*, 1851
5 Chester & Mort. *The Staffordshire Pottery Directory*, 1802
6 Shaw, Simeon. *History of the Staffordshire Potteries*, 1827
7 Plot, Dr Robert. *Natural History of Staffordshire*, 1686
8 Pigot & Co. *The Staffordshire Directory*, 1828-9
9 *Slater's National Commercial Directory (Midlands)*, 1862
10 *Kelly's Post Office Directory for . . . Staffordshire*, 1868
11 *Kelly's Post Office Directory for Staffordshire*, 1892
12 Pigot & Co. *Commercial Directory*, 1818-20
13 Smart, J. *Directory of Wolverhampton, Wednesbury & Bilston*, 1827
14 Pigot & Co. *National Commercial Directory*, 1835
15 Bridgen, J. *Wolverhampton Post Office Directory*, 1847
16 William Salt Library, Stafford: The Quarter Sessions Recognizance Registers, Q/S. Pr 2/2.
17 Hackwood, F. W. *Odd Chapters in the History of Wednesbury*, 1920
18 Bagnall, J. N. *A History of Wednesbury*, 1854
19 Meteyard, Eliza. *The Life of Josiah Wedgwood*, 1865-6
20 Tunnicliff, William. *A Survey of Staffordshire*, 1787
21 Ryles, T. *A Map of Burslem about the Year 1720*
22 Cooper, R. G. *English Slipware Dishes, 1650-1850*, 1968

THE POTTERIES

BURSLEM. Dr Plot, writing in 1686, stated that 'the greatest Pottery they have in this County is carried on at Burslem near Newcastle-under-Lyme, where for making their severall sorts of pots, they have as many different sorts of Clay, which they dig round about the Towne, all within half a miles distance, the best being found near the coale . . .' (7). Previously (7) he had given details of the tall butter-pots made here for the Uttoxeter butter-market. According to a list of potters drawn up by Josiah Wedgwood, there were 42 potteries working in Burslem in 1710-15, a further 7 working in Hanley, and only 2 in Stoke. Prefacing this list, Josiah made out the following account, which probably refers to his grandfather's pottery at the Churchyard Works, Burslem (19):
'Men necessary to make an Oven of Black and Motled, per week, and other expenses;

	£	s	d
6 Men, 3 @ 4s p. week and 3 @ 6s.	1	10	0
4 Boys @ 1s 3d.	0	5	0
1 cwt. 2 qrs. Lead Ore, @ 8s.	0	12	0
Manganese	0	3	0
Clay, 2 Cart-Load, @ 2s.	0	4	0
Coals, 48 Horse-Loads, @ 2d.	0	8	0
Carre of do. @ 1½d.	0	6	0
Rent of Works @ 5L. p. annm.	0	2	0
Wear and tear of Ovens, Utensils, &c. 10L p. annm.	0	4	0
Straw for packing, 3 Thrave, of 24 Sheaves to the Thrave, @ 4d.	0	1	0
The Master's Profit, besides 6s. for his Labor.	0	10	0
	£ 4	5	0

Adams, John, maker of black & mottled wares 1710-20 (19) (21).
Adams, John, (1624-87) made black, mottled, and slipwares (1).
Adams, Ralph, potter, on Ryles' map of 1720 (21).
Adams, Thomas I, recorded as potter at Burslem pre-1563.
Adams, Thomas II, described as a potter in his will of 1629 (*VCH* p 123)
Adams, William, described as a master potter in his will of 1617.
Bagley, William, potter, 1787 (20).
Bagnall, —, butter-pot maker in Wedgwood's list of 1710-15 (19).
Ball, Isaac, listed in Tunstall Court Rolls 1671 (1), married Sara Edge on 24 December 1696 at Stoke (1) and is probably

responsible for a number of posset pots dated 1696-1700.

Bath, William, coarse earthenware mfctr, Queen St, 1834 (3).

Beech, H., butter-pot maker in Wedgwood's list of 1710-15 (19).

Bold, James, recorded as potter in 1757 (16).

Bucknall, Robert, mottled ware maker in Wedgwood's list of 1710-15 (19).

Burn, William, owner of Pot Works on Ryles' 1720 map (21).

Cartlich, S & J, are listed as potters in 1787 (20).

Cartlich, Samuel, is listed by Wedgwood 1710-15 (19) and by Ryles (21) 1720.

Cartlich, Thomas, listed as potter on Ryles' map of 1720 (21).

Cartwright, Thomas, butter-pot maker in Wedgwood's 1710-15 list (19).

Cornes, Thomas, recorded as potter in 1747 (16).

Cornes, William, listed as potter of Longport, Burslem, in 1834 (3).

Daniel, John, called earthpotter in Tunstall Court Rolls (1) 1693.

Daniel, John, occupier of smug pot works on Ryles' 1720 map (21).

Daniel, Ra., potter of Hot Lane in Wedgwood's 1710-15 list (19).

Daniel, Robert, listed as potter on Ryles' map of 1720 (21).

Daniel, Thomas, received 'a pasture called Brownehills and another called The Hill in Burslem, containing three acres with the right to dig clay' as recorded in 1616 Tunstall Court Rolls (1). His son Thomas was also recorded as an inhabitant of Burslem in 1671 (1). The name 'Thomas Daniel' is occasionally found impressed on to butter-pots.

Daniel, Thomas, listed as a potter in 1787 (20).

Fletcher, Ralph & Richard, listed as inhabitants of Burslem in 1671. Possett pots dated 1682-97 probably made by one of these (1).

Fulkner, Joseph, listed as a potter in 1764 (16).

Green, John, listed as potter in 1787 (20).

Hales & Adams, listed as potters, Cobridge, in 1787 (20).

Harrison, William, listed by Wedgwood, 1710-15 (19).

Heath, John, listed as potter on Ryles' map of 1720 (21).

Locker, Maria, listed as potter on Ryles' map of 1720 (21).

Locket, Thomas, listed as a potter in Wedgwood's list of 1710-15 (19).

Malkin, Burnham, listed as a potter in 1787 (20).

Malkin, Clark, listed as a potter on Ryles' plan of 1720 (21).

Malkin, Isaac, Richard, & Thomas, all listed by Wedgwood as makers of mottled and blackwares 1710-15 (19).

Malkin, Samuel, 1668-1741, notable slipware potter, & parish clerk of Burslem. The site of his pottery was excavated 1939 by Ernest Allman, sherds bearing his signature and dated 1712 discovered.

Major production consisted of moulded dishes with proverbial or religious designs (1).

Mare, Hugh, listed as potter in Wedgwood's list of 1710-15 (19).

Mitchell, John, listed as a potter on Ryles' plan of 1720 (21).

Mitchell, Thomas, whose pottery was 'not worked' when Wedgwood made his 1710-15 list, was listed as a potter by Ryle in 1720 (19) (21).

Onion, Richard, listed as a potter on Ryles' map of 1720 (21).

Parrott, Richard, listed as a potter on Ryles' map of 1720 (21).

Simpson, John, mentioned in 1671 Tunstall Court Roll (1), and in Wedgwood's list of 1710-15 (19) as a maker of 'Red Dishes & Pans'. Possibly he was the maker of a number of circular and octagonal plates bearing the initials 'I.S.'. Two further potters of this name also occur in Wedgwood's list.

Simpson, Joseph, listed as a potter on Ryles' map of 1720 (21).

Simpson, Richard, listed as a maker of 'Red Dishes, etc' by Wedgwood 1710-15 (19).

Simpson, William, mentioned in 1671 Tunstall Court Roll (1) and also in Wedgwood's list of 1710-15 (19). His name appears on a posset pot dated 1685.

Shaw, Aaron, listed as a potter in 1731 (16).

Shaw, M, listed as a potter in 1731 (16).

Shaw, Ralph, tried to patent a sgraffito technique but failed to do so in face of strong opposition from other potters. Died between 1754 and 1759. A cradle in Hanley Museum is inscribed 'Made by Ralph Shaw, Oct, 31, Cobridge gate, M. T. 1740' (or 46). (1).

Smith, John & Joseph, listed as potters in 1787 (20).

Tunstall's Pottery was not being worked when Wedgwood made his list in 1710-15 (19).

Tunstall, J. & William, were both listed as Earth Potters in 1731 (16)

Warburton, Joseph, listed as a potter by Wedgwood 1710-15 (19).

Wedgwood, Aaron, listed as a maker of 'Dt. and Black' wares by Wedgwood in 1710-15 (19).

Wedgwood, Gilbert, 1588-1678, potted at the Overhouse, Burslem, (1).

Wedgwood, Thomas, 1617-79, son of the above Gilbert, had a son also called Thomas, 1660-1716, a grandson called Thomas, 1687-1739, all of whom worked at the Churchyard House, Burslem, where the more famous Josiah served his apprenticeship.

Wood, John, listed as a potter in 1787 (20).

Wood, Robert, 1650-1717, slipware potter. A posset pot in the Hanley Museum is inscribed 'The best is not to good for you Robbort Wood' (1).

Gazetteer

Hammersley, R. is listed as a potter at Ffenton Culvert in 1732 (16).

STOKE-ON-TRENT. According to Simeon Shaw (*History of the Staffordshire Potteries*, 1829) there were three manufactories for coarse brown pottery at Penkhull, near Stoke 'one of which belonged to Mr Thomas Doody' (1, p 173). The following are all taken from source 16 unless otherwise stated.

Allen, Christopher, Earthpotter, 1762-3.

Booth, Enoch, Potter, 1734.

Brian, Richard, Potter, 1744.

Bridgewood, Nathaniel, Potter, Boothen, Stoke (3, p 553).

Brindley, James, Potter, (20, p 38).

Glass, Joseph, Potter, 1749.

Meer, Richard, married Maria Pilsbury at Stoke on 2 August 1675. His name, alternatively spelled Meir, occurs on Staffordshire slipwares dated 1682-1708.

Meir, John, married Joyce Asson at Stoke on 23 September 1672. A trailed slipware Staffordshire cradle is inscribed 'JOHN MEIR 1708 MADE THI . .' (1, p 148).

Moreton, Aaron, Potter, 1735.

Pope, Mathew, Potter, 1769.

Poulson, William (d 1746), one of two Stoke potters listed by Josiah Wedgwood (1, p 181).

Shenton, Joseph, Earthpotter, 1764.

Simpson, Moses, Potter, 1744.

Smith, Thomas, Potter, 1735.

Standley, Charles, Potter, 1735.

Toft, Albert, Earthpotter, 1764.

Ward, —, the other Stoke potter listed by Wedgwood, 1710-15 (19).

HANLEY

Bagnall, Sampson, 1720-1803, listed as a potter in 1787 (1) (20).

Boon, Joseph, listed as a potter in 1787 (20).

Brooke, Richard, said to have worked kiln here in 1540 (*VCH*, p 164).

Chatterley, C. & E., listed as potters in 1787 (20).

Ellis, John, listed by Wedgwood as butter-pot maker 1710-15 (19).

Moses, Samuel senr, & Samuel jnr. listed as potters in 1733 (16).

Glass, Henry, listed as potter in 1739 (16).

Glass, Joseph, maker of 'Clowdy and a sort of dishes painted with dift. color'd slips, and sold at 3s. and 3s. 6d. p doz.' (19). This name occurs on a cradle in the Fitzwilliam Museum, Cambridge.

Keeling, Edward, listed as a potter in 1787 (20), and 1800 (5).

Keeling, John, listed as a potter in 1763 (16).

Mare, Hugh & John, both listed as makers of black & mottled wares in Wedgwood's list of 1710-15 (19).

Marsh, Richard, listed as maker of 'Motled and Black, Lamprey Pots and Venison Pots' in Wedgwood's list of 1710-15 (19).

Moston, Aaron, listed as a potter in 1763 (16).

Neale & Wilson, listed as potters in 1787 (20).

Perry, Samuel, listed as a potter in 1787 (20).

Pool, Joseph & William, both listed as potters in 1733 (16).

Sandford, Moses, listed as a maker of 'Milk Pans and Small Ware' in Wedgwood's list of 1710-15 (19).

Simpson, William, listed as a maker of 'Clowdy and Motled' wares in Wedgwood's list of 1710-15 (19).

Turner, Samuel, listed as a potter in 1745 (16).

Wright, Thomas, listed as a potter in 1787 (20).

Wright, William, listed as a 'Coarse Earthenware Manufacturer' in 1828 (8).

LANE END

Buxton, George, listed as a potter at Vauxhall in 1834 (3).

Rivers, William, listed as a Practical potter in 1834 (3).

MEAR HEATH

Moore, Benjamin, listed as a potter in 1747 (16).

SHELTON

Astbury, John, 1690-1743. Said by Simeon Shaw (6) to have made red earthenware teapots with white applied decoration, toy figures, etc, and also to have introduced Devon clays to The Potteries and discovered the use of calcined flint. In his will, printed in R. Adam's 'Notes on some North Staffordshire Families', 1930, he bequeathed his 'tools, implements, etc. in the trade of a Potter' to his son Joshua.

Dakin, Thomas, baptised at Stoke 3 March 1710. (1). A posset pot in the Victoria & Albert Museum is inscribed 'Thomas Dakin made this cup for Mary Scull Tharp her friend 1710'.

Glass, Joseph, listed as a potter in 1744 (16).

Heath & Bagnall, listed as potters in 1787 (20).

Keeling, Anthony, listed as a potter in 1787 (20).

Keeling, John, listed as an earth potter in 1762 (16).

Middleton, John, died 1744; James Shettell of Stoke was apprenticed to him for a fee of £10 on 18 May 1719. (1).

Skerratt, Thomas, potter, and the above Joseph Glass mentioned in the Quarter Sessions Registers in connection with the theft of ducks in 1749 (16).

Taylor & Pope, listed as potters in 1787 (20).

Toft, John, listed as earth potter, Skelton (Shelton) in 1762 (16).

Twemlow, G., listed as a potter in 1787 (20).

Whitehead, Christopher Charles, listed as potter in 1787 (20).

Yates, John, listed as earth potter in 1762 (16).

TUNSTALL

Baggaley, Thomas, listed as an earthenware mfctr in 1802 (2).

Breeze, John, listed as an earthenware mfctr in 1802 (2).

Broughton, William, listed as a potter of Roylance Street in 1851 (4).

Brummitt, George, listed as a potter of Paradise Street in 1834 (3).

Cartlich, Samuel & Thomas, listed as earthenware manufacturers 1802 (2).

Daniel, John, listed as a potter of Kidsgrove, Tunstall, in 1756 (16).

Daniell, John, listed as earthpotter in 1693 Court Roll (1).

Griffe, Gervase, mentioned as dish-maker in Tunstall, *VCH*, Vol VIII, 99.

Lindop, John, listed as maker of blackware in Green Lane, 1802 (2).

Read, William, listed as potter in Paradise Street, 1834 (3).

Rathbone, Thomas, listed as potter in Woodland Buildings, 1834 (3).

POTTERIES WITH SITES AS YET UNKNOWN

Bird, William, 1717-65, son of William and Ann Bird. See Plate, p 52.

Heath, Job, b 1678, married Elizabeth Taylor at Stoke on 28 April 1701. A slipware posset pot bearing his name and the date 1702 is in the Ashmolean Museum, Oxford (1).

Taylor, George, married Elinor Taylor at Stoke on 29 April 1687. His name and the date 1692 occur on a slipware posset pot, and his name alone on a dish in the Glaisher Collection in the Fitzwilliam Museum, Cambridge (1), (22).

Toft. The Toft family produced the finest range of late seventeenth century slipware dishes, all showing excellent workmanship and a developed sense of design. The name occurs in the Parish Registers of Stoke (from 1638) and Burslem, the Hearth Tax Rolls for Shelton, Bucknall, Fenton, and Stanley, in 1666, and for the Returns from Rushton Spencer and Leek (1).

Thomas Toft. Dishes dated 1671, 74, 77, and 98. On 21 April 1663 he married Ellena Bucknall, the following of their children being baptised at Stoke: Matthias (1663), John (1664), Thomas (1670), James (1673), and Cornelius (1677) (1). He died a pauper, and was buried on 3 December 1689.

Ralph Toft. Dishes dated 1676, 77, and a posset pot dated 1683. Probably a brother of the above Thomas, he married Christabel Hatton at Stoke on 19 December 1669 (1).

James Toft. Dishes dated 1695 and 1705. Son of Thomas and Ellena Toft, being born in 1673.

Wright, John. Dishes, similar to those of the Tofts, dated 1705-7. Possibly it was he who made the posset pot in the British Museum inscribed 'ANN DRAPER THIS CUP MADE FOR YOU AND SO NO MORE I W:1707' (1).

POTTERS IN THE VICINITY OF THE POTTERIES

CAVERSWALL. In Keates' *Potteries & Newcastle Directory* of 1869, the name of Frederick Bates, Flowerpot & Brick Maker, Weston Coyney, Caverswall, is recorded.

GOLDEN HILL. Golden Hill, 1 mile north of Tunstall, formed part of the parish of Wolstanton until it became a parish in its own right in 1841. In 1802 it was recorded (note 2) that 'Manufacture consists chiefly of coarse black, chequered and portobello wares of which considerable quantities are here made'.

Baggaley, Abraham, earthenware manufacturer (2) 1802

Capper, John & Thomas, earthenware manufacturer (2) 1802

Collinson, John, earthenware manufacturer (2) 1802

Collinson, John, black & brown earthenware manufacturer (3 & 4) 1834-51.

Moss, Thomas, said to have made pottery here, *VCH Staffs*, Vol VIII, 99.

Tunstall, Thomas, earthenware manufacturer (2) 1802

Walker, Thomas, earthenware manufacturer, Newfield, (4) 1851

IPSTONES. Possible kiln remains including saggers, kiln furniture, sherds of pitchers, vinegar kegs, mugs, bowls, milk pans, etc, found here at Hay House Farm, Belmont, Ipstones. See *N. Staffs Field Club Trans* 1941-2, LXXVI, 41-2, article by J. D. Johnstone. An advertisement (1, p 16) dated 16 Sept 1797, for a coarse pottery to let between Leek and Cheadle may possibly refer to this site.

NEWCASTLE-UNDER-LYME. Potters recorded here in Poll lists 1774-92

Gazetteer

(30 potters) and 1837 (40 potters). Possibly these potters worked in the manufactories of The Potteries.

NORMICOT
Legg, Isaac, Coarse Earthenware Manufacturer, Furness (8, p 726) 1828-9.
Legg, Isaac, Earthenware Manufacturer, Meir Heath, Normicot, (3, p 628) 1834 & (4, p 37) 1851.
Legg, John, Earthenware Manufacturer (9, p 147) 1862

NORTON-IN-THE-MOORS. John Aiken's *Description of the Country around Manchester*, 1795, mentions a coarse earthenware pottery here (1, p 166).

MILWICH
Snape, William, Beer retailer and earthenware manufacturer, Garshall Green, Milwich (10, p 606) 1868.
Snape, Samuel, Beer retailer and flowerpot maker, Garshall Green, Milwich (11, p 240) 1892.

RED STREET, WOLSTANTON
Hollins, William, & Ford, George, made earthenware here until 22 August 1799 (1, p 112).
Moss & Henshall, Earthenware Manufacturers (2) 1802.
Myatt, Benjamin, Earthenware Manufacturer (1, p 188) 1818.
Riles & Bathwell, Earthenware Manufacturer (2) 1802.
Riles, Samuel; this pottery was offered for sale in 1815 (1, p 188).

POTTERIES IN SOUTH STAFFORDSHIRE
ARMITAGE
Fox & Co, Earthenware Manufacturers (9, p 130) 1862.

BILSTON
Bew, Robert, Earthenware Manufacturer, Lower Bradley Pottery (4, pp 145-8) 1851. This pottery was managed by Robert John Myatt at this period.
Brereton, William, mentioned as potter here in document in Birmingham Reference Library, 1801 (1, p 23).
Myatt, John, Earthenware Manufacturer, Bradley, Bilston (9, p 9) 1862.
Myatt, John & Son, Manufacturers of rockingham teapots, yellow ware, garden pots & chimney pots, porous cells & batteries of all sizes, Bradley Pottery, Bilston (10, p 478) 1868.

Starson, William, Potter, etc, Bradley, near Bilston (12, p 21) 1818-20.

Stinson, William, Potter, at Bradley near Bilston, 1818, Parson & Bradshaw's Directory.

Turner, Alex & Son, Earthenware & Stoneware Manufacturers, Bradley (11, p 41) 1892.

Turner, William P., Earthenware water filter manufacturer, Bradley (9, p 9) 1862.

Wilde, John & Son, Manufacturers of coarse black earthenware, 1827-34 (13, p 87; 8, p 703; 3, p 229). Stoneware also from 1835 (14, p 396).

A collection of Bilston pottery is now in Bilston Museum, consisting of jugs, bowls, & vases with olive green, yellow, or ochre-coloured glazes and either incised lines or feathery leaf patterns in slip as decoration. Some are impressed 'MYATT'.

KINGSWINFORD, BRETTELL LANE

Edge, Samuel, Earthenware Mfctr, coarse black & stone (3, p 269) 1834.

Green, James, Earthenware Mfctr, coarse black & stone (4, p 188; 9, p 63) 1851-62.

Green, James, Red Earthenware Manufacturer (10, p 492) 1868.

Hampton, J., Earthenware Mfctr (1, p 123) 1860.

Handley, Joseph, Black & Stoneware Mfctr (4, p 188) 1851.

Meese, Thomas, Black & Stoneware Mfctr (4, p 188; 9, p 63) 1851-62.

Smith, Francis & Sons, Black & Stoneware Mfctr (3, p 269; 14, p 657) 1834-5.

Smith & Hodnett, Black & Stoneware Mfctr (4, p 188; 9, p 63) 1851-62.

Woodward, David, Black & Stoneware Mfctr (14, p 657) 1835.

KINGSWINFORD, BRIERLEY HILL

Barnbrook, John, Black & Stoneware Mfctr (3, p 269; 14, p 657) 1834-5.

Evans, Richard, Black & Stoneware Mfctr, Moor Lane (3, p 269) 1834.

Green, Benjamin, Black & Stoneware Mfctr (1, p 123; 14, p 657) 1818-35.

Green, Mrs J., Earthenware Mfctr, Delph (1, p 123) 1860.

Parish, T. Earthenware Mfctr (1, p 123) 1818.

Southall, T. Black & Stoneware Mfctr (3, p 269) 1834.

Squires, Charles, Earthenware Mfctr (10, p 493) 1868.

Wassall, Charles, Black & Stoneware Mfctr, Moor Lane (4, p 188) 1851.

Wassall, Henry, Black & Stoneware Mfctr, Moor Lane (4, p 188) 1851.

Westwood & Moor, Black & Stoneware Mfctr (4, p 188; 9, p 63) 1851-62.

White, Thomas, Earthenware Mfctr, The Delph Pottery (1, p 123; 9, p 63) 1860-96.

KINGSWINFORD, THE LEYS

Carder, George, Stone & Earthenware Mfctr, Leys Pottery (1, p 123) 1860-92.

KINGSWINFORD, RAVENSICH

Stinson, Joseph, Coarse black & stoneware Mfctr (3, p 269; 14, p 657) 1834-5.

KINGSWINFORD, THORNS

Onions, John, Coarse black & stoneware Mfctr (3, p 269; 14, p 657) 1834-5.

Read, William, Coarse black & stoneware Mfctr (3, p 269; 14, p 657) 1834-5.

Thorns, John, is mentioned as a potter in a deed dated 13 January 1801, now housed in Birmingham Reference Library (1, p 123).

OLD SWINFORD

Meir, John, recorded as a potter of Old Swinford, Staffs, on 10 July 1744 (16).

TAMWORTH

Gibbs & Canning, Brick & Tile Maker, & glazed stoneware, pipe, and terracotta works, Glascote, Tamworth (9, p 150).

Hyde, Henry, Earthenware Maker, Glascote, Tamworth (14, p 452).

TIPTON. Dr Plot (1686) states that 'Potters clays for the more common wares there are at many places, particularly at Horsley Heath in the Parish of Tipton'.

Evans, Susana, Potter, Lea Brook, Tipton (9, p 159).

Evans, Thomas, Earthenware Mfctr, Lea Brook, Tipton (10, p 679).

WEDNESBURY. Dr Plot (1686) says that 'in Monway field . . . there are two sorts [of clay] gotten . . . Of these they make divers sorts of vessels at Wednesbury, which they paint with slip, made of a redish sort of Earth gotten at Tipton . . .' The Wednesbury parish registers also refer to potters between the years 1712-29.

Mills, Thomas, potter, recorded as creditor in a quit claim (1, p 238) 1740.

Perry, Joseph, mentioned in a deed of 1749 (1, p 238).

Rolistan, James, potter (17, pp 52-3).

About 1800 'The last potters removed from the Parish . . . and went to reside in the Staffordshire Potteries' (18), but c 1886 a Mr Hepplewhite, making 'a class of art ware not unlike that of Doulton's . . . vases, flagons, cups, and many other forms of vessels (17, p 52-3), revived the industry here for a few years, marking his wares 'Oaklands'. There is no mention of this enterprise in the 1892 county directory. **M**

SUFFOLK

Numerous small potteries during late eighteenth and early nineteenth centuries, most making drain-pipes and other coarse horticultural wares. Kelly's 1883 *Directory of the Building Trades* lists William Aldous, Ingate St, Beccles; William Balaam, 64-6 Rope Walk, Ipswich; George Chambers, Wickham Market; Hall Goulding, Haverhill; George Newson, Yoxford; George Reuben Wright, Old Kiln, Woolpit, Bury St Edmunds.

WATTISFIELD. R. G. Haggar's 1950 *English Country Pottery* dates first records of pottery to 1646-89, when a 'pott-maker' was resident. Present pottery apparently founded in 1734 when John Death leased site from John Cogisdale, Death and family continuing until 1808, when Thomas Watson took over. Throughout nineteenth century the Watsons made functional wares such as gotches, bread pans, milk steens, frying-pans and wash-bowls, and later rustic wares. Advertisement in 1896 directory calls them, 'Manufacturers of the famous TERRA-COTTA RUSTIC WARE. Lovers of anything pretty and artistic for ferns should write for specimens'. Watson family still work Wattisfield pottery to this day.

SURREY
by Mr Felix Hollings

POTTERIES OF HAMPSHIRE-SURREY BORDER

Potteries formerly existed to north-east of Farnham in belt extending up to several miles from Hampshire-Surrey border, here formed by River Blackwater. Expanding considerably in nineteenth century, industry first arose through adjacent special clay producing off-white pottery. All medieval and most of sixteenth- and seventeenth-century output is off-white; but about beginning of eighteenth century ordinary redware superseded it. Demand for off-white wares induced early potters to establish themselves even several miles from clay sources in Farnham Park and Tongham, both lying between Farnham and Ash. Clay occurs in narrow outcrop of Reading Beds in this area. Other local pits provide ordinary potters' clay, and are known to have been regular sources for nineteenth-century potters in Farnborough and neighbourhood. These potteries fall in area of largely sandy and often waterlogged heaths, large parts being shown on eighteenth-century maps as 'peat moors', though turf rather than peat was generally found here and nineteenth-century potters favoured this fuel. There is also considerable acreage of woodland on these heaths, and hereabouts, from which potters could obtain brushwood and cordwood.

Comparing sixteenth- and seventeenth-century pottery from kiln-sites with pottery found in London, it appears certain that this area supplied London market with off-white wares, and equally certain that more kiln-sites are yet to be discovered. In early nineteenth century the pottery was conveyed to London via Basingstoke Canal and Thames, but later by horse and cart.

ALDERSHOT (SU 873503 & SU 872504). These sites are shown on local tithe map as potteries in early nineteenth century, but neither is shown on the First Edition 6in Ordnance Survey map of 1871. Local directories say W. Collins worked pottery in High Street, 1850s-60s.

ASH (SU 895505). A medieval and, subsequently, a mid-late seventeenth century pottery, were found in 1965 near now demolished cottage. No trace of a kiln, but numerous wasters and some kiln furniture recovered from new garden and nearby school grounds. All medieval and about 90 per cent of seventeenth-century pottery was off-white, output of latter consisting largely of bowls and platters, various sizes of pipkin, and a few cups and other small vessels. Commonest glaze colour greenish-yellow, but true green and yellows also used. Documentary evidence, though not directly connected with site, gives prominence to family of potters called Watts, apparently active throughout seventeenth and early eighteenth centuries in Ash and adjoining parish of Pirbright. On First Edition

213

1in Ordnance Survey Map 'Ash Crock Kilns' are marked at SU 904509, though this site not yet investigated.

BRAMLEY. Verbal report states that pottery formerly worked here, closing when clay ran out.

CHEAM. A major centre of Surrey pottery industry during late medieval period, but inactive from then up to 1840, when Messrs Waghorn of Ewell opened pottery. Second pottery built in 1869 (Jewitt), making flower-pots, rustic fern-stands, vases, chimney-pots, etc, sometimes stamped 'Henry Clark, Cheam Pottery'.

COVE (SU 859555). Seventeenth-century pottery existed almost on site of Alma public house, redeveloped in 1967. Many waster sherds, mainly in off-white wares, found in gardens of new houses on site, suggesting mid-late seventeenth-century date. Ordnance Survey 6in map of 1871 shows two further potteries: Hill House Pottery (SU 861555) and West Heath Pottery (SU 855559), one of which was operated by David Yeomans between 1850s and c 1920.

CROOKHAM (SU 798526). Nineteenth-century pottery formerly worked at Grove Farm, and many redware waster sherds found in field behind farm.

DORKING. Will of Mathew Day, Potter, of Dorking entered in Prerogative Court of Canterbury in 1675 (Folio 23), must confirm seventeenth-century pottery. In 1969 eighteenth-century waster heap discovered behind Woolworth's in High Street (TQ 166495) included Metropolitan type slipwares, including dishes dated 173-, and wide range of other wares, with iron-flecked fabric similar to that of Sussex. Further pottery is shown on early nineteenth century tithe map (TQ 168474) as being empty, and on 1871 Ordnance Survey Map as 'Potkiln Cotts'.

FARNBOROUGH (SU 876566). Site situated in grounds of Farnborough Hill Convent, within ¼ mile of pottery acquired in 1809 by William Smith (see biography by his grandson, George Sturt of Farnham). Site not yet fully excavated, but evidence points to continuous production from fifteenth to seventeenth centuries. Floors of buildings or working areas and at least two kiln-sites dating from late sixteenth century found in 1969, plus large waster dump containing several complete vessels. Site's outstanding feature was production of 'Farnham Greenware' or 'Tudor Green' pottery, among which are jugs and drinking vessels identical with examples found on many London excavation sites, including Temple. Sixteenth-century output covers numerous domestic vessels—pipkins, storage jars, bowls, jugs, platters, chamber-pots, chafing dishes, butter-pots, and dripping pans—and money-boxes, costrels, and candlesticks. Except for coarsest vessels, fabric is off-white, with yellow or green glaze. Medieval pottery is entirely off-white, but frequently reduced to pale grey. Although confined mainly to ordinary wares, such as jugs, cisterns, cooking-pots, and large pans, it also included fragments of delicate lobed cups and mugs in Tudor Greenware, which appear from their context to date from late fifteenth century. This prolific site probably supplied the 229 pots carted from Farnborough to 'stywes' of Windsor Castle in 1391 (see Salzman, *Building in England to 1540*, 276).

FARNHAM. In 1858 Absalom Harris, formerly apprentice to George Cobbett of Shorley Pottery, Beauworth, Hants, took over small pottery at Charles Hill, Elstead, Farnham, where he made coarse red-wares from local Gault clay. To avoid rising rents, etc, he moved in 1866 to new site in Glenbervie Enclosure of Alice Holt Forest, where he built kiln and house, again working Gault clay; but new site proved unsuitable, particles of lime in the clay causing pots to blister in kiln and making them unsaleable. After seven years at Glenbervie, Absalom moved to Clay Hill, Wrecclesham, Farnham, where pottery works to this day. Up to 1880s pottery made wide range of litharge-glazed redwares, including plant, rhubarb, paint, chimney, and lard-pots, together with drain-pipes and tiles. In 1880 came revival of 'Farnham Greenware', copies of medieval and early post-medieval Surrey greenwares being made with litharge-based lead glaze stained bright green by adding copper oxide. From this copying arose 'Art Pottery', made in collaboration with Farnham School of Art, and lasting until just before 1939. Now pottery concentrates on horticultural wares, specially terrace jars and strawberry pots.

FRENSHAM. Manning & Bray's 1814 *History of Surrey* mentions that pottery in Churt area was using clay from Tongham, maybe that listed in 1855 directory under 'Natl. Langridge, potter & Farmer, Churt'.

FRIMLEY (SU 890566). Pottery shown on 1871 Ordnance Survey map, but not traced when site was developed recently.

HAWLEY (SU 861581). Seventeenth-century pottery, which, on style of its vessels, is thought to have closed c 1660 after limited life of about thirty years. Seventeenth-century cottage was later built above working surface on which part of kiln survived and has been preserved. Pottery's range was wide, much the same as Farnborough's, except for inclusion of fair number of cups and mugs (the latter glazed both sides and usually of high quality) and apparent exclusion of large storage jars. Yellow and green glazes predominate on off-white fabric for about 80 per cent of output.

MYTCHETT (SU 888555). Present occupier says pottery started here in 1780 by Mrs Smith. Certainly pottery is shown on 1871 Ordnance Survey map, and waster sherds found in garden.

PIRBRIGHT (SU 946544). Pottery was found at Stanford Farm through documentary sources. Farm was acquired in 1665 by John Watts, member of Ash family of potters, and contemporary field names suggest that pottery already existed at this date. Waster sherds in farm gardens confirm seventeenth-century date for site, with output of wares very similar to those of Ash, but with a higher proportion of redware, no doubt because it was farther from source of white clay.

Rocque's 1762 map of Surrey shows pottery in grounds of early nineteenth-century Pirbright Lodge (SU 938552), but site is grassed over now, and shows no sign of its former use. Further site, on edge of Brookwood Crematorium (SU 953558), is shown as pottery on early nineteenth century tithe map, and wasters have been found there. Probably this is pottery of Messrs Harding & Cheeter, potters, listed in 1855 directory.

SUSSEX

Urban potteries among most interesting in England, producing variety of wares for south-eastern counties; but little published on them, except for J. M. Baines's *Sussex Pottery*, 1948.

BEEDING. The Norman family operated pottery at Holmbush, Lower Beeding, near Colgate from c 1860s-1890s. In 1897 Messrs Jesse & Henry Norman were listed as makers of terracotta; brownware; and seakale, rhubarb, & chimney-pots.

BOSHIP POTTERY. Spirit flask in Victoria & Albert Museum, London, inscribed as made by John Siggery at Boship Pottery in 1794. During late nineteenth century worked by Henry Whenham, and for period after 1900 used by B. W. H. Bridges for making reproductions of the early Sussex wares.

BURGESS HILL. Number of potteries round about, probably most important being that of Meeds family, worked by James Meeds from 1840s-c 1870 when it passed to William & Frederick Meeds. According to *The Connoisseur*, 33, 15, works closed in 1912.

The other potteries were situated on St John's Common, and included Richard Berry, 1870s-90s; John Gravett, 1860s-80s; Richard & Nathan Norman, 1860s-90s.

BREDE. According to Horsfield's 1834 *History of the County of Sussex*, pottery first established about 1755, but earliest documentary evidence occurs in Brede Parish Registers of 22 May 1767, when 'John Eldridge of this Parish, potter' married Elizabeth Rummins. During late eighteenth century pottery land acquired by Henry Richardson of Brede, but by late 1790s pottery itself was being run by Thomas Weller, a potter who had recently moved into the area. Thomas had five sons and two daughters, who emigrated to America in 1840s with sole exception of John Weller (1806-1891). He remained at Brede Pottery, taking over at his father's death. Of John Weller's twelve children four continued to work for some time at pottery, Aaron becoming a thrower, James working the clay, Edward doing general work, and Luke delivering the goods by horse and cart. The supply of clay ran out in 1892, forcing the pottery, then worked by Aaron and his son Enoch John, to close down. Works were demolished. Pottery made at Brede included tongue and milk pans, chamber-pots, pitchers, pipkins and flower-pots, together with ornamental snakes, hens and chickens, and hedgehogs, a Brede speciality.

CHAILEY. According to *Catalogue of the Glaisher Collection* earthenware was made here in 1791 by Robert Burstow, but by early nineteenth century pottery had passed to the Normans (see *Sussex Archaeological Collections*, 46, 28) as bowl inscribed 'Richard Norman Chailey, 1827' testifies. From c 1850 to c 1870 pottery was operated by Messrs John & Richard Norman, Messrs Ephraim & Richard Norman then continuing it. Closed in early twentieth century.

DICKER. *Catalogue of the Glaisher Collection* says 'Crock kiln and brick kiln' belonging to William Cuckney sold here in 1779. During latter half of nineteenth century Lower Dicker pottery was worked by Uriah Clark. Closed early this century.

DITCHLING. Pottery on Ditchling Common near Hurstpierpoint worked in the mid-nineteenth century by G. Chinery, and closed, according to Jewitt, in 1870.

EAST GRINSTEAD. *The Connoisseur* 33 (1912), 15 noted barrel inlaid 'H. F. Foster' and 'Dec th 1865. 23 East Grinstead' (see plate p 86), and apparently this Henry Foster's son was working there in 1912. Second potter also worked here: George Lynn, potter, of High Street is recorded in 1883 directory.

HASTINGS. Medieval kiln found, but earliest post-medieval reference dated 30 January 1773, when Henry Richardson of Brede appealed against Poor Rate assessment of Parish of St Clement. He was originally rated at £4 for 'the Pott Manufactury belonging to his House in the occupation of his Mother in Law, Mrs Sweetlove over and besides the £9 for the Said House', but after his appeal rating was dropped to £9 for house alone. Pottery presumably still working in 1784, when John Sargent, potter, appealed against his own Poor Rate assessment.

Silverhill Pottery. *The Cinque Ports Chronicle* of 1839 contained following advertisement: 'To potters & Brickmakers. To be let or sold . . . either together or separately THE SILVERHILL POTTERY AND BRICKYARD situated at Silverhill, about a mile and a quarter from Hastings and St. Leonards . . . The buildings are new, extensive and on the most improved principle . . . To view apply to Mr Edlin at the Tivoli tavern adjoining the premises'. This pottery, thought to have been built by Mr Eldridge of St Leonard's Brewery, became property of Frederick Tree following this sale, passing ten years later to his foreman, John Pelling. In 1879 pottery again changed hands, passing to James Walder, who also operated brick and tile works at Crowhurst and Battle. Production ceased in 1886 due to shortage of clay and rising transport costs for fuel, and buildings were demolished in 1895. During mid-nineteenth century Silverhill Pottery made crocks, pans, and drainpipes in redware, but concentrated on tiles and chimney-pots under James Walder.

RYE. Rye Pottery. Believed to have developed from brickyards at Cadborough owned by James Smith near end of eighteenth century. His son, Jeremiah Smith described in Pigot's *Directory of Sussex* of 1840 as 'brickmaker, lime burner and potter' at Cadborough, but unlikely to have had more than business interest in works as he was one of largest hop-growers and flock-masters in Sussex, also seven times Mayor of Rye. At this time pottery tenanted by William Mitchell, who worked there with two sons Henry and Frederick making coarse redwares. From about 1850, however, his younger son, Frederick, began to experiment, producing 'Rustic Wares', which were ornamented with details cast in coloured clays from moulds of his own manufacture. This ware greatly admired locally, and awarded bronze medal at Hastings and St Leonards Industrial Exhibition of 1867. Following year Frederick left his father and started his own works. Rye Pottery continued until 1871, closing after William Mitchell's death.

Belle Vue Pottery. After leaving Rye Pottery Frederick Mitchell built new works for 'Rustic Wares', vessels made with mixture of Dorset and local clays and having moulded ornament in form of hops, snakes, branches, etc. After only four years at new pottery Frederick died, but his widow and nephew, Frederick Thomas Mitchell, continued to make art wares. Mrs Mitchell concentrated on historical wares, such as her 'Trojan Ware', copying pottery excavated by Schliemann at Mycenae, for example, while Frederick II developed 'Palissy Ware', imitating naturalistic productions of famous sixteenth-century French potter. Pottery passed out of the Mitchells' hands in 1920, when Mrs Mills became owner.

WARWICKSHIRE
ASTON. Apparently seventeenth-century pottery industry existed at Aston, a suburb of Birmingham, for names 'Clay putts' (1647) and 'Potters Croft' (1661) are both recorded in this parish (see *The Place-names of Warwickshire*, 341-2).

BAGINGTON. This village, some 3 miles south of Coventry, possessed a 'Potter pytte' as early as 1544 (*The Place-names of Warwickshire*, 362).
CHILVERS COTON (SP 352906 & SP 343898). Place-name 'Pot Kiln Close' and 1604 reference to 'Chilverscotton at Potters Coton' (PNW, 79) strongly indicated pottery industry in this area, confirmed by recent series of excavations. In 1967 P. Mayes and R. G. Thomson excavated twenty-seven pottery kilns and wares, ranging in date from first half of thirteenth to early sixteenth centuries. A note showing development of Midlands kilns through two, three, four and five firemouth varieties appeared in *Medieval Archaeology*,

Vol XII (1968), 209, and full details of this important site now eagerly awaited.

COUGHTON. Name 'Potters Pytte' recorded here in 1544 (PNW, 368).

NUNEATON, *see* Chilvers Coton.

POLESWORTH. In his *Catalogue of the Glaisher Collection* Bernard Rackham gives account of vessel in buff fabric with red slip decoration inscribed 'Polesworth Pottery, R. G. 1801', sole present evidence for existence of pottery.

STOKE. Although fourteenth- or fifteenth-century pottery kiln discovered in 1910, industry apparently dormant until late nineteenth century, when Robert Wakefield opened pottery for general horticultural wares such as flower-pots, seakale-pots, etc (Jewitt). Further pottery in village in 1880s, operated by Messrs Hawkins & Sons.

STONELEIGH. At Stoneleigh, some 4 miles from Coventry and 2 from Bagington was a 'Pottersfield' in 1538 (PNW, 365).

WESTMORLAND
WEATHERIGGS POTTERY. At Clifton, near Penrith, built on part of Broughton Estate by Mr Binings in 1855. In 1865, brothers James and Jeremiah Schofield took over pottery, but James soon emigrated to Australia and third brother, John, took his place. John Schofield worked pottery up to his death in 1917, when his widow became manageress, continuing until 1937. Weatheriggs then operated by Arthur Schofield, John's son, but when he died in 1952 works passed to H. Thornburn, present potter. Mr Thornburn has been connected with pottery since 1916, his father working there before him. During its earlier years pottery produced butter, cream, and barm-pots; hen-and-chicken money-boxes; and salt kits, etc; as well as drain-pipes and bricks. Since Second World War traditional local markets have declined rapidly, but with growth of tourism in Lake District new market has developed for more ornamental wares such as slipware salt kits, flower-pots, bowls, jugs, mugs, etc, and limited number of grained wares.

WILTSHIRE
Most interesting product is elaborate South Wiltshire ware dis-

cussed in Chapter 3, but history and development remains obscure.

CHILMARK. Pottery at Ridge, near Chilmark, some 11 miles west of Salisbury, was worked in 1860s by Mrs G. Harvey, who later sold it to William Blandford, listed as owner in 1895.

CHIPPENHAM. During mid-nineteenth century pottery worked here by J. Taylor in London Road.

CROCKERTON (ST 862423). Following discovery of extensive scatter of sherds in 1966 D. Algar and Salisbury Museum Research Committee excavated one of Crockerton kiln-sites, finding base of single-flued wood-burning kiln, probably late sixteenth century. Kiln (p 147) consisted of stone-lined oven pit 2ft deep by 6ft in diameter with 2ft high plinth of 4½ft diameter in centre. At one side was shallow stoking pit from which single firemouth entered annular flue of kiln, flames from which rose upwards through series of radiating firebars to enter firing chamber. Wares consisted of large pans, wide mouthed jugs, meat dishes, floor and ridge tiles, in red fabric with greenish-brown glaze (see *Post Medieval Archaeology*, 2 [1968], 187-9). Apparently potteries continued here until early nineteenth century, for Colt Hoare mentions 'Crockerton, where a large pottery is at present situated' in his *Ancient Wiltshire* (Vol 1, 51) published early nineteenth century.

MARLBOROUGH. Two coarse redware potteries here during second half of nineteenth century viz : Symons Colthurst & Co (Zabulon Lee, manager), Dodsdown Yard, Wilton, Marlborough; and Edward Ponting, Jr, Garsdon Brickworks (makers of bricks, tiles, and wares of every description).

SWINDON. J. Turner operated pottery at Stratton St Margaret, Swindon, during mid-late nineteenth century.

WESTBURY. W. Greenland, Eden Vale, Westbury, produced coarse redwares during 1860s and 70s.

YORKSHIRE

BURTON IN LONSDALE. Potteries here, 12 miles from Lancaster, well situated on small detached coalfield to north-west of county. Most lay on banks of River Greta, where coal, coal-measure fireclay, and pot-clay could all be dug near surface. First potteries at 'Black Burton' (popularly named) started in mid-late eighteenth century to serve growing population of North Lancashire, and surrounding Pennine dales. While transport was poor, potteries flourished, but with coming of railways, which could import Staffordshire pottery speedily and cheaply, potteries declined. Closure of local coalmines in early 1920s added difficulty. Last pottery closed in 1945. Information gathered from O. Grabham's *Yorkshire Potteries, Pots and Potters* of 1915, local directories, and reminiscences of Mr Bateson of Waterside Pottery.

BAGGALEY POTTERY, GRETA BRIDGE, BURTON. Founded by John Baggaley in 1750s; succeeded on death in 1788 by son John, who died 1812, and grandson George, born 1780. In early nineteenth century John Baggaley III, George's son, passed pottery to relative, Edward Coates, licensee of 'Punch Bowl Inn' nearby. On death of Edward Coates c 1880, pottery and inn left to son Thomas, who sold pottery to Mr Bateson of Waterside Pottery in 1920s. Pottery finally closed in 1945. It had two kilns, one for stonewares and another for earthenwares. Only early piece extant is knife-pot with finely slip-trailed inscription 'Knives & Forks, 1797', now in Yorkshire Museum, York (cat no 72/a).

GRETA BANK POTTERY, BURTON. Founded in 1850, and worked by T. Burton, Mr Greenets and Mr Parker in late nineteenth century. Producing brown and black wares in 1918 under G. Kilshaw, but closed soon after.

TOWN END POTTERY, BURTON. Probably established in early eighteenth century by Thomas Bateson, though potter called Gibson may have had earlier pottery. Thomas's son, grandson, and great-grandson continued tradition until c 1853, when pottery taken over by William and John Parker. John Parker running pottery single-handed late 1880s until closure shortly after First World War. Produced brown and black ware domestic pottery.

CASTLEFORD. Eagle Pottery started in 1854 by company of workmen styled John Roberts & Co, producing, as Jewitt remarked, 'only the most common classes of earthenware'. By 1878 converted to glass-bottle works.

CRAYKE. In late 1930s remains of two kilns found in garden of E. M. Rutter, close to parish church. One kiln was about 6ft in diameter with single flue, and floor formed originally of yellow clay, subsequently relined with sandstone slabs, and finally topped with 5-6in layer of calcined clay. Second kiln, 34ft away, consisted of burnt area bounded by circle of small boulders. This was completely surrounded by mass of partly burnt clay containing quantities of pottery and resting on 6in layer of charcoal ash. Remains consisted of jugs and other vessels in local reduced greenware, attributed by G. Dunning to sixteenth century. Kilns were probably of clamp type, which is quite possible even at this date. (See excavation report in *Yorkshire Archaeol Journal*, Vol 40, 90.)

HALIFAX. Potteries situated on steep eastern side of valley from Halifax up to Denholm, and at junction of coal measures with Pennine gritstones—well placed for coal, fireclay, and potclay nearby and market in booming wool-towns of industrial West Riding. Declined in late nineteenth century under influx of cheap Staffordshire whitewares, but final closure delayed until 1964, and then for want of potter not market. Potteries here may be readily divided between Halliday and Catherall families. Hallidays worked Puel Hill, Bate Hayne, and Howcans potteries in succession from 1640s to 1880s, while Catheralls founded most of remainder. According to local tradition, Jonathan Catherall, a Welshman, first started pottery at Keelham, near Denholm, in mid-eighteenth century, and documents confirm this. Jonathan Catherall belonged to famous Catherall family of Buckley Potteries, North Wales, which explains similarity in wares from both potteries. See J. Walton. 'Some Decadent Local Industries', *The Halifax Antiq Soc Papers*, 1938 vol, 19.

AINLEY TOP POTTERY, HALIFAX. Worked by Joseph Kitson from 1826 until his death in 1836, when son Edward took over. When Edward moved to Grimscar brickworks in 1868, Titus Kitson became manager of pottery, working there until it was demolished in 1890.

BLACKLEY POTTERY, HALIFAX. Started in 1810 by Joseph Kitson, who moved to Ainley Top Pottery in 1826. Made coarse redwares, similar to those of other Halifax potteries.

BRADSHAW HEAD, HALIFAX. Redware pottery founded by Samuel Catherall, grandson of Jonathan Catherall of Soil Hill, about 1830, but he and partner closed down works two years later.

DENHOLME POTTERY, HALIFAX. Samuel Catherall, son of Jonathan Catherall of Soil Hill Pottery, started Denholme Pottery in 1875, his widow and son, John Catherall, succeeding in ownership. On 14

August 1893, John Catherall sold the working plant and stock to Nicholas Taylor, former workman, renting premises to him at £30 per annum. Mr Taylor must have been renting pottery previously, however, for Kelly's 1891 *Directory of the West Riding* lists 'Nicholas Taylor, Denholme Pottery', without mentioning the Catheralls. In December 1898, Nicholas Taylor left pottery after disagreement with Ezra Catherall, John's only son and heir, on responsibility for repairs to structure; but returned in 1900 and took out fifteen-year lease on it. Modern machinery and steam-power were installed, and probably new kiln built, but this outlay strained his finances and he was forced into deed of assignment in February 1907. Pottery continued unsuccessfully under various new proprietors for next few years, and closed permanently soon after.

Denholme wares consisted largely of white-slipped redware pancheons, redware plates with slip-trailed bands about rims, breadcrocks, jars, and plant-pots. While Nicholas Taylor was at pottery, both as workman and owner, great range of finely thrown wares such as slip-trailed mugs and puzzle jugs were also made. Some of his pieces now in Yorkshire Museum, York, are genuinely dated between 1855 and 1905, but he was also responsible for so-called Woodnam House jug in that collection, dated 1719 and sold fraudulently to the then curator of Yorkshire Museum, anxious to enlarge his collection.

PUEL HILL, BATE HAYNE, AND HOWCANS, HALIFAX. About 1640-50 the Hallidays, local family of potters and pipe-makers, built kiln at Puel Hill, bleak and exposed Pennine hilltop near Halifax. Kiln recently excavated by G. Bryant of Halifax (see *Post Medieval Archaeology*, Vol 1 [1967], 117). Kiln not used for long, however, for late in seventeenth century Hallidays leased site from Dearden family at Bate Hayne, more sheltered spot on steep hillside below Puel Hill, and built new pottery. In 1775 Abraham and George Halliday started another pottery at Howcans, little further along hillside, Bate Hayne kiln being continued by brother Isaac until death in 1780s. (Bate Hayne farm occupied by Halliday family until 1872, but not as pottery.) On Isaac's death, his younger son John apprenticed to uncle George Halliday at Howcans for seven years. By indenture of apprenticeship, dated 24 August 1789, George Halliday of Howcans agreed to 'teach, learn, and inform him, the said Apprentice, . . . the Trade, Art, or Mystery of Throwing and Making Pots or Earthenware of which the said Master now useth, after the Best Manner of Knowledge that he may'. About 1830 John, son of Abraham Halliday, began to manage pottery. He is mentioned in various directories as 'Earthenware Manufacturer, Howcans' up to 1845, when 'Firebrick maker' was added to his entry. When John died in 1850s, sons George and William continued to make both pottery and bricks until closure of pottery in 1889. Good range of Howcans redwares and slipwares at Yorkshire Museum, York, and Halifax and Bradford Museums.

SIDDAL, HALIFAX. Established by Mortons of Salendine Nook in late eighteenth century. John Morton described in 1789 as earthenware manufacturer of Sinderhills, Southowram, while in 1798, John Morton & Sons assessed for their pot-ovens at Sinderhills. Pottery apparently worked by Morton family until closure in 1860s, except for period 1850-58 when Titus Kitson senior ran it.

SMALL CLUES, HALIFAX. Between 1800 and 1810 James Robinson, a dissolving partner of Catheralls of Soil Hill, acquired land and three cottages from Spencers at Bradshaw, built kiln and founded Small Clues Pottery—trading as James Robinson & Co. Later, when W. Wade made partner, name changed to Robinson & Wade, which it remained until Robinson's death. After husband's decease Mrs Robinson operated pottery, being partnered by previous Town's apprentice at Small Clues, called Greenwood. But soon Mr Wade returned to pottery, running it single-handed up to closure in 1879. Range covered usual domestic and horticultural redwares of area, plus plant-pots and stands in decorated slipware, some of which can be seen in Yorkshire Museum, York, and Bolling Hall, Bradford.

SOIL HILL, HALIFAX. In 1770 Jonathan Catherall moved pottery from Keelham near Denholme to Soil Hill, Ovenden, near Halifax. Valuation of 1797 mentions house and 'Pott oven', which he built on starting his pottery. After his death on 11 August 1807, pottery was continued by son John and family. John's son Samuel returned to work here after abortive attempt to start pottery at Bradshaw Head and was responsible for fine slipwares made at Soil Hill up to death in 1887.

About 1880 pottery passed from Catheralls' possession, Mr Wilcock taking over and trying to run it himself. Apparently no potter, he soon converted property into chicken farm, still without success. In 1883 John Kitson, member of well established Yorkshire potting family, bought and reopened pottery, working it up to death in 1892. His widow and children tried to keep pottery in operation, but eventually sold it to Isaac Button in 1897. Pottery buildings now over a century old, and in poor condition, so Mr Button demolished old works and built new pottery further down hillside. New pottery extremely well designed, though small, and introduced many new features into Yorkshire pottery industry: for first time kiln was down-draught instead of up-draught, and clay-pan was heated from below by exhaust gases from kiln passing through on way to chimney. Mr Button worked at Soil Hill pottery from rebuilding to time of his death, when it passed to son Isaac, who retired from pottery in 1964, last of the Halifax potters.

Throughout eighteenth and nineteenth centuries Soil Hill pottery made redwares and slipwares in usual range of Halifax shapes, including knife-boxes, candle-holders, and domestic and horticultural wares. Examples in Yorkshire Museum, York, and Bradford and Halifax museums. Twentieth century pottery from Soil Hill still continued earlier traditional wares, including pancheons, puzzle jugs, stew-pots, etc, but made greater range of ornamental wares, eg sgraffito wares. For these Mr Button threw ornamental vase and cup shapes, gave them a coat of contrasting slip, and while still unfired, sold them to local people to decorate for themselves for a hobby, pots being returned to pottery for final firing and glazing. This accounts for many of the strange Soil Hill wares still to be found in the area.

WOODMAN HOUSE POTTERY, HALIFAX. Blackware pottery was built at Woodman House in 1868 by Titus Kitson, who potted there until 1908, when pottery was sold to Titus Kitson, jr, and Oliver and H. K. Whitworth. New owners worked pottery up to 1920, when economic climate caused sale to Mr Wilkinson, who only continued business for further three years before renting it to Oliver Kitson and Mr Bushell for few years more. By 1931 both Woodman House and Woodman House Pottery were demolished, no further blackwares being produced there.

HULL. Pottery for coarse earthenware operated at Stepney Lane from early 1820s to early 1880s by Joseph Mayfield and successors, also proprietors of Stepney Paper Mills.

LITTLETHORPE. First pottery to work alluvial clay deposits of River Ure at Littlethorpe, near Ripon, opened by James Foxton & Co in early 1830s. The Foxtons continued to make pottery and bricks up to beginning of this century, when Mr Hymas bought works. As Mr Hymas was not potter himself, leased works to James Green for few years. Then works sold to Mr Richardson, who introduced own staff. At this time pottery employed nineteen, including four throwers, with a number of wheel-turners, clayboys, and labourers. Wares were chiefly 'bigwares': huge pancheons, bread-crocks, drain-pipes, and horticultural pots, latter made up to 36in high by 36in diameter by Albert Kitson, probably finest bigware thrower in England.

On Mr Richardson's death in 1920 small company from Ripon took over pottery, selling it in 1922 to George Curtis, former clayboy who had been trained at Littlethorpe. Mr Curtis still works pottery, but expects to close down within next few years. Main products, horticultural wares, for which Littlethorpe clays are particularly suited—plant-pots, wall-pots, strawberry-pots, garden urns, etc. (Information from Mr Curtis of Littlethorpe Pottery.)

MEXBOROUGH. According to White's 1822 *Directory of the West Riding* two earthenware potteries worked coal-measure clays here, one under James Atherton and other under Peter Barker. But major pottery in early nineteenth century was Messrs Ford and Beevers' Rock Pottery, so called because workshops were built against outcrop of local sandstone. Produced brown and yellow wares, and redware garden-pots. Before 1839, works were enlarged and better quality ware made by Messrs Reed & Taylor of Ferrybridge Pottery.

MIDHOPE. Like Halifax, lies at junction of coal measures with gritstones of Pennines, so possessing good supplies of coal, fireclay, and potclay. Derbyshire mines nearby provide glazing materials required. Although number of minor potteries worked in mid-nineteenth century at Unsliven Bridge, Hand Bank, and Bate Green, main pottery was situated at Midhope Stones at side of Little Don.

In September 1720, William Bosville of Gunthwaite leased to George Walker of Hunshelf and Robert Blackburn of Alderman's Head, Langsett, plot of land at Nether-mill-Green, Midhope Stones, for erection of pot-house and other buildings. Robert Blackburn died in 1727, but widow, Mary, assigned lease to her servant William Gough. By agreement of 14 December 1728, Mary Blackburn confirmed her husband's permission to build three houses by riverside, joined by pottery workshop, also to build wall on north side of site, by which the clay-house was supported. Thomas Dyson and John Kay were tenants of above houses, and perhaps worked in pottery. On 28 June 1762, William Gough sold lease of site and buildings to John Taylor of Dike-side, Nether Midhope. Probably unsuccessful, Taylor, on 5 July 1965, assigned lease to John Whiteley of Woodseats, Yeoman, to settle debt under bond. John Whiteley, not a practical potter, apparently let pottery to John Lindley.

In 1770s John Wilson wrote, 'the pottery is now let to two persons who carry on the work and sell pots to people who make it their business to expose them to sale in the country and towns adjacent'. In 1793 John Whiteley's widow sold remainder of lease to Edward Appleyard of Sheffield Park, but John Lindley continued to work there until death in 1801. From then till expiration of original lease in 1819, Thomas Fawley of Midhope Stones tenanted pottery, but had no great success, as potteries of Swinton area were in course of great expansion, with advantages of greater financial backing and access to excellent transport facilities. In 1819, when pottery returned to ownership of Lord of the Manor, William Appleyard, son of Edward Appleyard the lessee, sold off machinery and loose tools, and removed all stock in trade to Sheffield Park. History of next few years uncertain, but when Midhope was enclosed in 1828 commissioners sold 'seven dwelling houses and gardens, with warehouse and other building thereto belonging used as a pottery' to John Haigh for £280. White's 1833 *Directory* says Messrs Thickett & Co of Midhope were makers of brown earthenware; but this company soon failed through competition of Swinton potteries, for when Luke Moorhouse bought property in 1845 it was described as 'formerly used as a Pot-House'.

Wares made consisted of slipware and redware in form of initialled bottles, barm-pots, honey-pots, mugs, and pressed slipware plates. Some good-quality whiteware also made in late eighteenth and early nineteenth centuries. Fine collection of Midhope Pottery in City Museum, Sheffield, was collected by J. Kenworthy, author of lengthy *History of the Midhope Potteries*, published in Sheffield, 1929, from which these notes have been drawn.

OSMOTHERLEY. Coarseware pottery reputed to have worked here in late eighteenth and early nineteenth centuries, but little evidence except for brief entry by Jewitt.

POTOVENS. Established in late fifteenth century on perimeter of Outwood, area of coarse scrub to north of Wakefield, with coal-measure clays, fireclays, coal and stone within easy reach. While transport facilities were limited potteries slowly expanded, but declined throughout eighteenth century in face of Halifax potters (geological advantages) and Leeds potters (factory techniques). In 1709 at least eight potteries working, but all closed before 1785. See *Post Medieval Archaeology*, Vol 1, 1967.

The author excavated Potovens kilns between 1963 and 1966, discovering the following:

Gazetteer

Kiln 1. Situated beneath present garden of 7 Imperial Avenue, Wrenthorpe, was operated from early seventeenth century by Jacob Willans, then son Thomas, and grandson Robert (described as one of chief potters in village in 1709). Still working in 1759, pottery had closed by 1785, as had rest of Potovens potteries. Produced cups, bowls, pancheons, cisterns, etc.

Kiln 2. Remains of stone-built multi-flued kiln of early sixteenth century discovered in middle of Bunker's Hill, Wrenthorpe, in 1964. Later excavations showed kiln had produced decorated Cistercian wares, only a few being in lighter 'reversed Cistercian' fabric.

Kiln 3. In 1964 substructure of seventeenth century kiln found in croft of seventeenth-century cottage at top of Bunker's Hill, Wrenthorpe. Produced red and yellow-ware cups, plates, and bowls.

Kiln 4. Disturbed foundations and floor of late sixteenth- and early seventeenth-century kiln making cups, costrels, etc, discovered while cutting trench near Malt Shovel Hotel, Wrenthorpe, in June 1964.

Kiln 5. Used for pipe-making in late seventeenth century by man with initials 'E.G.', probably member of Gill family.

Kiln 6. In croft of seventeenth-century cottage on Roger Lane, Wrenthorpe, 5ft diameter floor of single-flued pottery kiln found during building operations in 1964. Mid-seventeenth-century kiln had produced slipware plates, and redware bowls, etc.

Kiln 7. From documentary evidence it appeared likely that 155 Wrenthorpe Road, Wrenthorpe, was pottery worked by Glover family from early seventeenth century. Excavations in 1965 proved this, revealing seventeenth-century clamp-kiln in croft at rear of house. Earliest recorded potter to work on this site was Robert Glover, whose son, Robert II, and grandson, Robert III, continued work until 1679. In that year Robert Glover III leased his 'new house . . . a small garden, and a structure called a Cupp-oven built upon it'. On termination of this 21-year lease Robert's son, Robert Glover IV returned to pottery, working it to mid-eighteenth century; but by 1759 owed over three years rent to Duke of Leeds, and had certainly closed down by 1785. Produced blackware cups and skillets, yellow-ware plates, bowls and chamber-pots, and redware dishes.

Gazetteer

Kiln Sites. Heavy deposits of kiln waste, disturbed kiln structure, etc, on following sites make it likely that kilns once operated there, even though kilns not found :

Site 8. School Lane, late seventeenth and early eighteenth centuries,

Site 9. 27 School Lane, mid-eighteenth century,

Site 10. 143 Wrenthorpe Road, seventeenth century,

Site 11. Wrenthorpe Village Hall, seventeenth century,

Site 12. Brandy Carr Road, Kirkhamgate, late sixteenth to late seventeenth century,

Site 13. 142 Wrenthorpe Road, late sixteenth to late eighteenth century.

SILCOATES, POTOVENS. When new pavilion was being built on playing fields of Silcoates School in 1960, large quantities of Cistercian-ware wasters were discovered. Subsequent excavations by K. Woodrow, school's history master, showed that this 14-acre site had been extensively used for pottery production during early sixteenth century.

POTTERTON. In 1963 students of Leeds University Extra Mural classes in Archaeology found site of pottery in front garden of Potterton Grange. Excavations brought to light remains of circular six-flued kiln in which range of Cistercian wares had been made, many being in light 'reversed Cistercian' fabric. No documentary evidence available to date kiln, but magnetic tests carried out by Research Laboratory for Archaeology, Oxford, suggest early sixteenth century. Pottery recovered now in Leeds City Museum. See 'A Cistercian Ware Kiln of the Early Sixteenth Century at Potterton, Yorkshire', *The Antiquaries Journal*, vol XLVI (1966), 255.

SILKSTONE. Earliest evidence for pottery at Pot House, Silkstone, is bottle made for Richard Bailey, inscribed 'R.B. 1779', now in British Museum (cat no D110). Presumably bottle made by John Taylor, for churchyard at Silkstone has gravestone to his memory : 'John Taylor, Potter, of Silkstone, who died July 14th, 1815, aged 72 years, and Hannah, his wife, who died August 13th, 1815, aged 68 years'. This is last mention of pottery industry in Silkstone parish.

SWINTON. In 1745 Edward Butler founded pottery on Swinton Common, property of Marquis of Rockingham. Here, according to

Jewitt, was 'common yellow clay used for the purpose of making bricks, tiles, and coarse earthenware; a finer white clay for making pottery of a better quality, an excellent clay for making fire bricks, and also a white clay usually called "pipe-clay".' With these materials and local deposits of coal, Butler made bricks, tiles, and coarse earthenwares until 1765, when Messrs Malpass & Bremeld took over, developing works into great Rockingham factory.

YEARSLEY. The site of late fifteenth to early sixteenth-century pottery discovered and excavated at Soury Hill, Yearsley, by Suzan Brooke, MA, 1936-9. Remains of pottery, which probably supplied nearby Abbey of Byland, were discovered at depth of 5-9in. Cistercian type wares were made, sometimes in moss-green glaze. Good copies of contemporary French lobed cups, also in green lead glaze, also made here. Examples now in Yorkshire Museum, York.

Pottery was founded in Yearsley in mid-seventeenth century by John Wedgwood of famous Staffordshire family. In 1653 Coxwold Parish Register we read that on 'November 8th, John Wedgwood and Elizabeth Harrison was married'—first mention of any Wedgwood in parish though Harrisons were old-established Yearsley family. From mid-seventeenth century until death in 1682 John Wedgwood, together with son John, who died in 1707, made large cisterns, puzzle jugs, plates, and bowls. Victoria and Albert Museum has fine puzzle jug inscribed 'John Wedgwood, 1691', made at Yearsley. After John II's death pottery continued by son William, about whom song 'In Yearsley there are pancheons made, By Willie Wedgwood, that young blade', quoted by Jewitt, was written. In early eighteenth century William's son John transferred pottery to Heworth, York, where it continued into nineteenth century.

Pottery made was all northern reduced greenware type, Yearsley being southernmost kiln known to produce this type of ware. Examples in Fitzwilliam Museum, Cambridge, Victoria and Albert Museum, and Yorkshire Museum, York. See 'A Late Medieval Pottery Site At Yearsley', *Yorkshire Archaeological Journal*, vol 37 (1951), 345; and 'A Catalogue of English Country Pottery Housed in the Yorkshire Museum, York', *Yorks Phil Soc*, 1968.

YORK, HEWORTH MOOR. In early eighteenth century John Wedgwood of Yearsley moved into Walmgate in city of York, and founded pottery, probably at Heworth Moor. Register of St Maurice's Church, York, records that 'Mary, daughter of John Wedgwood, Potmaker, by Alice his wife was baptised August 7th, 1763'. When John died, a little later, his wife continued pottery, still making reduced greenware in Yearsley tradition; but pottery must have changed hands in late 1780s, for in the *York Herald* of 16 January 1790, we read :

Pottery.
At Mr. Ella's Brick and Tile Yard, Heworth Grange, nigh the City of York.

JOHN BOLLANS

Respectfully aquaints his friends, and the public in general, that he has taken and entered on the above Pottery, (lately occupied by Mrs. Wedgwood) where he intends making all kinds of Garden Pots, Chimney Pots, (as cheap as any other Pottery in the Kingdom), Druggist Pots and all kinds of Green Earthenware, in the neatest manner and on the most reasonable terms.

N.B. He purposes drawing the first kiln on February 1st, and having made considerable additions and new buildings to the pottery, he will be enabled to draw one every Monday throughout the year.

Orders from the county, addressed to JOHN BOLLANS, Goodramgate, York, will be forwarded with the greatest expedition.

Pottery continued through early nineteenth century, becoming property of John Webster in 1846, but he only worked it two years before selling out, following advertisement being placed in the 1848 *York Herald:*

House, Pottery and Brick kiln, now occupied by Mr. Webster, pot and tile maker, situated on Heworth Moor, on the York and Scarborough Road, about a mile from York, for Sale.

Apparently pottery never opened again after time of this sale.

Appendix 1

Potting Terms

As in most crafts, a great number of names and terms exist for the various tools and processes employed. These vary from area to area, workshop to workshop, and can often confuse those with only an academic knowledge of the subject. Most of the terms have been recorded personally by the author from conversation with the potters themselves, but where a written source has been consulted, its origin is quoted.

AGATE-WARE	See 'Ware'.
BAG WALL	A wall placed inside the kiln to prevent the concentrated heat from the firemouths striking the wares directly. This term is most commonly used in northern England.
BAT (1)	A disc of wood on which a pot may be thrown on the wheel. It forms a false wheelhead on which the pot may be lifted clear of the wheel with the minimum of trouble.
(2)	A fireclay slab used to form shelves or cupboards within the kiln.
BEATING	Wedging, or a quantity of wedged clay. This is a Halifax term, recorded from Isaac Button of Soil Hill Pottery, Halifax.
BISCUIT	Unglazed fired ware.
BLACKWARE	See 'Ware'.
BLISTER, OR BLOATING	The swelling or bubble occasionally formed within the fabric or glaze of a pot while in the kiln, by gases originating from impurities such as lime.
BLUNGER	A form of mill used to break down lumps of clay and water into a smooth slip.

P

233

BOBS	Small pellets of clay on which pots are stood during the glaze firing to prevent them sticking to the saggars. 'Bobbs' are mentioned in Dr Plot's *History of Staffordshire* of 1686.
BODY (1)	The main section of a pot.
(2)	The potter's name for the clay substance of which a pot is made. This term has been replaced in this volume by the alternative 'fabric', as used by the archaeologist, to avoid confusion with the shape of the pot.
BOWING	Handling, a North Devon term, recorded from Fishley Holland, formerly of the Fremington Pottery.
BUNG	A single stack of saggars or ware within the kiln.
BROWNWARE	See 'Ware'.
CHARGING	Packing a kiln with ware.
CLAYAIN	A storage-place for clay. A North Devon term recorded from Fishley Holland, formerly of the Fremington Pottery.
CLAYPAN	See 'Sunpan'.
COCKSPURS	See 'Spurs'.
COILING	The process of building up a pot with successive ropes of clay placed one upon another and smoothed together.
COLLARING	Reducing the diameter of the top of a pot as it spins on the wheel.
COMBINED WATER	Water which is chemically combined with the clay, and which can only be driven off at temperatures between 400 & 500°C.
COMBING	A technique of slip decoration in which a dipped pot is decorated by a blunt-toothed comb of wood, bone, or leather.
CRANK-WHEEL	A potter's wheel powered by having a cranked shaft, rather like that of a brace and bit, turned by a labourer with a long rod.
CRAZING	The fine network of cracks found in the glaze of a pot where the glaze has contracted more than the fabric after firing.
CREAMWARE	See 'Ware'.
CROWN-WHEEL	A type of potter's wheel in which the power is supplied to the shaft by means of a series

of cast-iron gear wheels turned by a handle at the side of the wheel frame.

CUPBOARDS — An arrangement of shelves and boxes built up of quarries or bats (2) inside the kiln to support the wares.

DAMPER — The draught control of a kiln.

DESS — A mass of clay in process of being trodden by way of preparation. This term came from Mr Bateson, formerly of the Burton-in-Lonsdale potteries.

DIPPING — The method of applying slip or glaze to a pot by immersing it in the particular solution required.

DISC-WHEEL — A potter's wheel having a flat disc mounted on its shaft just above ground level, which is kicked round by the potter, thus powering the wheel.

DRAUGHT (1) — A single knuckling-up when throwing. Recorded from Fishley Holland, formerly of the Fremington Pottery, North Devon.

(2) — The supply of air to the kiln.

DRAWING — Withdrawing the fired wares from the kiln.

DUNTING — The cracking of the ware in the kiln due to an over-rapid rate of cooling after firing.

EARTHENWARE — See 'Ware'.

FABRIC — The term most commonly used by the archaeologist and ceramic historian for the clay substance of which a pot is made.

FEATHERING — A method of slip decoration in which different colours of wet slip are drawn into one another by the use of a fine point, such as the tip of a feather.

FIRECLAY — A coarse yellow or grey clay having the property of withstanding very high temperatures without losing its shape.

FIRING — Burning or stoking a kiln.

FLAKING — The peeling or scaling of slips or glazes due to their relatively small contraction compared to that of their supporting fabric during or after firing.

FLASHING — The process of giving a sudden burst of heat to the kiln when at maximum temperature to melt the glaze.

FLATWARE	Any broad shallow ware, such as plates, saucers, or shallow bowls.
GALENA	A raw lead ore, chiefly lead sulphide, used as a glaze.
GRAINED WARE	A Westmorland term for Agate Ware, collected from Mr Thorburn of the Weatheriggs Pottery, Penrith.
GREAT WHEEL	A potter's wheel powered by means of a long belt passing from a small pulley on the shaft to a large hand-turned pulley wheel some feet away.
GREEN	A term used to describe an unfired (ie, raw) pot.
GREENWARE	See 'Ware'.
GROG	Powdered clay fabric added to an unfired clay fabric to improve its firing properties.
HOLLOW-WARE	Any deep vessels, such as jugs, cups, or mugs.
HOVEL	The roofed structure which encloses a kiln, keeping it dry, sheltering the stokers, and helping to ensure an even draught to each firemouth.
INCISING	Scratching decorative features into the surface of a dry pot.
INLAYING	An ornamental technique in which clay is rubbed into incisions in a fabric of a contrasting colour.
IRON OXIDE	The oxide most used by the potters to stain their glazes to a range of golden browns and blacks.
JOGGLING	A technique of slip decoration in which parallel lines of slip are first trailed across an area of wet slip of a contrasting colour. The whole piece is then given a series of twisting jerks, running the slip into a series of ornamental waves and swirls.
KICK-WHEEL	A variety of potter's wheel powered by means of a crank and foot pedal.
KNEADING	Mixing the clay into a plastic homogenous mass by hand or foot.
KNIFE TRIMMING	Trimming the foot of a vessel by paring off the surplus clay with a sharp knife.
KNUCKLING UP	The action of raising the walls of a vessel being thrown on the wheel by running the

clenched knuckles of each hand up the interior and exterior of the pot simultaneously.

LEAD — The basic constituent of most of the potter's glazes, used mainly in the form of galena, red lead, or litharge.

LEATHER HARD — The state of hardness in which the ware is dry enough to be handled without being deformed, but is not yet brittle.

LITHARGE — Lead monoxide, used by the potters to make their glazes.

LUTING — The process of joining two pieces of formed clay when still plastic, with the fingers.

MANGANESE OXIDE — Occasionally used as a glaze stain, producing a range of warm browns and purple-blacks.

MARBLING — Superimposing slips of various colours on leather-hard pots and running them together either by shaking or by the use of a sharp point or bristle to give a marbled finish (cf joggling).

MULLING — A North Devon term for wedging, from Fishley Holland, formerly of the Fremington Pottery.

OXIDATION — The process of firing a kiln in such a manner that the gases passing through it are rich in oxygen, thus causing the metallic elements in the clay and glaze to produce their oxide colours.

PARTING SHERD — A small piece of broken pottery placed between adjoining pots, or between a pot and a saggar to prevent them being stuck together by the glaze during firing.

PASSER — The labourer who wedged the clay and weighed it into balls ready for throwing before passing them to the thrower. This term was used at the Buckley Pottery, Flintshire, and appears to have been introduced to the Halifax potteries by J. Catherall, who moved from Buckley to Halifax in the late eighteenth century.

PEELING — See 'Flaking'.

PIN DUST — A Sussex term for powdered brass used to prepare a green glaze, recorded by Mainwaring Baines in his *Sussex Pottery* of 1948.

PLACING	Packing the pottery into the kiln.
PUG MILL	A mill which compresses, slices, and mixes plastic clays into a uniform consistency.
PYROMETER	A technical instrument (usually worked by means of a thermocouple) for measuring the temperature of a kiln.
QUARRY	A slab of either sandstone or fireclay used to form cupboards or shelves within the kiln.
QUILL STRINGING	A Halifax term for a slip trailer, collected from N. Taylor of the Denholm, Howcans, and Denholm Chapel potteries, Halifax.
REDUCED GREENWARE	See 'Wares'.
REDUCTION	The process of firing a kiln so that the gases passing through the firing chamber are smoky and incompletely burnt. The carbon present during this operation reduces the oxides in the fabric and glaze to their metallic forms, so that an iron-rich fabric, for example, would fire to a grey colour when reduced, rather than its normal oxidised red colour.
REDWARE	See 'Ware'.
RIB	A template of wood, metal, or pottery, used to finish a pot when throwing on the wheel.
RING PROP (1)	A small ring of clay 1-3in across, having three spikes pinched vertically round its circumference on which a glazed pot might be stood during the firing.
(2)	An L-sectioned strip of clay about 9in long curved to the radius of a pancheon rim, used in great numbers to form vertical bungs of pancheons in the kiln.
RING SAGGAR	A bottomless saggar used to support pancheons, plates, and bowls in the kiln before the introduction of the ring prop (see p 13, Stoke-on-Trent Museum Archaeological Society's *Report* No 3).
SAGGAR	A container, usually made of fireclay, in which the smaller wares are packed in the kiln, thus preventing them from sticking together when the glaze melts, and protecting them from the direct heat of the flames.
SCALING	See 'Flaking'.
SCRYING	Washing and sieving clay to remove the

stones, etc. This is a Sussex term recorded by Mainwaring Baines in his *Sussex Pottery*, 1948.

SETTING   Packing the ware into the kiln.

SGRAFFITO   A technique of slip decoration in which a coating of slip is carefully scratched away to reveal the contrasting colour of the fabric beneath.

SHEARING SPADE   A wooden spade with an iron blade used to turn clay in the sunpans of the Halifax potteries.

SHERDS, OR SHARDS   Small pieces of broken pottery.

SLIP   Clay dissolved in water to the consistency of thick cream.

SLIPWARE   See 'Ware'.

SLURRY   A rough mixture of clay and water.

SNAILHORN WARE   A Halifax term for agate-ware, supplied by N. Taylor of the Denholm, Howcans, and Denholm Chapel potteries, Halifax.

SOAKING (1)   The steady firing of a kiln at maximum temperature to allow the heat to penetrate through all the wares.

(2)   The process of softening clay by soaking it in large open-air clay pans filled with water.

SPINNING   A Sussex term for throwing. See Mainwaring Baines *Sussex Pottery*, 1948.

SPOON   A North Devon term for a rib, from Fishley Holland, formerly of the Fremington Pottery.

SPRIG   A moulded detail of decoration applied to the green pot.

SPURS   Triangular clay supports for placing glazed ware in the saggars.

STONEWARE   See 'Ware'.

STOUKING   A Staffordshire term for the process of fixing handles, lugs, spouts, etc. See Dr Plot's *History of Staffordshire* of 1686.

SULPHATION   The formation of whitish or yellowish patches on the surface of the glaze, caused by sulphur in the fuel (as in coal), or in the glaze (as in galena). This trouble was rare in the normally well ventilated updraught kiln but common where galena glazes were fired in closed un-pierced saggars or in electric kilns.

SUN KILN ⎫ SUNPAN ⎭	A large open-air tank up to 30ft wide by 6oft long in which slip was evaporated to a plastic state by the action of the wind and sun.
TENMOKU	A black iron glaze often shot with streaks of a pale rust colour. Although this glaze is best known from the stonewares of Japan, the same glazing results were occasionally accidentally achieved on high-fired redwares in this country (eg, the Cistercian wares of northern England).
TERRACOTTA	Fine unglazed redware, mainly used for architectural details and garden ornaments.
THROWING	The process of shaping pots on the potter's wheel.
TRAILING	A method of slip decoration in which coloured slips are piped on to the wares through a fine nozzle.
TURNING	Trimming the walls or feet of a pot as they spin on the potter's wheel.
WARE	Pottery products in general.
Agate-ware	A fabric made of clays of two or more contrasting colours coarsely mixed to produce a marble-like effect. (Not to be confused with marbling, a *Surface* decoration in slip.)
Bargee-ware	A type of pottery made in the late-nineteenth and early twentieth centuries that had a red fabric ornamented with sprigs of white clay and dabs of Wenger colours. So called from its popularity with the bargees of the Midlands waterways.
Blackware	Earthenwares, usually with a red-firing fabric, having a dense black lead glaze.
Brownware	This term has been used by various writers to describe (1) a redware glazed to a brown colour, or (2) a stoneware glazed with salt to a warm brown orange-peel finish.
Earthenware	Pottery with a porous fabric, fired to c 1,000°C.
Greenware	Pottery made from an earthenware fabric which fires to a cream colour due to its iron-free state, and which has been given a lead glaze stained to a brilliant green with copper.
Reduced Greenware	Redware (see below) fired in a reducing

	atmosphere with little or no oxygen to produce a slate grey colour, and thus appearing olive green under a yellow lead glaze.
Redware	Pottery made from a red-firing earthenware fabric, fired in an oxygen-rich atmosphere. It is often glazed to orange, brown, or black by the use of a lead-based glaze.
Slipware	Pottery decorated with slips.
Stoneware	Pottery which is impervious to water, vitrifying at temperatures usually in excess of 1,200°C.
Welsh-ware	Slipware of extremely high quality, usually decorated with complex feathered designs.
Whiteware	Pottery made from a white-firing earthenware fabric, normally only produced in pottery factories.
Yellow-ware	Pottery made from a yellow or buff-firing earthenware fabric, often appearing butter-coloured beneath a lead glaze.

Appendix 2

Names of Vessels

The names of different items of pottery vary considerably through-out England: a baking bowl, for example, may be a pancheon, a fuggin, or a cawdern. In this appendix the various local terms have been gathered together and classified to avoid confusion. Where a written source is available, this is quoted, but otherwise it may be assumed that the particular term is in common usage among the potters or their customers.

ALEMBIC

A tall conical vessel used for distilling. It had a closed top in which the hot vapours rising from the pottery cucurbit, or boiler, beneath were condensed. The base of the alembic, supported by the broad rim of the cucurbit, was completely open, and had a characteristic internal upturned rim in which the distillate was collected before being run off through a small spout pierced through the side of the vessel.

APPLE ROASTER

See 'Ovens'.

BAKER

A Cornish term for a shallow dish used for baking. In use a wood fire was first lit on top of a flat stone, and allowed to burn clear. The ashes were then pushed to one side and the food, covered by the baker, placed on the slab. The baker was then covered with hot ashes and fresh turves and so remained until the food was finally cooked. This cooking technique was used in Cornwall up to the late nineteenth century (see *Medieval Archaeology*, 1962, 290).

242

BAKING DISH   A shallow pressed-ware dish, often decorated with trailed slip, used for general baking purposes from the early eighteenth century. In Yorkshire these were often used to bake Yorkshire puddings in or to roast the meat (See J. Kenworthy. *Midhope Potteries* [1928]).

BALLOT-BOX   An antiquarian term for a salt-kit.

BARM-POT   A pot used in northern England for the storage of yeast. It is usually cylindrical, with a hollow beneath the rim to help tie down a paper or cloth covering over the mouth of the jar.

BEDPANS   Most pottery bedpans are copied from pewter originals. They have a shallow bowl, perhaps 12in across and 3in deep, with a wide inturned rim. From one side projects a wide tubular handle, serving the double function of urinal and spout for emptying.

BENISONS   Nests of bowls, varying from 1pt to 1 peck in volume, each fitting snugly inside the others. See Bourne, G.

BIGPANS   See 'Pans'.

BOWL   An open vessel with shaped sides (ie, not a pancheon).

BREAD-POT, BREAD-CROCK   A pot for the storage of bread. Those of the South and West of England are usually about as broad as they are high, and have two opposed handles at the rim, and a lid in the form of a shallow truncated cone with a central strap handle. The pots of the Midlands and North-east are taller, with curved sides, and a disc-shaped lid with a hollow central knob thrown into it; whereas those of the North-west are cylindrical, with similar lids to those of the Midlands (see pp 63-71).

BUNG-HOLE POTS   Large pottery cisterns equipped with a spigot hole at the base, made in Northern England from the late fifteenth to the late nineteenth century.

BUSSA   A variety of pan used for pickling pilchards in Devon & Cornwall.

BUTTER POT (1)   A tall cylindrical unglazed pot made in

Burslem, Staffordshire, for the storage of butter for sale. By an Act of Parliament (13 & 14 Charles II, cap 26, 1661) these pots were to weigh less than 6lb, yet contain 14lb of butter, and not be porous enough to imbibe much water, for that could be counted in the weight of the butter.

(2)   A tall cylindrical pot used during the eighteenth to the twentieth centuries for salting down butter for domestic use.

CAUDLE-POT   A pot for serving caudle, an oatmeal gruel enriched with spices and wine. The pot is shaped like an over-sized mug and usually has two opposed handles, though multi-handled examples are known.

CAWDERN   See 'Pan'.

CHAD-POT   A Buckinghamshire term for a fire-pot (see Thomas Wright. *The Romance of the Lace Pillow*).

CHAFING DISH   A shallow bowl-shaped vessel mounted on a tall pedestal base and having a number of knobs or spikes projecting above the rim to hold a secondary bowl or plate of food. The dish was filled with burning charcoal, a number of holes being pierced through its walls to supply the necessary draught; and the heat from the charcoal would be sufficient to carry out simple cooking operations or food-warming at table.

CHICKEN FEEDERS   Pots made in a variety of designs which have a hopper arrangement for supplying a small trough with grain, from which the chickens can feed unattended.

CHURN   A pottery version of a wooden plunger-churn, usually made in the nineteenth century with a ceramic body and lid, but a wooden plunger.

CLOAM   A North Devon term for earthenware in general.

CLOUGH   A meat-salting pan (see Morton's *Natural History of Northamptonshire*, 1712).

CLOUT   A Derbyshire term for a large brown-glazed mug.

COSTREL	A squat bottle having two pierced lugs for suspension at the shoulders.
CREAM-POT	A pot of 3-4 gallons capacity used to hold cream.
CUCURBIT	See 'Alembic'.
DICKY POT	A Bedfordshire term for a fire-pot.
DUTCH OVEN	See 'Oven'.
FIRE-POT	The firepot was shaped like a small chamber-pot with a single handle, but had a row of small holes pierced through its walls just below the rim. It was filled with hot ashes, often bought from the baker, and placed at the feet or under the skirts of the Midlands lace-makers, who were obliged to sit in one place for long periods. It was also used in a similar manner during long church services in winter. A full pot would maintain its heat for about half a day, but could be revived periodically by careful use of the bellows.
FISH-DISH	From the sixteenth century to the eighteenth shallow leaf-shaped dishes, about 15in long and 2-3in deep, were used for cooking fish. Usually they have a single pulled handle attached to one side, and the walls at each end are pulled out to form spouts.
FOUNTAIN	This pot, used for feeding chickens, was a domed vessel without a bottom, having a small hole pierced through its wall about an inch from the base. In use the pot was up-turned and filled with water, a deep saucer was then placed over it, and the whole fountain swiftly inverted. The water rose in the saucer until it came to the level of the hole in the dome, where it remained until the water supply was finally exhausted. In this way the chickens were supplied with water for up to two or three days with very little trouble.
FROG MUG	A drinking mug, most common from the eighteenth century to the twentieth, which has inside it a realistically modelled frog that emerges slowly as the pot is drained, startling the drinker.

FUDDLING CUP | A trick cup, usually made from a number of individual cups joined together. The drinker had to discover a method of drinking without being either drenched or befuddled. Most examples are of early eighteenth-century Staffordshire origin.

FUMING POT | A bowl-shaped vessel, standing on a tall pedestal base, and having its upper section pierced to produce an open lantern-like top. These pots, termed 'stink-pots' during the Plague (see W. G. Bell. *The Great Plague in London, 1665,* 2nd edition 1951, 106, 155, & 285), were probably used to hold some form of pot-pourri to scent rooms (see *Surrey Archaeol Collections,* LVIII [1961], 17).

GALLIPOT (1) | A small pot used to hold medicines, having a hollow beneath the rim to enable a fabric or paper cover to be secured in place with string.

(2) | A paint-pot, North Devon.

GOTCH | An East Anglian term for a jug.

GREATCROCK | A large pot used for pickling pilchards in North Devon.

GULLYMOUTH | See 'Pitcher'.

HAM PAN | A large pot, oval, or pear-shaped in plan, in which a whole ham could be placed for salting. These vessels usually had wooden lids, pierced for ventilation.

HEDGEHOGS | Pottery models of hedgehogs were made during the nineteenth century, particularly at the Brede Pottery, Sussex.

HEN & CHICKENS | A variety of money-box made in the potteries of the North and Midlands during the eighteenth, nineteenth, and twentieth centuries, which had a large bird modelled on the top of the box and a circle of smaller birds modelled below.

HOG POT | A cylindrical jar used to salt pork.

JOLLY-BOYS | A North Devon variety of fuddling cup.

KNIFE BOX | A pottery version of a wooden knife box, being made up of clay slabs in an exactly similar manner to the wooden originals.

KNIFE POT | A pot made either on the wheel or from thin

slabs of clay in which cutlery was stored vertically.

LADING POT — A cylindrical pot of about ½ gallon capacity with a single large handle, used in northern England to bale water from the boiler to fill the bath or the wash-tub.

LONG TOM — See 'Pitcher'.

LOVING CUP (1) — A two-handled cup, usually in a semi-classical shape with a pedestal base and an inverted bell-shaped bowl. These cups were often used in Nonconformist Love-feasts during the late eighteenth and throughout the nineteenth centuries.

(2) — An antiquarian term for any two-handled cup.

MEAS CUP — A single-handled blackware mug made in South Yorkshire and Derbyshire during the eighteenth and nineteenth centuries.

MEAT DISH (1) — From the late sixteenth century to the eighteenth most meat dishes were rectangular, some 12in wide by up to 18in long, and 2-3in deep. Normally two handles protruded from one of the long sides (see *Medieval Archaeology*, Vol VIII [1964] 209).

(2) — Later meat dishes were usually in the form of shallow pressed-ware baking dishes.

OVENS (1) — Bread ovens were made in Devon and Cornwall from the early post-medieval period at the latest, up to the late 1920s. In shape they were similar to large beehives, but with closely fitting doors cut in their front faces. A wood fire was first lit inside the oven and the temperature built up until the top would produce sparks from any stick rubbed over it. The ashes were then taken out, the inside rapidly mopped clean with a damp cloth on a stick, the food inserted, and the door sealed in position with wet clay. After a certain time had elapsed, as proved by experience, the door was pulled free, and the cooked food removed.

(2) — A second type of oven was the Dutch Oven (Northern England) or Apple Roaster (Somer-

set). These ovens were made from half a large pan, with a narrow shelf formed round the internal curved wall, and either handles or knobs fitted to the back surface. The object to be roasted was placed inside and the oven slid across the hearth to face the open fire.

OWL — A term used in South and South-west England to describe a costrel.

OWL JUG — A slipware jug in the form of an owl, the head of which lifts off to form a cup. These are usually of Staffordshire origin, dating from the early eighteenth century.

OWLSHEAD — A North Devon term for a costrel, brought about by the resemblance of the short round costrels with their two rounded lugs to the head of an owl.

PAINTPOT — A pot, rather like a chamberpot in shape, with a small loop handle at the rim into which the painter inserts his left thumb, thus allowing the pot to be held easily in one hand and leaving the other free to wield the brush.

PAN — A shortened form of 'pancheon'. In North Devon pans progress in size from widebottoms to cawderns, bigpans, and, largest of all, washpans.

PANCHEON — An open vessel in the form of a straight-sided truncated cone, used for general baking or washing purposes.

PARTING CUP — A romantic antiquarian term for any form of multi-handled cup.

PIG — Hollow pigs with heads that lifted off to form cups were made in Sussex during the nineteenth century, the idea being that a 'hogshead' could be drunk with ease. The older examples have a red fabric and heads which rest on the snout alone, whereas the more recent examples have a light-coloured fabric and heads which rest on both the snout and the tips of the ears when separated from the body.

PIGGIN — A shallow cylindrical pot with a flat vertical

248

Names of Vessels

handle, copying the shape of the cooper-made baler.

PILL — A costrel (particularly from the Verwood pottery) in Hampshire, Wiltshire, and Dorset.

PINCHGUT — See 'Pitcher'.

PITCHER — A South-country term for a jug. In North Devon these are classified as pinchguts, 4pt; gullymouths, 5½pt; thirtytales 7pt; Long Toms, 2 gallons.

PLANT-POT — A straight-sided vessel, normally unglazed, with a drainage hole at the base, exactly like the present-day product.

PORK-PAN — A deep pan with vertical sides, used for salting pork. This term is mainly used in the South.

POSSET POT — A pot, often bearing a lid, two handles, and occasionally a spout, used when drinking posset, a hot drink of milk flavoured with wine, ale, treacle or honey, and spices. Frequently these pots are extremely well decorated in slips or applied decoration.

POTTLE — A four-pint pot.

POTTY — A ball of clay about ½in in diameter used for various games in northern England.

RHUBARB-POT — A large bottomless pot over 1ft in height and diameter, domed over at the top to leave a hole about 6in wide that is covered by a separate lid. This pot is placed over the rhubarb plant to force it.

SALTER — A North Devon term for an oval meat-salting pan.

SALT-KIT — A jar, completely domed over to a finial knob, having a circular hand-hole covered by a broad hood cut into the side. Used in the North for the storage of cooking-salt.

SEAKALE-POT — A pot similar to a rhubarb-pot used to force seakale, mainly in Southern England from the mid-nineteenth century.

SPITTOONS — Open bowls filled with sawdust, used mainly in public houses.

SQUIBBER — A tub to hold waste clay. See Bourne, G.

STINK POT — See 'Fuming Pot'.

TAW — See 'Potty'.

Q

249

THIRTYTALES See 'Pitcher'.

TYG An ornamental mug, frequently decorated with slip-trailing and applied pads of clay, having a number of highly ornate handles that are often hollow, concealing drinking-spouts.

WASH PAN See 'Pan'.

WHISTLE Pottery whistles were made at many eighteenth- and nineteenth-century potteries in the North, many of them being given away to the children of prospective customers to attract their parents. Larger whistles in the form of pigeons were made in Sussex, where they are believed to have been mounted in chimneys where the strong draught would cause them to whistle, scaring off evil spirits.

WIDEBOTTOM See 'Pan'.

Bibliography

Most of the sources quoted in the text refer to single pots found in excavations, etc, and are dealt with under 'Notes in the Text'. In this bibliography the works listed either give further background information on the potteries or contain additional material and photographs of the wares made in them.

Baines, J. M. *Sussex Pottery* (Hastings 1948)

Barton, K. J. 'Some Evidence for Two Types of Pottery Manufactured in Bristol in the Early Eighteenth Century', *Trans of the Bristol & Gloucs Archaeol Soc*, 80 (1961), 160-8, and 'Buckley Potteries 2, Excavations at Prescot's Pottery', *Flintshire Hist Soc Publications*, 16 (1956), 63-87

Bemrose, G. *Nineteenth Century English Pottery & Porcelain* (1952)

Board of Agriculture, Reports of, usually entitled *A General View of the Agriculture of the County of* . . . (c 1800)

Bock, G. V. 'Volks Kunst in Rheinland', *Führer und Schriften des Rheinischen Freïlichtmuseums in Kommern No 4*

Bourne, G. *William Smith, Potter & Farmer, 1790-1858* (1920)

Bradley, R. J. *Castle Hedingham Pottery, 1837-1905* (1968)

Brears, P. C. D. *Catalogue of the English Country Pottery Housed in the Yorkshire Museum, York* (1968) and *The Farnham Potteries* (Farnham 1970)

Brooke, S. 'A Late Medieval Pottery Site at Yearsley', *The Yorkshire Archaeol Jnl*, 37 (1951)

Chaffers, W. *Marks and Monograms on Pottery & Porcelain* (1863)

Church, Sir A. *English Earthenware* (1885)

Cooper, R. G. *English Slipware Dishes, 1650-1850* (1968)

Crawley, J. *The Potteries of Sunderland & District* (Sunderland 1961)

Bibliography

Emmison, F. *Tudor Food & Pastimes* (1964)

English Ceramic Circle *Proceedings* (1933 to date)

Grabham, O. *Yorkshire Potteries, Pots, & Potters* (1916)

Haggar, R. G. 'Country Pottery & Porcelain', *Concise Encyclopedia of Antiques* 2 (1955), and *English Country Pottery* (1950)

Hobson, R. L. *Catalogue of the Collection of English Pottery in the British Museum* (1903)

Hodgkin, J. E. & E. *Early English Pottery with Names & Dates* (1891) and *Examples of Early English Pottery* (1896)

Holland, W. F. *Fifty Years a Potter* (1958)

Honey, W. B. *English Pottery & Porcelain* (revised by R. J. Charleston 1962)

Hughes, G. B. *Victorian Pottery & Porcelain* (1959)

Hurst, J. G. 'Tudor Green Ware' etc, *Winchester Excavations 1949-60* (Winchester 1964)

Jewitt, L. *The Ceramic Art of Great Britain* (1878)

Kenworthy, J. *The Midhope Potteries* (Sheffield 1928)

Kiddell, A. J. B. 'Wrotham Slipware & the Wrotham Brickyard', *Trans of the English Ceramic Circle*, 3, part 2 (1954), 51-7, and '2 Wrotham Pottery Tile Slabs', *ibid*, part 2, 290-1

Kleyn, J. de. *Volksaardewerk in Nederland 1600-1900*, N.V. Zeist (1965)

Leach, B. *A Potter's Book* (1945)

Leicester Museums. *A Catalogue of the Permanent Collection of English Ceramics* (Leicester 1953)

Lewis, G. *A Picture History of English Pottery* (1956)

Lomax, C. *Quaint Old English Pottery* (1909)

Medieval Archaeology (1956 to date)

Musty, J. 'Note on the Post Medieval Kiln Sites supplying the Salisbury Area', *Wilts Archaeol & Nat Hist Magazine*, 63 (1968), 51

Newton, E. F. & Bibbings, E. 'Seventeenth Century Pottery Sites at Harlow, Essex', *Essex Archaeol Soc Trans*, 25, part 3, New Series (Colchester 1960) 358-77

Parkinson, M. R. *The Incomparable Art*, Manchester (1969)

Plot, Dr R. *The Natural History of Staffordshire* (1686)

Post Medieval Archaeology (1967 to date)

Post Medieval Ceramics Research Group *Broadsheet* (1964-6)

Rackham, B. *Catalogue of the Glaisher Collection in the Fitzwilliam Museum, Cambridge* (1935), *Catalogue of the Schreiber Collection in the Victoria & Albert Museum* (1915 & 1930), *Early Staffordshire Pottery* (1951), 'Farnham Pottery of the Sixteenth

Bibliography

Century', *Surrey Archaeol Collections* 52 (1952), *Medieval English Pottery* (1924)

Rackham, B. & Rhead, H. *English Pottery* (1924)

Ralegh Radford, C. A. & Hallam, A. D. 'The History of Taunton Castle', *Proc of Somerset Archaeol Soc* (Taunton 1953)

Reeks, T. & Ruddler, F. W. *British Pottery & Porcelain in the Museum of Practical Geology*, 2nd ed (1871)

Rhead, G. W. & F. A. *Staffordshire Pots & Potters* (1906)

Savage, G. *English Pottery & Porcelain* (1961)

Shaw, S. *The History of the Staffordshire Potteries* (1829)

Sidebotham. *Catalogue of the Greg Collection of English Pottery*, now in the City Art Gallery, Manchester (1923)

Solon, M. L. *The Art of the Old English Potter* (1885), and 'On some fragments of English Earthenware', *Derbyshire Archaeol & Nat Hist Soc*, 9 (1889)

Taggart, R. E. *The Frank P. & Harriet C. Burnap Collection of English Pottery*, Kansas, 2nd ed (1967)

Victoria County Histories, The

Walton, J. 'Some Decadent Local Industries', *Halifax Antiq Soc Trans* (1939) 19

Watkins, C. M. 'North Devon Pottery & its Export to America in the Seventeenth Century', *United States National Museum Bulletin*, 225 (Washington 1960)

Wedgwood J. C. & Ormsbee T. H. *Staffordshire Pottery* (1947)

Woodfield, P. 'Yellow Glazed Wares of the Seventeenth Century', *Trans of the Birmingham Archaeol Soc*, 81 (1966)

Acknowledgements

The writer wishes to express his thanks and appreciation to all those who have helped to make the present volume possible, particularly to the curators and librarians, too numerous to mention, who have offered him every assistance at their disposal during his researches.

Grateful acknowledgement must also be made to those potters who have given freely of their time to discuss a multitude of technical and personal details and to demonstrate their impressive skills. They include Mr G. Curtis of the Littlethorpe Pottery, Ripon; Messrs A. & R. Harris of the Farnham Pottery; Mr H. Thorburn of the Weatheriggs Pottery, Penrith; Mr R. Bateson, formerly of the Burton-in-Lonsdale potteries; Mr W. F. Holland, formerly of the Fremington Pottery; and the late Mr I. Button of the Soil Hill Pottery, Halifax.

Sincere thanks are also due to Mr W. Davey, Miss D. Griffiths, Mr F. Holling, Miss R. H. Healey, and Mrs E. H. Rudkin for allowing the author to publish their specialist contributions on particular areas, and also to Miss R. Allan, Mr A. Booth, and Mr S. Moorhouse for supplying further notes and general information.

The writer is also indebted to Miss P. E. Bridges, Mr D. Davidson, Mr R. Milligan, and Mr K. Stubbs for the preparation of the photographic plates, and to the various individuals and institutions acknowledged in the List of Illustrations who have kindly granted their permission to reproduce items from their respective collections.

Peter C. D. Brears

254

Index

Index

Whistling Syke, 172
White, Thomas, 211
Whitehaven Potteries, 172
Whitehead, Christopher Charles, 207
Whiteman & Co, 174
Whiteware, 241
Whitley, John, 227
Whitney Bottom Pottery, 200
Whitney-on-Wye, 188
Whitworth, H. K., 226; Oliver, 226
Wickham Market, 212
Widebottoms, 71, 250
Wigton, 172
Wilcock, Mr, 225
Wilde, John & Son, 210
Wildenhill, 189
Wilder Street Pottery, 200
Wilhelm, Christian, 36
Wilkinson, John, 172; Mark, 226
Willans, Jacob, 228; Robert, 228;
    Thomas, 228
Williams, Philip, 198
Williamson, Thomas, 173
Willis, G. 189
Wilson, Brothers, 193; Thomas, 185
Wilton, 221
Wiltshire Potteries, 220-1; decorative
    wares, 47, 122, 129
Winchester, pottery from, 24
Winchcombe Pottery, 185
Wolstanton, 209
Wood, John, 204; Robert, 204;
    Thomas, 183

Wood-firing kilns, 146-51, 187
Woodman House Pottery, 74, 226
Woodside, 188
Woodward, David, 210; Robin, 197;
    Thomas, 197; William, 198
Woolpit, 212
Woolwich, 189
Worcester, pottery from, 24
Wrecclesham Pottery, 147-9; kiln at,
    149-51
Wright, Edward W., 174; George,
    183; George R., 212; John, 182-
    3; Thomas, 206, 208; William,
    183, 206
Wrotham, decorative wares, 49, 117,
    122; potters, 190; tygs, 50, 85,
    164
Wroxham, 195
Wychwood, 198

Yardley Gobion, 197
Yates, John, 207
Yearsley Pottery, 121, 231
Yellow-wares, 31-7, 61, 241
Yeomans, David, 214
York, pottery at, 61, 231-2; pottery
    from, 36, 39, 121, 163
Yorkshire Potteries, 221-32
Young, James, 173
Youngs, Richard, 185
Yoxford, 212

Zillwood, Mr, 48

266